AUTISM

AUTISM

DIAGNOSIS, CURRENT RESEARCH AND MANAGEMENT

Editor

Edward R. Ritvo, M.D.
Department of Psychiatry,
University of California School of Medicine,
Los Angeles

Co-editors

Betty Jo Freeman, Ph.D.,
Edward M. Ornitz, M.D.,
Peter E. Tanguay, M.D.,
all of the Department of Psychiatry,
University of California School of Medicine,
Los Angeles

S P Books Division of
SPECTRUM PUBLICATIONS, INC.
New York

Distributed by Halsted Press
A Division of John Wiley & Sons

New York   Toronto   London   Sydney

SPECTRUM PUBLICATIONS, INC.
86-19 Sancho Street, Holliswood, N.Y. 11423

Distributed solely by the Halsted Press division of John Wiley & Sons, Inc., New York

Library of Congress Cataloging in Publication Data
Main entry under title:

Autism--diagnosis, current research, and management.

(Series on child behavior and development ; v. 2)
Consists of papers presented at a two-day seminar
held Jan. 1975 by the UCLA Extension Division.
1. Autism--Congresses. I. Ritvo, Edward R.
II. California. University. University Extension.
III. Series. [DNLM: 1. Autism--In infancy and child-
hood. W1 CH645 v. 2 / WM203 A9393]
RJ506.A9A92   618.9′28′982   76-1931
ISBN 0-470-15039-4

To
MAX RITVO, M.D.
(1897-1962)
My Father
Professor of Radiology, Harvard, Tufts, and
Boston University Medical Schools
and

JOSEPH WEINREB, M.D.
My Uncle
Director, Worcester Youth Guidance Center
Worcester, Massachusetts (Retired)
Professor of Child Psychiatry
Vanderbilt University Medical School (Retired)
I wish to dedicate this book
with love and respect
to two men whose charity and wisdom,
dedication and skill as physicians
and patience as gifted teachers
I have chosen for my personal
and professional ideals
and whom I strive to emulate.

Editors
and
Contributors

Editor

EDWARD R. RITVO, M.D.
Associate Professor
Mental Retardation and Child Psychiatry
 Program
Department of Psychiatry
UCLA School of Medicine

Co-editors

BETTY JO FREEMAN, Ph.D.
Assistant Professor
Medical Psychology, Mental Retardation
 and Child Psychiatry Program
Department of Psychiatry
UCLA School of Medicine

EDWARD M. ORNITZ, M.D.
Associate Professor
Mental Retardation and Child Psychiatry
 Program
Department of Psychiatry
UCLA School of Medicine

PETER E. TANGUAY, M.D.
Assistant Professor
Mental Retardation and Child Psychiatry
 Program
Department of Psychiatry
UCLA School of Medicine

Contributors

LORIAN BAKER, Ph.D.
Staff Research Associate
Mental Retardation and Child Psychiatry
 Program
Department of Psychiatry
UCLA School of Medicine

LAWRENCE BARTAK, M.D.
Lecturer
Department of Child Psychiatry
Institute of Psychiatry
University of London, England

DENNIS P. CANTWELL, M.D.
Assistant Professor
Mental Retardation and Child Psychiatry
 Program
Department of Psychiatry
UCLA School of Medicine

BARBARA FISH, M.D.
Professor
Mental Retardation and Child Psychiatry
 Program
Department of Psychiatry
UCLA School of Medicine

REBECCA FLAHARTY, M.A.
Demonstration Teacher
Mental Retardation and Child Psychiatry
 Program
Department of Psychiatry
UCLA School of Medicine

FRED FRANKEL, Ph.D.
Research Psychologist
Mental Retardation and Child Psychiatry
 Program
Department of Psychiatry
UCLA School of Medicine

EDWARD GELLER, Ph.D.
Associate Professor
Assistant Chief
Neurobiochemistry Research Laboratory
Veterans Administration
Brentwood Hospital and UCLA School of
 Medicine

VICKI GRAHAM, M.A.
Demonstration Teacher
Mental Retardation and Child Psychiatry
    Program
Department of Psychiatry
UCLA School of Medicine

MATTHEW L. ISRAEL, Ph.D.
Director
Behavior Research Institute
Providence, Rhode Island
Assistant Clinical Professor
Mental Retardation and Child Psychiatry
    Program
Department of Psychiatry
UCLA School of Medicine

COLLEEN JAMISON, Ph.D.
Project Psychologist and Professor of
    Educational Psychology
California State University at Los Angeles

CONNIE LAPIN, B.A.
Speech Pathologist
Second Vice President
Los Angeles Chapter
National Society for Autistic Children

HARVEY LAPIN, D.D.S.
Second Vice President
National Society for Autistic Children
Past President
Los Angeles Chapter
National Society for Autistic Children

MARILYN LOWELL, M.A.
Research Associate
Mental Retardation and Child Psychiatry
    Program
Department of Psychiatry
UCLA School of Medicine

FLORENCE NEEDELS, M.S.
Project Director and Consultant
Los Angeles County Schools Autism
    Project
Lawndale, California

ELLEN RICHEY, M.A.
Demonstration Teacher
Mental Retardation and Child Psychiatry
    Program
Department of Psychiatry
UCLA School of Medicine

MICHAEL RUTTER, M.D., D.P.M.,
    M.R.C.P., F.R.C. Psychiatry
Professor of Child Psychiatry
Institute of Psychiatry
University of London, England

JAMES Q. SIMMONS, III, M.D.
Associate Professor and Chief of Child
    Psychiatry
Associate Program Director
Mental Retardation and Child Psychiatry
    Program
Department of Psychiatry
UCLA School of Medicine

M. ANNE SPENCE, Ph.D.
Assistant Professor
Department of Biomathematics and
    Department of Psychiatry
UCLA School of Medicine

RUTH CHRIST SULLIVAN
Director
Information and Referral Service of the
    National Society for Autistic Children
Huntington, West Virginia

ALEXANDER J. TYMCHUK, Ph.D.
Assistant Professor
Medical Psychology
Mental Retardation and Child Psychiatry
    Program
Department of Psychiatry
UCLA School of Medicine

ARTHUR YUWILER, Ph.D.
Associate Professor
Chief
Neurobiochemistry Research Laboratory
Veterans Administration Brentwood
    Hospital, and UCLA School of Medicine

Preface

It was a typically sunny Saturday morning in Southern California, January 25, 1975. A crowd of 600 people flocked into the UCLA Student Union—a most unusual crowd since they had not come to watch another UCLA basketball victory. Rather, they were there to attend a two-day Extension Division seminar on the subject of "Autism: Diagnosis, Current Research, and Management", which could hardly be considered a crowd-puller.

The seminar participants—including parents of autistic persons—of varied backgrounds and professions all shared a common enthusiasm and motivation to learn more about the disease autism, and how each, working within his own professional parameter, could best help autistic persons.

This volume contains all the papers presented that weekend. Also included are seven additional chapters which could not be scheduled into the two-day seminar. In view of the tremendous amount of recent research in the field, we realized that it would be impractical to attempt an exhaustive presentation of all relevant material. Hence, we exercised our professorial prerogatives and decided on which areas to focus and which areas to omit. For those readers interested in exploring specific topics in more detail, the authors have cited references after their chapters.

The UCLA Extension Division's seminar was presented in collaboration with the National Society for Autistic Children. (The Society is composed of parents of autistic persons and professionals interested in autism.) One of its goals is to help educate people who work with autistic persons and alert them to the needs of their patients' families. We wish to acknowledge our appreciation for their direct and continuing support.

More information concerning the Society is included in the chapters by Mrs. Sullivan and Dr. and Mrs. Lapin.

The editors and most of the contributors to this volume are on the staff of UCLA's Neuropsychiatric Institute and members of the Division of Mental Retardation and Child Psychiatry, UCLA School of Medicine. Our collaborative efforts over many years have been sceintifically directed and administratively supported by Dr. George Tarjan, Director of the Division. Without his continuing support we could not have developed our multidisciplinary clinical, research, and training programs focused on autism. Thus, we wish to acknowledge our debt of gratitude to him on behalf of ourselves, our patients, and their families.

We also wish to thank our editorial assistant, Mrs. Rose Weisler, for her expert and patient help in translating our thoughts into written form.

Research reported in this volume was supported in part by the following Grants:

1. State of California Department of Mental Hygiene
2. McGregor Fund, Detroit, Michigan
3. MH-13517
4. MCH-927
5. Drew H-181
6. HD-04612, 00345, 04364, 05615
7. The Grant Foundation
8. USPHS—Career Scientist Development Award MH-47361 (Dr. Tanguay)
9. USPHS MD-26047
10. Veterans Administration Research Service
11. USPHS HD-01-058 and AM-08775
12. NIH, FR-3
13. U.S. Office of Education, OEGO-72-3974 (603)
14. Harriett Ames Charitable Trust, New York and New York State Department of Mental Hygiene (Dr. Fish)
15. NIMH Special Research Fellowship 1F0-3MH52205-01
16. NIMH MH-17039-0452
17. Easter Seal Research Foundation
18. SRS 59-P-45192
19. MC-08467
20. NIMH HSM-42-133
21. Benevolent Foundation of Scottish Rite Freemasonry, Northern Jurisdiction
22. HEW-EHA Title VI-B—No. 19-00000-1423-4-04
23. Office of Los Angeles County Superintendent of Schools, Division of Special Education

Foreword

It is a privilege to introduce a book which describes the clinical experiences, the ideas, and some of the research results of a number of my colleagues on autism—an enigmatic disorder which is one of the greatest tragedies that can confront children and their parents. It is apparent that a very successful conference has been committed to this volume and important differences of opinion among the participants have been expressed here. These differences are necessary for progress toward the solution of the mysteries of this syndrome.

The Mental Retardation and Child Psychiatry Program was established at the Neuropsychiatric Institute of UCLA in the late 1960s, and became fully functional in the early 1970s; the academic base of the program originated in the Department of Psychiatry. The construction and the essential operational funds were provided by the federal government and by the State of California's Department of Mental Hygiene. I acknowledge with gratitude these generous contributions. However, the accomplishments of the program and the quality of this book reflect more directly the intellect, sensitivity and diligence of the faculty than the results of the construction or the sources of funding. It is in this spirit that I pay homage to the editors and to the authors.

I especially welcome the chapters written by individuals who are not members of the UCLA Mental Retardation and Child Psychiatry Program whose contributions add much to the book.

When my late friend, Stanley W. Wright, and I thought about the program we hoped to develop, certain basic concepts were foremost in our minds. We wanted to assemble outstanding scientists and clinicians who could focus on the prevention and amelioration of mental retardation and related conditions. We thought even the most basic research targeted on these goals could flourish best in an atmosphere in which those who work primarily in laboratories could consistently encounter the clinical symptoms of the ultimate beneficiaries. We also thought the quality of clinical practice could be significantly enhanced by close proximity to scientific work. Consequently, one of our overriding principles focused on the close integration of research, professional education, and clinical practice. This book attests to the spirit of that approach.

We noted early the close relationship between autism and other forms of impaired cognitive functioning and planned to devote an important portion of our resources to autism. We were also searching for a solution which would enable parents to enter our services through a single door, independently of the nature of their child's mental or emotional problem, or the presence or absence of a specific diagnosis. Such an approach would minimize the parents' burden at the time of initial contact; it would eliminate the need for some classification of the child by them, even before receiving any professional guidance. Our studies uncovered very close relationship between traditional child psychiatry and the field of mental retardation, which will be of benefit to all our patients.

George Tarjan, M.D.
Professor of Psychiatry
Director
Mental Retardation and Child Psychiatry Program
The Neuropsychiatric Institute
University of California, Los Angeles

Contents

PART I

Introduction

CHAPTER ONE

Autism: From Adjective to Noun

EDWARD R. RITVO

In 1906, Eugene Bleuler, a Swiss psychiatrist, introduced the adjective "autism" into the psychiatric literature. He had been studying the thought processes of patients diagnosed as having dementia praecox, a condition he relabeled with another term he introduced into the psychiatric literature, schizophrenia. He used the word autism to describe the quality of his patients' psychotic ideation in which they referred everything in the world to themselves.

In 1943, Leo Kanner, a child psychiatrist at Johns Hopkins University, described a group of severely disturbed children who shared certain clinical features; one was an inability to relate to other people. Employing Bleuler's adjective, he described these patients in the title of his initial paper as having "Autistic Disturbances of Affective Contact."

Over the next several decades, much controversy arose in the literature regarding the nature of the illness Kanner had described. Different clinicians and researchers diagnosed these children according to the specific aspects of the disease which they thought most important. Kanner, adhering to descriptive nosology, coined the diagnostic term "early infantile autism." "Childhood schizophrenia" was used by Lauretta Bender (1947) and others who postulated that these children represented the earliest expression of the adult form of the disease. "Symbiotic psychosis" was a diagnostic term coined by Margaret Mahler (1952) based on her interest in resonating mother-child pathology. Rank (1949) referred to these children as having "atypical ego development" based on his psychoanalytic understanding of the disease. Other investigators, taking a more eclectic viewpoint, tried to integrate the various notions of etiology. For example, Goldfarb (1961) set

3

up a continuum of cases ranging from childhood schizophrenia, organic type, to childhood schizophrenia, non-organic type.

As the 1940s and 1950s unfolded, clinical centers were established by advocates of these different theoretical positions. Each diagnosed patients, conducted research, and advocated treatments consonant with his views. Treatments ranged from the individual psychoanalysis of the patient to concurrent psychoanalysis of mother and child, outpatient psychotherapy, institutionalization of the patient combined with psychotherapy, electro-shock treatment, the use of psychotropic drugs, treatments based on operant conditioning principles, special educational approaches, megavitamin therapy, and sensory deprivation.

The clinical situation at the end of the 1950s could best be characterized by the old story about the blind men and the elephant. Each was allowed to touch a part of the animal. When asked to describe what they thought it was, each expressed a different view based on the part he had touched. They could come to no agreement as to the overall nature of the beast. So it was with autism. Each group of investigators focused on what it thought was the most significant aspect of the beast, evolved a general picture, and recommended treatment from its perspective.

Unfortunately, particularly for the patients, none of the various treatment methods passed the "test of time." None empirically altered the course of the disease; none yielded solid evidence to support the theoretical positions from which it evolved (Ornitz, 1973).

Our first efforts were directed towards gathering fresh clinical data from an unbiased point of view. We wanted to crystalize a phenomeno-logically-based description of the disease. We could then construct hypotheses to explain which pathological process or processes could account for the symptoms and design experiments to test them.

In order to organize our research, we needed to formulate a working model of a disease, and agreed to use the term "autism" as a *noun* to refer to it. We hypothesized that a dysfunction of the central nervous system existed in all patients and caused their deviant development and specific symp-tomatology. We further postulated that the personality deficits observed in these children were secondary to their organic brain pathology. We recognized the possibility that the primary organic pathology of the brain could be caused by a variety of specific etiologic agents.

A model for this type of disease concept is epilepsy. Epilepsy is characterized by transient disturbances in central nervous system func-tioning which produce an alteration of consciousness and associated be-havioral symptoms. It can be caused by a variety of specific etiologic agents operating either alone or in combination. In all its forms, a common "clinical syndrome" exists in terms of the disruption of brain function as manifested on the EEG and by seizures.

What type of "organic" pathology could be present in autism as the final common pathway of one or more etiologic factors? First, it must be quite subtle, since it had avoided detection by routine neurological tests administered to many of these children by competent neurologists. Second, since the symptomatology fluctuated over time and in degree, it most likely involves the modulation or regulation circuits within the central nervous system. Recent research had begun to pinpoint several areas of the brain which act as filters to modulate perceptual input, maintain homeostatic regulation of sensory and motor functions, and coordinate responsiveness of other parts of the central nervous system. The most well-known such areas are the reticular activating system, and the vestibular system (Ornitz, 1969, 1970, 1974, Ornitz and Ritvo, 1968a, 1968b).

This theoretical position led to a number of hypotheses which could be tested experimentally, utilizing a variety of observational and neurophysiologic techniques. We next proceeded to design such experiments to test the validity of our hypotheses.

The results of this research are described in subsequent chapters of this book. Based on this evidence and the research of many others, I feel we can say with certainty that autism is a *physical disease of the brain*. Whether the specific etiologic agent is known to be associated with the "autism"—as can be demonstrated in certain cases of PKU and CNS Rubella Syndrome—or whether it is unknown, these patients share a neuropathophysiologic process which interferes with developmental rate, and the modulation or integration of sensory input within the brain. These malfunctions then lead to other symptoms typical of the disorder—disturbances of motility, disturbances of language, and disturbances of personality development expressed by psychosis and the inability to relate to others.

Other research has proven that autism has been identified by trained diagnosticians in various countries and cultures. Social-class studies have also indicated that autism occurs in children whose parents come from all social classes and races within defined geographical areas.

Follow-up studies are just beginning to appear in the medical literature. They will eventually answer the question as to the natural history of the disease. Since we do not know the specific cause, nor neuroanatomical or neurobiochemical pathology involved, specific etiologically-based therapy is unavailable. However, symptomatic treatment has been developed for autistic children. Many children formerly thought to be retarded and uneducable, are now making giant strides towards realizing their potentials and adapting to society despite their handicap. Special educational approaches, operant conditioning-based programs, and psycho-therapeutic support can now be applied in specific cases where indicated. Each of these therapeutic modalities will be reviewed in subsequent chapters. Research is expanding in these areas at an exponential rate. In the years ahead, we hope to have identified the specific etiologic factors which lead to the disease autism. We will then be able to design rational therapeutic interventions to prevent the occurrence of the disease itself or to erase or mitigate its symptoms. This prospect supplies continued energy to those dedicated professionals exploring this frontier.

REFERENCES

Bender, L. (1947). Childhood schizophrenia, clinical study of one hundred schizophrenic children. *American Journal of Orthopsychiatry* 17:40-56.
Bleuler, E. (1950). *Dementia Praecox or the Group of Schizophrenics* Translated by N. Lewis, New York: International Universities Press.
Goldfarb, W. (1961). *Childhood Schizophrenia* Cambridge, Mass.: Harvard University Press.
Kanner, L. (1943). Autistic disturbances of affective contact. *Nervous Child* 2:217-50.
Mahler, M.S. (1952). On child psychosis and schizophrenia, autistic and symbiotic infantile psychosis. *Psychoanalytic Study of the Child* 7:286-305.
Ornitz, E.M. (1969). The disorders of perception common to early infantile autism and schizophrenia. *Comprehensive Psychiatry* 10:259-75.
——— (1970). Vestibular dysfunction in schizophrenia and childhood autism. *Comprehensive Psychiatry* 11:159-73.
——— (1973). Childhood autism: A review of the clinical and experimental literature. *California Medicine* 118:21-47.
——— (1974). The modulation of sensory input and motor output in autistic children. *Journal of Autism and Childhood Schizophrenia* 4:197-216.
——— and Ritvo, E.R. (1968a). Perceptual inconstancy in early infantile autism. *Archives of General Psychiatry* 18:76-98.
——— Ritvo, E.R. (1968b) Neurophysiologic mechanisms underlying perceptual inconstancy in autistic and schizophrenic children. *Archives of General Psychiatry* 19:22-27.
Rank, Beata. (1949). Adaptation of the psychoanalytic technique for the treatment of young children with atypical development. *American Journal of Orthopsychiatry* 19:130-139.

CHAPTER TWO

Medical Assessment[1]

EDWARD M. ORNITZ
EDWARD R. RITVO

Of all the syndromes now classified as developmental disabilities, "autism" is one of the most difficult to understand. Wide differences in severity, periodic changes of the symptoms (Ornitz and Ritvo, 1968), confusing and inconsistent nosology, and the lack of specific physical signs make diagnosis a difficult procedure. The behavior of autistic children is bewildering to parents, and thus it is often difficult to obtain an adequate developmental history. Unless the physician suspects autism and knows which symptoms and signs to elicit, the diagnostic process may be thwarted from the outset. Too often parents are told, "Let's wait. He is just slow in developing and will probably catch up soon."

Initial parental concern arises at different ages. A particularly observant mother may comment to her pediatrician that her two-month-old reacts very differently than her other children did. At the other extreme are parents who do not seek medical attention until their child is six or seven. The majority of patients are usually first evaluated when two to three years old. The most frequent initial complaint is that of a delay in speech development, earlier and more subtle symptoms having been overlooked or denied. Thus, autism must always be included in the differential diagnosis when evaluating any child with a developmental disability.

DIAGNOSTIC TERMINOLOGY

The syndrome was first identified by Kanner (1943) when he described a group of children as having "autistic disturbances of affective contact." In

---

[1]Parts of this chapter will be published separately in the *American Journal of Psychiatry*, ©1976, the American Psychiatric Association.

1944, he adopted the term "early infantile autism," and drew attention to the fact that symptoms occurred in early infancy (Kanner, 1944). The term "autism" and its synonyms—childhood autism, primary autism, infantile autism, and autistic child—have become the most commonly accepted ways of referring to this condition.

"Atypical development" and "atypical ego development" have been used by psychoanalytically oriented investigators to describe similar patients. The term "symbiotic psychosis" has also been used to describe children who are similar in many ways, but who may relate differently (Reiser, 1963; Mahler, 1965). At times, these patients cling tenaciously to their parents. Since this clinging behavior can alternate with emotional unresponsiveness, this term does not necessarily describe an independent disorder.

The labels "pseudo-retarded" and "pseudo-defective" have been used to emphasize the differences between *typical* or *simple* mental retardation and autism (Bender, 1956). Many recent studies have demonstrated that the large majority of autistic children have intellectual and cognitive delays. Thus, these terms are not sufficiently specific to be clinically useful (Lockyer and Rutter, 1969). The more general and less well-defined terms infantile psychosis, childhood psychosis, and early onset psychosis, are also used extensively (Kolvin, 1971; Rutter, 1967; Creak, 1963). They emphasize psychological damage to the developing personality of the child and, depending on the investigator, may or may not overlap with autism.

Finally, a term which is also widely used for similar patients is "childhood schizophrenia" (Bender, 1956; DeMyer et al., 1971; Fish et al., 1968). Semantic confusion and controversy exist with regard to the use of this label. Certain investigators view autism as phenomenologically quite distinct from adult forms of schizophrenia (Kolvin, 1971; Wing, 1966). Others postulate a continuum of disease process from childhood to adult forms (Bender, 1956, 1971; Havelkova, 1968; Ornitz, 1969, 1970). The distinctions and similarities between patients labeled autistic and schizophrenic will be discussed later. Articles referring to "childhood schizophrenia" and "schizophrenic children" will be cited in this review if the clinical features of the patients conform to those described in the following section.

CLINICAL FEATURES OF THE AUTISTIC SYNDROME

Age of Onset

Autism is most likely present at birth. Since the first symptoms may not be recognized or recalled by parents, two courses of the illness have been reported. In the first, deviant behavior was noted shortly after birth even though mothers may not be able to specify the subtle nature of their infants' "strange behavior." The infants may cry infrequently, not respond to companionship nor apparently need stimulation. They become limp or rigid when held, often being described as "very good babies" who never fuss. On the other hand, they may be intensely irritable and overreactive to any form of stimulation, and may have flaccid muscle tone (Harper and Williams, 1975).

In the second course of development, the parents report relatively normal development up to eighteen to twenty-four months, at which time they first note symptoms. The obvious appearance of symptoms invariably occurs before thirty months of age (Kolvin et al., 1971). In our experience, the subsequent clinical course is the same regardless of the age at which symptoms are first reported. A recent report of better prognosis when the apparent onset is delayed (Harper and Williams, 1975) suggests that symptoms are not recognized at birth in milder forms of the illness.

Very careful history taking usually elicits the fact that subtle signs did indeed occur during the first year of life. These may be forgotten, overlooked or denied due to parental anxiety or unfamiliarity with normal development.

The Behavioral Characteristics of Autism

The behavioral symptoms of autism can be separated into five subclusters. These include: (1) disturbances of perception, (2) disturbances of developmental rate, (3) disturbances of relating, (4) disturbances of speech and language, and (5) disturbances of motility.

Disturbances of Perception

Disturbances of perception are most likely due to an underlying neuropathophysiological process which is common to all autistic patients (Ornitz and Ritvo, 1968). It results in faulty modulation of external sensory input (Ornitz, 1969; Bergman and Escalona, 1949), distortion of the normal hierarchy of receptor preferences (Goldfarb, 1956), and an impaired ability to use internal sensory input to make discriminations in the absence of feedback from motor responses (Hermelin and O'Connor, 1970).

The failure of adequate modulation of sensory input constitutes a striking and unique aspect of autism (Goldfarb, 1963; Ornitz, 1971). Behaviorally it appears as hypo- or hyperresponsive states which alternate in the same child.

When hyporeactivity to auditory stimuli occurs, the patient does not react to either verbal commands or sounds. There may be no startle response to very loud sudden noises and delayed attending to those (personal observation) and other sounds (Condon, 1975). Visually, no reaction may be noted to new persons or objects in the environment and the patient may walk into objects as if he did not see them. A similar lack of response to tactile and painful stimuli frequently occurs during the first two years of life: objects placed in the hand fall away; painful stimuli such as bruises, cuts or injections may evoke no reaction.

Contrasting starkly to such hypo-reactivity are decidedly exaggerated reactions to the same stimuli. When in this state, patients show heightened *awareness* and heightened *sensitivity* to stimuli. They may also seek out stimulation. Behaviors such as making sounds by scratching surfaces while putting the ears close to listen, being distracted by background stimuli of marginal intensity, rubbing, banging or flicking at the ears, and teeth-grinding are all activities which induce auditory input. Visually, they may regard their hand and finger movements and scrutinize fine details or surfaces and have brief episodes of intense staring. They may induce tactile input by rubbing surfaces of furniture or fabrics. Many behaviors suggest they are actively inducing vestibular and proprioceptive stimulation. For example, whirling, rocking, and head-rolling are common. Repetitive hand-flapping also may provide proprioceptive input.

One can often observe distress induced by routine stimuli in all sensory modalities. When in such a state a child may become severely agitated by a siren, a vacuum cleaner, or a barking dog. He may cup his hands over his ears in an attempt to shut out such intense sounds (Goldfarb, 1963; Bergman and Escalona, 1949). Sudden changes in illumination or confrontation with an unexpected object may elicit similar fearful reactions. In the tactile mode, a severe intolerance for certain fabrics can suddenly appear. Also the introduction of rough-textured table foods may evoke distress. The child who whirls himself may at other times show a pronounced aversion to vestibular stimulation induced by rough-house play, riding in a car or in an elevator.

Autistic patients have been described as showing a preference for "proximal receptors" (touch, smell and taste) rather than "distal receptors" (auditory and visual) (Schopler, 1965). They also have been shown to have fewer eye movements and spend less time regarding visual displays than do non-autistics (O'Connor, 1971). Many who have normal or even advanced form perception (Ritvo and Provence, 1953) make poor use of visual discrimination when learning (Ottinger et al., 1965). It has been observed that they are more dependent than normals on feedback from their motor responses to make sense out of perceptions (Hermelin and O'Connor, 1970).

Disturbances of Development Rate

Autistic children show deviations from the normal sequential motor, language and social milestones (Fish, 1959, 1960). In particular, the even course of normal development is disrupted. For example, an autistic child may sit without support precociously but be delayed before he will pull to a stand. Sequences of spurts and plateaus are characteristic as are "special abilities" of some otherwise very retarded autistic children. These observations can be used to distinguish them from other types of severe retardation.

Disturbances of Relating

Behaviors which indicate disturbances of relating are due to arrests or developmental delays in personality formation. Behaviors indicative of such ego pathology include poor or deviant eye contact (McConnell, 1967), delayed or absent social smile, delayed or absent anticipatory response to being picked up, apparent aversion to physical contact, a tendency to react to only a part of another person, disinterest in playing games with others, and delayed, absent, or overreactive stranger anxiety. Disturbances in relating may be subtle and intermittent. Experiments conducted under well-controlled laboratory conditions suggest that disturbed relatedness is not fundamental to autism but is secondary to disturbances of perception (Churchill, 1972; Reichler and Schopler, 1971). Disturbed relatedness to objects is expressed by flicking, twirling and spinning toys, rather than using them in an apperceptive manner. This observation led Kanner (1943) and others to conclude that these children wanted "to maintain sameness in their environment" (Eisenberg and Kanner, 1956). We believe that they are upset by observing different perceptual sets and hence, try to maintain "sameness." With increasing age, disturbances of relatedness lead to rigidity and inflexibility in the use of play material (Frith, 1972), inability to form peer relationships, and intermittent responsiveness to parents.

Disturbances of Speech and Language

Speech and language development may be totally delayed (muteness) or fixations can occur along the normal course of development (Shapiro et al., 1972; Griffith and Ritvo, 1967). Echolalia is a common feature and is usually accompanied by misuse or reversal of pronouns. Echoing of feelings as well as words occurs. When functional speech develops, it is usually atonal and arrhythmic, lacking inflection and failing to convey subtle emotion. The atonal and poor affective quality of speech in young autistic children usually persists into adulthood even in those few cases in whom communicative language develops (Fish, 1960; Churchill, 1972).

Disturbances of Motility

The strange and bizarre appearance of many autistic children is due to their peculiar mannerisms and motility patterns. These may be complex, repeated serially (stereotypies), and do not appear to be involuntary movements typical of seizure patterns. Motility disturbances may appear intermittently in some autistic children while they may be continuously present in others (Sorosky et al., 1968).

The most typical motility disturbances involves the hands and arms. The hands usually are moved within the visual fields. Laboratory studies have demonstrated that the motility disturbance of the hands (hand-flapping and oscillating) occurs at the same frequency over time and that groups of patients flap at the same rate (Ritvo et al., 1968). Furthermore, these behaviors are relatively unaffected by environmental factors such as the presence of other persons or toys (Ornitz et al., 1970). These studies have led us to the conclusion that the motility disturbances can best be understood as expressive of a central nervous system dysfunction. The possible significance of the relationship between motility and perceptual disturbances to a neuropathophysiologic dysfunction in autism has been explored (Ornitz et al., 1974). Toe-walking is frequently observed intermittently while running, but may also be continuous.

Motility disturbances of the trunk or the body include staccato lunging and darting movements, body-rocking and swaying, and head-rolling or head-banging. They are neither constant nor have the persistent, irritable quality typical of children labeled "hyperactive." In fact, the motility patterns of autistics are usually interrupted by episodes of immobility and posturing. For example, patients less than three years of age may be observed to arch the back and hyperextend the neck for several seconds.

When examining a patient, we have them look at a spinning top. This frequently elicits motility disturbances such as hand-flapping, posturing and twirling.

A detailed behavioral description of symptoms is important in order to avoid mis-diagnosis. Non-specific descriptions such as "the child shows bizarre behaviors" are insufficient. To enhance the accuracy of diagnosis, our clinical experience indicates that at least three separate diagnostic examinations at weekly intervals should be conducted by the physician. Parental descriptions of the child, while necessary, are clearly not sufficient to establish the diagnosis.

DIFFERENTIAL DIAGNOSIS

For clinical and research purposes, we reserve the diagnosis "autism" for patients who clearly show, prior to thirty-six months of age, irregularities of development and disturbances of the modulation of sensory input, relatedness and language as described in the previous section. The presence of these symptoms is necessary and sufficient to establish the diagnosis. Motility disturbances, while frequently present, are not necessary to establish the diagnosis. Seventy-six percent of a group of seventy-two autistic patients we reviewed had a history of hand-flapping (unpublished data).

When reviewing the differential diagnosis, one must consider specific diseases which are known to occur in association with autism. These include, for example, phenylketonuria, congenital rubella, other specific organic brain syndromes, mental retardation, and seizure disorders. Also, one must differentiate diseases with overlapping symptomotology. These include environmental deprivation (maternal deprivation and hospitalism), anaclitic depression, developmental aphasia, and sensory deficits. Also, in this latter category are syndromes which have been described in the research literature under the rubrics of disintegrative psychosis (Rutter, 1972), "late onset" psychosis (Kolvin et al., 1971), acquired autism (Rendle-Short, 1971) and childhood schizophrenia, non-organic type (Goldfarb, 1963).

In Table I, we have shown possible etiologic and phenomenologic inter-relationships among the clinically and behaviorally defined syndromes of autism, primary cognitive and intellectual retardation and psychologically induced psychosis (severe ego pathology). This model is based on the hypothesis that the syndrome of autism results from CNS pathology of a specific type. This neuropathophysiology may occur on an idiopathic basis or in conjunction with specific diseases of known etiology which affect the CNS. The same neuropathophysiologic process underlying autism may also produce cognitive and intellectual retardation and disrupt ego development producing secondary psychosis. According to this model, primary ego pathology (psychosis) can produce cognitive and intellectual retardation and vice versa, but neither of these alone can "cause" autism.

Idiopathic CNS Dysfunction

This is the category in which most young autistic children have to be placed. However, as an individual patient grows older, there is an increasing likelihood that evidence of specific CNS pathology will become

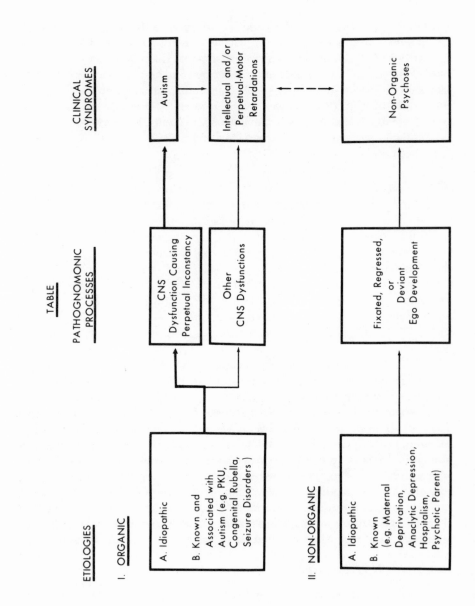

TABLE

ETIOLOGIES   PATHOGNOMONIC PROCESSES   CLINICAL SYNDROMES

I. ORGANIC

A. Idiopathic

B. Known and Associated with Autism (e.g. PKU, Congenital Rubella, Seizure Disorders)

CNS Dysfunction Causing Perpetual Inconstancy

Other CNS Dysfunctions

Autism

Intellectual and/or Perpetual-Motor Retardations

II. NON-ORGANIC

A. Idiopathic

B. Known (e.g. Maternal Deprivation, Anaclytic Depression, Hospitalism, Psychotic Parent)

Fixated, Regressed, or Deviant Ego Development

Non-Organic Psychoses

manifest by the onset of specific signs or symptoms (e.g., seizures), and the designation "idiopathic" revised.

Major Sensory Deficits

Specific sense organ pathology can precipitate severe emotional reactions and developmental arrests in infants and young children. This combination of sensory deficits and secondary ego disturbances may result in a clinical picture which can be confused with autism. Therefore, since disturbances of language are part of the syndrome of autism, specific otologic and audiologic examinations should be carried out (See Chapter 5). Complete or partial blindness is often accompanied by "blindisms" (Keeler, 1958). These mannerisms include gesturing with the arms and hands. They do not have the repetitive stereotyped characteristics of hand-flapping as seen in autism and they occur in response to environmental stimuli. Furthermore, blind children usually develop interest in their environment and do not have disturbances of relating typical of autism. When their visual deficit is recognized and if other CNS pathology does not interfere, they can develop quite normally. Interestingly, autism has been reported in association with retrolental fibroplasia but not with other types of visual impairment. Since retrolental fibroplasia is associated with generalized brain damage, autism in these cases probably results from the CNS impairment, and not from the visual deficit per se.

Developmental Aphasia

In both developmental aphasia (Wing, 1966) and autism, abnormal responses to sounds, delay in the acquisition of language, and difficulties in articulation occur (Churchill, 1972). Due to their difficulties with expressive and/or receptive language, aphasics may secondarily develop disturbances of relating and social responsiveness. They do not, however, manifest perceptual disturbances (sensory hyper- and hyporeactivity) characteristic of autistics. They can relate by non-verbal gestures and expressions, are sensitive to gestures and expressions of others, and can learn to point toward desired objects (Rutter et al., 1971). When they do acquire speech, it does not show the lack of "communicative intent and emotion" and delayed echolalia (Griffith and Ritvo, 1967) characteristic of autism. Thus, the language disability of speaking autistic children is more severe and more deviant than that of aphasic children (Bartak et al., 1975).

Cognitive and Intellectual Arrests and Delays

Clinical experience with autistics and recent follow-up studies demonstrate that low scores on developmental tests or reports of "untestability" during the early years are associated with retarded intellectual functioning later in life (Lockyer and Rutter, 1969). The majority of autistics cannot perform many IQ test items (See Chapter 3). The notion that autistics have a primary affective deficiency which interferes with expression of their assumed normal or superior intellectual and cognitive potentials has given way to the recognition that their intellectual deficiencies are every bit as real as in patients with "primary retardation." Accumulating clinical experience indicates that two-thirds to three-fourths of all autistic patients will perform throughout life at retarded levels (Rutter, 1970). Thus, "mental retardation" and autism can clearly co-exist.

Specific Organic Brain Syndromes

Some children with autism also have evidence of specific organic brain syndromes (Eaton and Menolascino, 1967). Attempts to link autism with Schilder's Disease and Heller's Syndrome have not been successful since the natural history and clinical course of these degenerative diseases is different. Autism has been reported *in association with* prenatal and perinatal complications, neonatal conditions associated with brain damage (e.g., retrolental fibroplasia), infantile spasms, cerebral lipidosis, metabolic diseases (e.g., phenylketonuria), Addison's Disease, celiac disease, and infectious diseases (e.g., congenital rubella) (Chess, 1971; Schain and Yannet, 1960). A series of patients with rubella has been studied extensively and 8 percent to 10 percent had specific symptoms indicative of autism. Contrari-wise, a number of patients first diagnosed autistic have been shown to have had congenital rubella.

Seizure Disorders

Alterations in consciousness and behaviors due to epileptic seizures must be distinguished from autism, particularly since momentary posturing and bursts of hand-flapping, frequently seen in the latter, may be confusing. Autism and seizures frequently co-exist (Creek, 1963; Kolvin et al., 1971) and one investigation has demonstrated that two electroencephalograms with sleep tracings are required to evaluate this possibility (Ritvo et al., 1970). Seizure disorders are more likely to become clinically manifest in autistic children as they become older. Twenty-five percent of a well-followed series of autistics first developed seizures between thirteen and nineteen years of age. Both grand mal and psychomotor seizures were noted to have developed. Most of these children had had normal EEGs and neurologic examinations earlier in life (Rutter et al., 1971).

Maternal Deprivation

It has been suggested that deficient human stimulation, e.g., "maternal deprivation," may cause autism (Spitz, 1945). The immediate and long-term sequelae of environmental deprivation in infants raised in institutions (Provence and Lipton, 1962) and at home have been well documented. While environmental deprivation has been shown to induce serious developmental disturbances, it does not produce the syndrome of autism. Deprived patients characteristically exhibit a uniform delay in the acquisition of motor skills, speech, and the adaptive use of toys. In contrast, autistics show uneven motor and speech development characterized by spurts and lags. Deprived infants may show unusual bursts of motor activity such as athetoid-type movements of the hands. However, these are not like the repetitive hand-flapping or other motility disturbances seen in autistics. Also, the whirling, toe-walking, darting and lunging movements of autistics have not been described in deprived patients. They do, however, engage in total body-rocking and hand-posturing. These are easy to interrupt or totally eliminate in contrast to the more intractable motility disturbances in autistics. They may also show abnormal relating and adapt poorly to being held. They may flick at toys, drop them, or fail to develop an interest in them. Autistics in contrast, usually use toys in peculiar ways such as spinning, feeling, or sighting along them. Deprived patients usually fail to seek out adults when given the opportunity. Unlike autistic children who do not appear to value eye contact, they may engage in intense visual regarding of adults. While autistic patients rarely develop active interest in playing games with others, deprived children participate although such interest develops later than in normals. Similarly, language development may be delayed, but they may catch up when deprivation is relieved. Once speech has been acquired, it does not have the atonal, arrhythmic, hollow sounding quality of autistic speech. Echolalia and misuse of pronouns has not been reported in deprived children nor have perceptual disturbances indicative of faulty modulation of sensory input. While autistics engage in tactile exploration, deprived patients show diminished tendencies to touch themselves or to mouth objects.

A difficult differential diagnostic problem occurs if a mother has had a post-partum depression or other serious emotional disorder during her child's first year. If an adequate surrogate was not provided, the child may have developed an environmental deprivation syndrome. On the other hand, the ill mother might have given birth to an autistic whose inability to relate and respond positively aggravated pre-existing disturbances in the mother.

Anaclitic Depression

Anaclitic depression develops after the sixth month when there is an interruption of a previously adequate maternal-infant relationship (Spitz, 1946). The interruption may be due to death, psychological withdrawal, or temporary maternal absence. Such infants become weepy, demanding and clinging. If the mothering person does not return within a few weeks, this stage may presage psychomotor retardation, language delay, weight loss and persistent crying. After two or three months these are replaced by quiet whimpering, facial rigidity, and finally, lethargy and apathy. Perceptual symptoms, developmental spurts and lags, language, and motility disturbances characteristic of autism are not seen in anaclitic depression. Their failure to relate to adults is characterized by apathy and withdrawal.

Relationship of Childhood Schizophrenia to Autism

The diagnosis of childhood schizophrenia has been applied to a wide spectrum of patients. These range from autistics (as defined in this chapter) to children without severe developmental or intellectual disabilities but who have psychotic level ego functions. Clinical subtypes have been defined by Bender (1956, 1969, 1971), (pseudo-retarded or autistic, pseudo-neurotic, pseudo-psychopathic), Fish (1959), (according to language and intellectual development), and Goldfarb (1961) (organic, non-organic). Their use of the term implies that there is a continuum of schizophrenic illness from the prenatal period (maturational lag at the embryonic level re: Bender) to adulthood with different ages of onset (autism, onset prior to three years; childhood schizophrenia, onset three years to adolescence; adult schizophrenia, onset adolescence or later).

In contrast, Rutter (1972) has suggested that the term childhood schizophrenia is confounding and should be abandoned. In his view, any patient, regardless of age, whose clinical picture fits the classic description of schizophrenia should be so labeled. He considers autism a separate disease which is first manifested during the first three years of life. Once established, it should then remain the primary diagnosis regardless of increasing age and change in symptoms. He also identifies a separate group of children in whom psychotic ego development occurs between the ages of three and five after an apparently normal course of development and labels these rare cases "disintegrative psychosis."

In support of the position that a continuum of one disease process including autism and childhood schizophrenia exists are clinical reports that when some "typically autistic" preschoolers reach ages eight to twelve, their clinical picture changes to fit criteria of childhood schizophrenia (Brown and Reiser, 1963). Also, there are reports of typically autistic children who, as adults, clinically exhibit schizophrenia (Bender, 1969) and some adult schizophrenics whose histories indicate they were typically autistic when preschoolers (Darr and Worden, 1951).

We have been able to observe several such cases. One boy, at four years of age, clearly met our criteria for autism (developmental delays and disturbances in the modulation of perception, relatedness, language and motility). He was seen again at age nine and asked why he rocked and put his hands up before his face. He said, "The floor is coming up at me" and "The walls are moving in on me." Another bright verbal boy had a similarly documented early history of autism. At age nine, when asked why he flapped his hands before his face he said, "I am pushing the thoughts back in my mouth." When young, his motility disturbances included hand-flapping and he was obviously trying to consciously explain, albeit on a psychotic level, the persistence of this symptom.

In support of the alternative hypothesis, namely that autism and childhood schizophrenia are distinct syndromes and should be carefully separated, Rutter (1972) details the following differences: (a) familial factors (none in autism, present in schizophrenia), (b) ages of onset, (c) symptomotology, and (d) natural history and course of the disease.

For heuristic purposes, we are exploring theoretically, and in the laboratory, possible neuropathophysiological processes which may produce the symptoms common to both schizophrenia and childhood autism, whether they are the same syndrome or not (Ornitz, 1969, 1970). It is encumbent upon each physician to understand both the descriptive parameters of the two terms and that these nosological differences have more than just semantic meaning. Indeed, they have marked implications for total patient management and the application of specific supportive treatments. For example, developmentally retarded autistic patients with severe language disturbances as described in this review, respond best to a combination of behavior therapy and special education (Bartak and Rutter, 1973). On the other hand, the thought and affectual disorders typical of childhood schizophrenia respond best to a combination of psychotropic medication, psychotherapy, and milieu therapy (Goldfarb et al., 1969).

CONCLUDING REMARKS

Ontogeny recapitulates phylogeny in the history of diseases as well as man. Thus, since its conception a scant thirty years ago, autism has undergone many vicissitudes. It was conceived as an adjective (autistic disturbances of affective contact), relegated to symptom status (mental retardation with "autistic features"), made a step-child of a step-child (childhood schizophrenia, autistic type), and finally merged as a noun (the syndrome "autism").

In this chapter we have tried to survey those studies which were based upon serious scientific efforts and avoided those which simply expressed opinions. The current state of our medical art leads us to these conclusions: (1) Autism is a clinically and behaviorally defined specific syndrome. (2) It is manifested at birth or shortly thereafter and remains throughout the lifetime of the patient. (3) Its symptoms are expressive of an underlying neuropathophysiologic process which affects developmental rate, the modulation of perception (sensorimotor integration), language, cognitive and intellectual development, and the ability to relate. (4) No known factors in the psychological environment of a child can cause autism. (5) To establish the diagnosis patients must demonstrate, before the ages of thirty-six months, specific disturbances of developmental rate, perception, relatedness and language. Many, but not all, patients demonstrate typical motility disturbances. (6) Autism occurs on an idiopathic basis or in conjunction with other diseases which affect the CNS. (7) It afflicts children in all parts of the world, of all racial and ethnic backgrounds, and is found in families with the normally expected distributions of intelligence, social class, and personality factors. (8) No etiologically-based rational treatment is available which alters the course of the disease. (9) Complete medical and neurological evaluations are essential to establish the diagnosis and should be repeated at yearly intervals. Particular attention should be paid to the likelihood that seizure disorders may appear in individual patients as they grow older. (10) Supportive or symptomatic therapeutic measures (behavior therapy, special education and residential treatment) are helpful in the majority of cases. These should be monitored by a physician in charge and administrated by specialists and parents trained in these modalities. Periodic re-evaluations and updating of supportive therapeutic programs are necessary to keep abreast of clinical changes which can be expected to occur in the majority of cases. (11) The long-term prognosis, unfortunately, is guarded. Approximately two-thirds of all patients manifest intellectual and cognitive deficits severe enough so that they remain classified as retarded throughout their lives. (12) Further basic research into the neuropathophysiological process underlying the syndrome is needed if we are to develop a rational treatment program, the ultimate goal of our efforts.

REFERENCES

Bartak, L. and Rutter, M. (1973). Special educational treatment of autistic children: a comparative study: I. Design of study and characteristics of units. *J. Child Psychol. Psychiat.* 14:161-179.

Bartak, L., Rutter, M., Cox, A. (1975). A comparative study of infantile autism and specific developmental receptive language disorder: I. The children. *Brit. J. Psychiat.* 126:127-145.

Bender, L. (1956). Schizophrenia in childhood—its recognition, description and treatment. *Am. J. Orthopsychiat* 26:499-506.

—— (1969). A longitudinal study of schizophrenic children with autism. *Hosp. Community Psychiatry.* 20:230-237.

—— (1971). Alpha and omega of childhood schizophrenia. *J. Autism Child. Schizo.* 1:115-118.

Bergman, P. and Escalona, S.K. (1949). Unusual sensitivities in very young children. *Psychoanal. Study Child.* 3,4:333-353.

Brown, J.L. and Reiser, D.E. (1963). Follow-up study of preschool children of atypical development (infantile psychosis)—later personality patterns in adaptation to maturational stress. *Am. J. Orthopsychiat.* 33:336-338.

Chess. S. (1971). Autism in children with congenital rubella. *J. Autism Child. Schizo.* 1:33-47.

Churchill, D.W. (1972a). The relation of infantile autism and early childhood schizophrenia to developmental language disorders of childhood. *J. Autism Child. Schizo.* 2:182-197.

—— (1972b). Looking and approach behavior of psychotic and normal children as a function of adult attention or preoccupation. *Compr. Psychiat.* 13:171-177.

Condon, W.S. (1975). Multiple response to sound in dysfunctional children. *J. Autism. Child. Schizo.* 5:37-56.

Creak, E.M. (1963). Childhood psychosis. *Br. J. Psychiat.* 109:84-89.

Darr, G.C. and Worden, F.G. (1951). Case report twenty-eight years after an infantile autistic disorder. *Am. J. Orthopsychiat.* 21:559-570.

DeMyer, M.K., Churchill, K.W., Pontius, W. and Gilkey, K.M. (1971). A comparison of five diagnostic systems for childhood schizophrenia and infantile autism. *J. Autism Child. Schizo.* 1:175-189.

Eaton, L. and Menolascino, F.J. (1967). Psychotic reactions of childhood—a follow-up study. *Am. J. Orthopsychiat.* 37:521-529.

Eisenberg, L. and Kanner, L. (1956). Early infantile autism. 1943-1955. *Am. J. Orthopsychiat.* 26:556-566.

Fish, B. (1959). Longitudinal observations of biological deviations in a schizophrenic infant. *Am. J. Psychiat.* 116:25-31.

—— (1960). Involvement of the central nervous system in infants with schizophrenia. *Arch. Neurol.* 2:115-121.

Fish, B., Shapiro, T., Campbell, M. and Wile, R. (1968). A classification of schizophrenic children under five years. *Am. J. Psychiat.* 124:109-117.

Frith, U. (1975). Cognitive mechanisms in autism—Experiments with color and tone sequence production. *J. Autism Child. Schizo.* 2:160-173.

Goldfarb, W. (1956). Receptor preferences in schizophrenic children. *AMA Arch. Neurol. Psychiat.* 76:643-652.

—— (1963). Self-awareness in schizophrenic children. *Arch. Gen. Psychiat.* 8:47-60.

Goldfarb, W., Mintz, I., and Strook, K.W. (1969). *A Time to Heal—Corrective Socialization—A Treatment Approach to Childhood Schizophrenia.* New York: International Universities Press, Inc., 1969.

Griffith, R.J. and Ritvo, E.R. (1967). Echolalia: Concerning the dynamics of the syndrome. *J. Am. Academy of Child Psychiatry.* 6:184-193.

Harper, J. and Williams, S. (1975). Age and type of onset as critical variables in early infantile autism. *J. Autism Child. Schizo.* 5:25-36.

Havelkova, M. (1968). Follow-up study of 71 children diagnosed as psychotic in preschool age. *Am. J. Orthopsychiat.* 38:846-857.

Hermelin, B. and O'Connor, N. (1970). *Psychological experiments with autistic children.* Oxford, Pergamon Press.

Kanner, L. (1943). Autistic disturbances of affective contact. *Nerv. Child.* 2:217-250.

——— (1944). Early infantile autism. *J. Pediatr.* 25:211-217.

Keeler, W.R. (1958). Autistic patterns and defective communication in blind children with retrolental fibroplasia. In Hoch, P.H. and Zubin, J. eds, *Psychopathology of Communication* New York: Grune and Stratton.

Kolvin, I. (1971). Psychoses in childhood—a comparative study. In Rutter, M. ed, *Infantile Autism—Concepts, Characteristics and Treatment,* London: Churchill.

——— et al. Six studies in the childhood psychosis. *Br. J. Psychiat.* 118:381-419, 1971.

Lockyer, L., and Rutter, M. (1969). A five- to fifteen-year follow-up study of infantile psychosis—III. Psychological aspects. *Br. J. Psychiat.* 115:865-882.

Mahler, M.S. (1965). On early infantile psychosis. The symbiotic and autistic syndromes. *J. Am. Acad. Child Psychiat.* 4:554-568.

McConnell, O.L. (1967). Control of eye contact in an autistic child. *J. Child. Psychiat.* 8:249-255.

O'Connor, N. (1971). Visual perception in autistic children. In Rutter, M. (ed.): *Infantile Autism: Concepts, Characteristics and Treatment.* London:Churchill.

Ornitz, E.M., and Ritvo, E.R. (1968). Perceptual inconstancy in early infantile autism. *Arch. Gen. Psychiat.* 18:76-98.

Ornitz, E.M. (1969). Disorders of perception common to early infantile autism and schizophrenia. *Compr. Psychiat.* 10:259-274.

——— (1970). Vestibular dysfunction in schizophrenia and childhood autism. *Compr. Psychiat.* 11:159-173.

——— (1971). Childhood autism—A disorder of sensorimotor integration. In Rutter, M. ed, *Infantile Autism: Concepts, Characteristics and Treatment.* London: Churchill.

Ornitz, E.M., Brown, M.D., Sorosky, A.D., Ritvo, E.R., and Dietrich, L. (1970). Environmental modification of autistic behavior. *Arch. Gen. Psychiat.* 22:560-565.

Ornitz, E.M., Forsythe, A.B., and de la Pena, A. (1973). The effect of vestibular and auditory stimulation on the REMs of REM sleep in autistic children. *Arch. Gen. Psychiat.* 29:786-791.

Ottinger, D.R., Sweeney, N., and Loew, L.H. (1965). Visual discrimination learning in schizophrenic and normal children. *J. Clin. Psychol.* 21:251-253.

Provence, S. and Lipton, R.D. (1962). *Infants in Institutions.* New York: International University Press.

Reichler, R.J., and Schopler, E. (1971). Observations on the nature of human relatedness. *J. Autism. Child Schizo.* 1:283-296.

Reiser, D.E. (1963). Psychosis of infancy and early childhood as manifested by children with atypical development. *N. Engl. J. Med.* 269:790-798, 844-850.

Rendle-Short, J. (1971). A paedatrician's approach to autism. In M. Rutter ed., *Infantile autism: Concepts, characteristics and treatment.* London: Churchill.

Ritvo, E.R., Ornitz, E.M., and LaFranchi, S. (1968). Frequency of repetitive behaviors in early infantile autism and its variants. *Arch. Gen. Psychiat.* 19:341-347.

———, Ornitz, E.M., Walter, R.D. and Hanley, J., (1970). Correlation of psychiatric diagnoses and EEG findings: A double-blind study of 184 hospitalized children. *Amer. J. Psychiat.* 126:7.

Ritvo, S. and Provence, S. (1953). Form perception and imitation in some autistic children: Diagnostic findings and their contextual interpretation. *Psychoanal. Study Child.* 8:155-161.

Rutter, M. (1967). Psychotic disorders in early childhood. In Coppen A.J., Walk, A. eds., *Recent Developments in Schizophrenia—A symposium*. London: RMPA.

——— (1970). Autistic children—Infancy to adulthood. *Semin. Psychiat.* 2:435-450.

———(1971). Childhood schizophrenia reconsidered. *J. Autism and Child Schizo.* 2,4:315-337.

———, Bartak, L. and Newman, S. (1970). Autism—A central disorder of cognition and Language? In Rutter M. ed., *Infantile Autism: Concepts, Characteristics and Treatment*. London: Churchill.

Schain, R.J., and Yannet, H. (1960). Infantile autism. *J. Pediatr.* 57:560-567.

Schopler, E. (1965). Early infantile autism and receptor processes. *Arch. Gen. Psychiat.* 13:327-335.

Shapiro, T., Fish, B., and Ginsberg, G.L. (1972). The speech of a schizophrenic child from two to six. *Am. J. Psychiat.* 128:92-98.

Sorosky, A.D., Ornitz, E.M., Brown, M.B., and Ritvo, E.R. (1968). Systematic observations of autistic behavior. *Arch. Gen. Psychiat.* 18:439-449.

Spitz, R.A. (1945). Hospitalism—An inquiry into the genesis of psychiatric conditions in early childhood. *Psychoanal. Study Child.* 1:53-74.

——— (1945). Anaclitic depression—An inquiry into the genesis of psychiatric conditions in early childhood—1. *Psychoanal. Study Child.* 2:313-342.

Wing, J.K. (1966). Diagnosis, epidemiology, aetiology. In Wing, J.K. ed., *Early Childhood Autism*. Oxford: Pergamon Press.

PART II

Establishing The Diagnosis

CHAPTER THREE

Cognitive Assessment

B.J. FREEMAN
EDWARD R. RITVO

"Intelligence" and "IQ testing" are two of the most confounding concepts used by psychologists today. There is little agreement, even among experts in the field, as to their basic nature. For example, some argue IQ tests, irrespective of type, measure an innate quality which is stable from birth until death. Others maintain that IQ test scores measure only a sample of behavior on a given test at a given point in time. Despite such differences of opinion, however, it has been found that IQ tests have a definite heuristic and clinical value. This chapter will briefly review first, the development of IQ testing; second, a practical formulation of IQ which we have found clinically useful; third, how the concept of IQ has been applied to autistic persons; and fourth, how the authors utilize IQ tests for their own clinical and research purposes, at UCLA.

THE DEVELOPMENT OF IQ TESTS

IQ testing began in 1902 with the work of Alfred Binet. He had been asked to predict which preschool children would do well in the Paris, France, school system. Based on his observation that the early years of a child are characterized by the rapid growth and maturation of various attributes, traits, and attitudes, Binet hypothesized that these could be measured and used to define a child's "intellectual potential." He classified the process and rate at which these developments occurred. He assumed that they reflected intellectual or adaptive abilities and defined them as the parameters of mental development. He then studied large groups of children

27

of various ages and determined what their average level of performance was at specific chronological ages. This he called the *mental age*. He defined IQ, then, as a ratio of *mental age* to *chronological age*. In order to compare children at different ages, he multiplied IQ scores by 100, thus establishing a standardized score with a mean of 100. Binet's test was restandardized in this country in 1937, and again in 1960, by psychologists at Stanford University (hence, the name Stanford-Binet Test). In summary, as developed by Binet, and later revised by others, the IQ score is a statistically determined value representing the percent deviation of a given child's performance from that of many children of the same age on standardized tests. More specifically, for each item on the test, the percentage of children passing and failing has been computed, and normative curves determined. In the 1937 revision (Terman and Merrill, 1960), statistical adjustments for atypical variabilities of IQ scores at certain age levels were made.

The Stanford-Binet test (as restandardized in 1960) is still in widespread use today in the United States (Rosenberg, 1973). It is important for our purposes to emphasize that scores obtained on this test are highly related to a child's verbal skills. This is because, as previously noted, Binet attempted to develop a test to predict school success among Parisian children. Thus, he focused on verbal skills since they are crucial to a child's school performance.

Another type of IQ test widely used today, was developed by David Wechsler. It is based on a different theoretical framework than Binet's. Wechsler arbitrarily defined "areas of intellectual functioning" and divided them into two broad categories—verbal and performance. He then designed six tests for each of these areas and standardized each by administering them to large numbers of children and adults. After an individual is tested, his verbal and performance IQ scores are determined by adding the six subtest scores in each area. Finally, both the performance and verbal scores are summed to yield a full-scale IQ. Hence, a verbal IQ, a performance IQ, and an overall IQ are obtained.

A third type of IQ test has been developed for assessing infants. For example, the Cattell, the Bayley, and the Gesell all attempt to measure intellectual functioning prior to two years of age. Much controversy has arisen as to what these tests actually assess since they have not shown, on follow-up, to correlate well with a child's subsequent adult IQ scores as measured by the Stanford-Binet or Wechsler tests (Lewis and McGurk, 1973; Rosenberg, 1973). This lack of correlation between an infant's test and his adult test scores leads to at least two obvious interpretations. First, if one assumes that the tests are measuring the same qualities, then it could follow that IQ is not stable, but rather can change with age. On the other hand, if the IQ as measured by these tests is stable, then the assumption is that the tests are measuring different parameters.

A PRACTICAL FORMULATION OF IQ

For practical purposes, a field theory model of intelligence has been adopted. This assumes that an individual's behavior at any point in time is the result of multiple factors, such as genetic, current psychological state, neurological maturation, and specific learning experiences. Genetic transmission of herditary factors most likely set the upper limits of an individual's potential for achieving a score on any given intelligence test, just as hereditary factors set the upper limits on all physiological variables such as organ size, height, etc. General physiological and neurological maturation also set limits as do early learning experiences. Furthermore, we assume that when we obtain an IQ score for an individual on a given test, we are in essence sampling behaviors which he has acquired from past experience. Thus, we have solved by inclusion of all factors the dilemma that exists in the field regarding the basic nature of intelligence.

When focusing our attention on autistic children, we assume that they are as likely to have a normative distribution of hereditary factors as patients with any other disease, or normals. For example, the old notion that children who were born "deaf" were also "dumb" is false. Rather, we now know that infants who are unable to hear have a normal distribution of intellectual endowment factors. However, if their specific handicap—deafness—remains uncorrected, they will be unable to realize their intellectual potential and thus grow up "dumb." With these cases, it has been shown that developing secondary thought processing or language is a necessary, though not sufficient, quality to express intelligence. Support for this hypothesis, that intellectual endowment in autistic patients is normally distributed, comes from our clinical experience and studies which have demonstrated that autistic persons have test scores ranging from the profoundly retarded to normal levels (Ornitz, 1973).

HOW THE CONCEPT OF IQ TESTING HAS BEEN APPLIED TO AUTISTIC PERSONS

We shall now review previous studies of IQ testing of autistic patients. In 1974, DeMeyer et al. reported a study of 115 autistic patients who were then followed up for five years. A variety of IQ tests were used, which makes comparison of scores across patients difficult. In spite of these methodological issues, they noted that 94 percent of their patients had overall IQ's in the retarded range (defined by IQ's less than 68) at the time of initial evaluation, and that IQ's were correlated with overall clinical severity. On follow-up, patients who had had IQ's over 50 showed a greater increase in IQ when treated than did patients who had IQ's less than 50. In the higher IQ groups, performance scores were better predictors than the verbal scores; also, greater gains were noted in performance scores than in verbal scores. This contradicts previous reports that verbal IQ scores are better prognostic indicators of future behavior of autistics (Fish et al., 1968; Rutter et al., 1971). These discrepancies may be due to the fact that the patients were of different ages when initially evaluated. The median age of the patients in the DeMeyer study was 5 years, 4 months. As reviewed by Ornitz (1973), the overall prognosis for children who reached the age of five without communicative speech is very poor. Further support for this observation is provided by Lockyer and Rutter (1969). They noted that the performance IQ scores of young autistic children whom they followed were highly stable and also good predictors of performance in adolescence and in early adult life. From these observations, it would seem that for the IQ test to serve as a prognostic tool for the autistic patient, not only the *initial* IQ but the *age* at which it was determined must be considered.

Certain investigators have recently attempted to develop intelligence tests which are specific for autistic children. For example, Bryson (1970) reported an operant-based test aimed at assessing the ability of autistic patients to make visual, vocal, and fine motor responses to visual and auditory stimuli. Unfortunately, no test has yet been developed which successfully takes into account the specific neuropathophysiological handicaps of autistic children.

HOW WE UTILIZE IQ TESTS FOR CLINICAL AND RESEARCH PURPOSES

We have listed in Table I some of the cognitive and non-cognitive factors which must be assessed in determining the reliability and validity of any test, whether it be for a normal or an autistic. For years it was questioned whether autistics could be evaluated by previously standardized tests. The most obvious problem was that these tests had been developed for children who were cooperative. Autistic patients, unfortunately, for the most part will not sit still, will not follow directions, and in other ways are not readily adaptable to standardized testing situations. One way around this problem was to assume that the autistic child had normal intelligence, but that he could not be tested because of these behavior problems. This assumption was buttressed by the frequent observations that even regressed and obviously retarded autistic children occasionally said something or did something which made the naive tester conclude that they were "bright" or had cognitive skills hidden behind their "autistic walls" (Kanner, 1943; DeMeyer et al., 1974). This led to the notion that autistics may be "idiot savants," or have "islands of intelligence," or "splinter skills."

Table I.
Factors Influencing "IQ" Test Scores

I. Cognitive Factors

   A. Input System

      Visual, Auditory, Olfactory, Kinesthetic, Vestibular

   B. Memory and Integrative

      Rote and Conceptualization

   C. Output System

      Motor and Verbal

II. Non-Cognitive Factors

   A. General Neurophysiological Status

   B. General Medical Status

   C. Social and Cultural Milieu

   D. Socio-Educational Status

   E. Testing Situation

      Skill of Examiner, Tests Used

Our observations of literally hundreds of autistic patients over the past decade lead us to the conclusion that they have a basic neuropathophysiologic disturbance which underlies the syndrome of perceptual inconstancy. This in turn produces clinical symptoms which define the disease state, "autism." This basic neuropathophysiologic process interferes with the development and expression of cognitive abilities which in the normal child define his intelligence. Any testing in autistic children of IQ must account for this neuropathophysiologic process, its primary manifestations of perceptual inconstancy, and its secondary manifestations of autistic symptoms—i.e., disturbances of developmental rate, perception, language and relatedness—(Ornitz, 1973; Ornitz and Ritvo, 1968).

In order to mitigate the influence of these neuropathophysiological factors during psychological evaluations, we introduce behavior therapy techniques into the testing situation. These behavioral techniques are aimed at controlling non-cognitive behavioral factors of a disruptive nature. For example, it is impossible to meaningfully evaluate a patient who is hand-flapping and intermittently attending. However, if you introduce concrete reinforcements, e.g., candy for attention to task and non-hand-flapping, a meaningful evaluation can usually be obtained.

The second modification which we use is to pre-screen a patient for testing. Reviewing the patient's clinical data and a brief interview allow us to determine his general level of functioning. Then a test is selected which is standardized at this level. Thus, the patient's approximate level of performance, rather than his chronological age, determines test selection. This approach avoids reaching the false conclusion that the patient is "untestable except for certain islands of intelligence." For example, an eight-year-old, mute, autistic patient is "untestable" on the Stanford-Binet, since this test is dependent on the presence of verbal skills. A more appropriate test is an infant's intelligence scale, or a test which does not require expressive verbal responses. If tested on the Stanford-Binet, he may well show a "splinter skill" by scoring in the average range on one or two non-verbal items. This obviously cannot be taken as indicative of his "true" level of intellectual functioning. Our approach is to administer only tests which have been standardized for a child of approximately the same developmental level. Thus, many test items are applicable to the given patient and a better overall picture of the patient's abilities can be formulated.

First and foremost, we use IQ tests to provide useful input when designing a patient's therapy program. As previously mentioned, we first clinically assess developmental level and select only tests appropriate to this level. We usually use behavior-based techniques to administer the tests. A careful review of test profiles allows us to determine the skills a child possesses, what tasks he is able to master, and where his developmental arrests are. Then, educational and behavior therapy programs are designed from the developmental point of view. This type of developmentally-based behavioral analysis is particularly crucial when one is dealing with patients under four years of age. A case which illustrates this point is that of a two-year-old inpatient at the Neuropsychiatric Institute. On admission he was non-ambulatory, had severe developmental delays, no self-help skills, severe disturbances of perception, severe disturbances of relating, no speech or language, and motility disturbances (e.g., finger-flicking). Initially, on the Cattell Infant Intelligence Test, he attained a mental age of 9.6 months —an IQ equivalent of 37. An item analysis was used to design operant-based programs for his developmental arrests. After nine months of treatment, retesting on the Cattell yielded a mental age of 22.5 months for an IQ equivalent of 65. Thus, he moved up the developmental curve as measured by behavior acquisition, and his Cattell score reflected these changes.

We are now attempting to develop specific IQ tests to bypass the behavioral problems caused by perceptual inconstancy and resultant symptomatology. The development of such tests would represent a major break-through in allowing clinicians to better assess the current status of an autistic patient, to design specific behaviorally- and educationally-based therapies, and to provide more objective re-evaluations. This research goal we hope will be realized in the foreseeable future.

REFERENCES

Bryson, C.Q. (1970). Systematic identification of perceptual disabilities in autistic children. *Perceptual and Motor Skills* 31:239-246.

DeMeyer, M.K., Barton, S., Alpern, G.D., Kimberlin, C., Allen, J., Yang, E. and Steele, R. (1974). The measured intelligence of autistic children. *Journal of Autism and Childhood Schizophrenia* 4:42-60.

Fish, B., Shapiro, T., Campbell, M. and Wile, R. (1968). A classification of schizophrenic children under five years. *American Journal of Psychiatry* 124:109-117.

Kaluger, G. and Kaluger, M.F. (1974). *Human Development: The Span of Life.* St. Louis: Mosby.

Kanner, L. (1943) Autistic disturbances of affective contact. *Nervous Child* 2:217-250.

Lewis, M. (1973). Infant intelligence tests: Their use and misuse. *Human Development,* 16:109-118.

——— and McGurk, H. (1972). Evaluation of infant intelligence. *Science* 198:1174-1177.

Lockyer, L. and Rutter, M. (1969) A five to fifteen-year follow-up study of infantile psychosis. *British Journal of Psychiatry* 115:865-882.

Ornitz, E.M. (1973). Childhood autism. A review of the clinical and experimental literature. *California Medicine* 118:21-47.

——— and Ritvo, E.R. (1968). Perceptual inconstancy in early infantile autism. *Archives of General Psychiatry* 18:76-98.

Rosenburg, L.A. (1973). Psychological examination of the handicapped child. *Pediatric Clinics of North America* 20:61-77.

Rutter, M., Bartak, L. and Newman, S. (1971). Autism—A central disorder of cognition and language. In Rutter, M., ed., *Infantile Autism: Concepts, Characteristics and Treatment* London: Churchill.

Terman, L.M. and Merrill, M.A. (1960). *Stanford-Binet Intelligence Scale* Boston: Houghton-Mifflin Co.

CHAPTER FOUR

EPEC: Evaluation and Prescription for Exceptional Children

REBECCA FLAHARTY

Historically, the cause of early infantile autism and the type of educational program provided for autistic children have been viewed in two different ways. Those who consider autism to be primarily an emotional disturbance (Bettelheim, 1950) recommend educational environments which are warm, permissive, and accepting and in which academic teaching is not stressed. Such environments are designed to allow the child to regress emotionally to where he feels secure and comfortable. Formal demands upon the children are kept to a minimum and relatively few contingencies are placed on maladaptive behaviors. Specific educational goals are not established; rather it is assumed that when the child is ready and feels comfortable, he will learn.

Others (Ornitz and Ritvo, 1968a; Rimland, 1964; and Rutter, 1968) consider autism to be a physical disease, caused by neuro-pathophysiological disturbances. The disease is manifested primarily by disturbances of perception (Ornitz and Ritvo, 1968b) with accompanying disturbances in language, relatedness, and cognitive development. Educational programs based on this model provide intensive, structured activities in a multitude of skill areas to allow the child to develop to his fullest potential. Bartak and Rutter (1973) have shown that such an approach may result in significantly greater improvement in social responsiveness and meaningful speech, and significantly greater decrease in deviant behavior than can be obtained from programs which use only a relationship approach. The study left little doubt that direct teaching of skills and firm setting of limits and structure was the method of choice. Rutter and Sussenwein (1971) have advocated a developmental and behavioral approach to the education of autistic children. They utilized a behavior modification technique within a developmental context, and found a greater normalization of social relationships and less deviant behavior in the children treated in this manner. These and other studies supporting a behavioral/developmental approach to the education of autistic children have suggested the individualized "prescription approach" currently used at the NPI school. This approach has required that we use a comprehensive assessment procedure in order to identify specific teaching goals. In our search for such assessment procedures, we initially experimented with two types of assessment: behavioral analyses and standardized psychometric tests. We found that each of these methods had advantages, but neither alone met all of our requirements.

Behavioral analysis has two advantages: it is teacher administered and it is prescriptive. The teacher chooses a terminal goal or objective for the child and specifies all the components of the behavior which the child must acquire. If the behavior chosen is "speaking in sentences," for example, the necessary components to be evaluated and taught would include the ability of the child to imitate sounds, to shape these sounds into words, and to chain the words together to form sentences. The first sentence taught might be, "I want a (cookie, etc.)." This particular type of sentence is often chosen because it allows the child to express his wants and needs. Also, behavioral analysis is prescriptive in that it tells the teacher exactly what is the next step to be taught in the sequence.

Advantageous as this method might seem, it is not complete; it is not a *generative* system. Once the child has been trained to say, "I want a cookie" in response to, "What do you want?" he does not usually progress from that point to "I want a ball," "I want a candy," "I want a . . . ." The teacher must go through another task analysis and specifically teach him to substitute each new word for "cookie." Using only the method of behavioral analysis, each "sentence" would need to be individually and separately trained, and generalization and building on previous learning might not naturally occur. Also, each individual word taught within such sentences would have little or no meaning for the child, only the "sentence" as a whole would have limited meaning.

The second type of evaluative procedure used was standardized psychometric tests. Used alone, however, such standardized testing would be inadequate. Standardized tests often yield only a single number; an IQ score or an overall mental age. Not only does this fail to tell the teacher what the child can or cannot do, but it may seriously mislead an educator. A child who has fine motor and manipulative skills at the four-year level but conceptual and language skills at the two-year level would receive an overall mental age of three years when, in fact, none of his skills were at the three-year level. The teacher who began to plan a program for this child based upon his test scores would be doing the child a great disservice, demanding too much of him in some areas and too little in others.

Another disadvantage of standardized intelligence tests is that they are not comprehensive in nature. They frequently fail to tap many of the skills necessary for the everyday functioning of the child. In order to gain a comprehensive understanding of the child's most important deficits, it would be necessary to administer many different tests to each child. Additionally, standardized intelligence tests are applicable to a relatively narrow age range. Infant developmental tests are only valid from birth through two years of age, and most children's intelligence tests are valid from age three to age seven. No one test can be used from birth through seven years of age. This is a major drawback in using standardized tests with autistic children. As has been frequently noted, autistic children often exhibit widely scattered developmental levels. An autistic child who is functioning at the two-year level in most areas may have fine motor skills at the four- or five-year level, and expressive language skills at the one-year level. No one standardized test covers the entire range of these abilities. It would require the administration of two or more tests to tap this child's range of abilities.

A third disadvantage to using standardized intelligence tests to plan educational programs for autistic children is that they are not prescriptive. Because no specific information is given in terms of what the child is or is not able to do, it is difficult to use the actual test results to plan a program. Because these tests must be administered by a psychologist, the teacher does not usually have access to the actual test protocol. In addition the teacher does not have the opportunity to see the child performing each individual test item, nor to observe the circumstances surrounding the child's failure on any specific item.

THE EPEC:

Because no previously devised method of educational or psychological assessment fully met the needs of our program, it became necessary for us to devise our own evaluative procedures. Our procedure is designed to meet four criteria. First, it is one which can be administered by teachers without much specialized training; it allows the teacher to gauge the child's strengths and weaknesses and makes it possible for the teacher to observe *why* the child failed specific items. Second, it is comprehensive in nature, covering a multitude of different skill areas, and attempts to tap the majority of abilities necessary for the everyday functioning of the child. It is also comprehensive with respect to age—it covers tasks that normal children can perform from birth through the sixth year. Third, it yields a mental age, or level of functioning, in each skill area it taps, rather than providing only an overall mental age or IQ score. This information is used by the teacher to plot a profile of the child's abilities and to determine areas or patterns of strengths and weaknesses in the child's behavioral repertoire. It enables the teacher to make better decisions about the priorities in each child's educational program. Fourth, the test is prescriptive in nature. It not only tells the teacher what the child can do, but suggests what normal children should learn next.

Our evaluation procedure is entitled Evaluation and Prescription for Exceptional Children, or EPEC. In its current form, EPEC contains items for establishing the child's level of functioning in each of fifteen skill areas. The areas include preschool curriculum such as puzzles, blocks, numbers and colors, as well as commonly accepted areas of intellectual and physical development, such as fine and gross motor skills, receptive and expressive language, visual and auditory memory, play, socialization and cognitive skills. Items in each skill area were obtained from widely used developmental and standardized intelligence tests, e.g., the Stanford-Binet Intelligence Scale, the Gesell Developmental Schedules, and the Cattell Infant Development Scale. (The appendix to this chapter contains a reproduction of the EPEC Scales and a bibliography which indicates where the items were obtained.)

Based upon the many developmental levels obtained by the child, a profile of his or her abilities is outlined, indicating patterns of strengths and weaknesses. These patterns plus any isolated deficit areas determine the remedial programs for each child. At each developmental level the type of task which normal children learn next is indicated. EPEC does not prescribe specific teaching items but rather indicates goals to be met. The actual steps the child goes through to meet that goal are determined by task analysis and by the learning style of each individual child.

DIRECTIONS FOR FUTURE RESEARCH

In its present form, EPEC has no items based upon teacher intuition or "logical extensions" of test items. It has become obvious, however, that gaps and omissions are still present in the developmental continuum within some test areas. Normative studies are being undertaken to "fill in the gaps," to add items to the scale, and to confirm doubtful items derived from the tests. Concurrently, standardization data are being collected on the test as a whole in an attempt to validate the use of the test with normal children as well as with those who have handicaps.

Two further areas of research are planned. Correlational data comparing a calculated overall mental age from the EPEC with standardized test results are being statistically analyzed. Also, studies exploring the possible use of the EPEC as a method for equalizing the scatter of abilities exhibited by many autistic children have been initiated.

REFERENCES

Bartak, L. and Rutter, M. (1973). Special education treatment of autistic children: A comparative study. 1. Design of study and characteristics of units. *Journal of Child Psychology and Psychiatry* 14:161-79.

Bettelheim, B. (1950). *Love Is Not Enough* Glencoe: Free Press.

Ornitz, E.M. and Ritvo, E.R. (1968a). Neurophysiologic mechanisms underlying perceptual inconstancy in autistic and schizophrenic children. *Archives of General Psychiatry* 19:22-27.

——— and Ritvo, (1968b). Perceptual inconstancy in early infantile autism and its variants. *Archives of General Psychiatry* 18:76-98.

Rimland, B. (1964). *Infantile Autism, the Syndrome and its Implications for a Neural Theory of Behavior.* New York: Appleton-Century-Crofts.

Rutter, M. (1968). Concepts of autism: A review of research. *Journal of Child Psychology and Psychiatry* 9:1-25.

——— and Sussenwein, F. (1971). A developmental and behavioral approach to the treatment of preschool autistic children. *Journal of Autism and Childhood Schizophrenia* 1:376-397.

APPENDIX

APPENDIX

Summary of Evaluation and Prescription for Exceptional Children Levels

	Fine Motor	Puzzles	Blocks	Drawing Writing	Concepts General	Concepts Colors	Concepts Numbers	Body Image	Matching Skills	Visual Memory (obj. Const.)	Auditory Memory	Expressive Language	Receptive Language	Socialization and Play	Gross Motor
84 mo.															
78 mo.															
72 mo.															
66 mo.															
60 mo.															
54 mo.															
48 mo.															
42 mo.															
36 mo.															
30 mo.															
24 mo.															
18 mo.															
12 mo.															
6 mo.															

Fine Motor Skills

Task	Specific Criteria	Age	Notes	P	F
Lifts cup with handle	Predominantly using one hand	6 mo.			
Palmer grasp		6 mo.			
Removes peg from pegboard	Must remove 2 or more times	7 mo.			
Hand Preference	Present object at midline, 5 of 6 with one hand	8 mo.			
Pokes hole in pegboard (i)		9 mo.			
Pincer grasp	Uses ends of thumb and forefinger from above	10 mo.			
Places 1 peg in pegboard	Places peg in board at least twice	14 mo.			
Opens round box	After demonstration opens box	14 mo.			
Closes round box	After demonstration closes box	16 mo.			
Completes pegboard when urged	Hands peg to child one at time - may say "Put it there"	16 mo.			
Turns groups of pages in book		18 mo.			
Completes pegboard without urging	Gives all 6 pegs at once	18 mo.			
Folds paper	Any crease which remains in paper	21–30 mo.			
Closes rectangular box	After demonstration closes at least twice	22 mo.			
Cut w/Scissors – Snip only	After demonstration	24 mo.			
Turns single pages in book		24 mo.			
Unscrew lid of small jar		24 mo.			
Strings beads	2 or more	24 mo.			
Turns doorknob		24 mo.			
Cuts w/Scissors	One long cut or several snips	27–29 mo.			

Fine Motor Skills (cont'd.)

Task	Specific Criteria	Age	Notes	P	F
Close fist and move thumb	Imitate, only thumb wiggles	30–35 mo.			
Buttons one button	No time limit, no demonstration	30–35 mo.			
Strings beads	4 in two minutes	36 mo.			
Opposition of thumb and fingers	In order index, middle, ring, little	42–47 mo.			
Folds paper in triangle, twice	⬡ ◿ △	60 mo.			
Ties knot around pencil	Doesn't come undone	60 mo.			

Puzzles

Task	Specific Criteria	Age	Notes	P	F
Remove ⊙ piece from form puzzle		10 mo.			
Place ⊙ piece in form puzzle		14 mo.			
Place 2 ⊙ in Bayley Blue Board		17 mo.			
Places ⊙ in Rotated formboard	Remove circle, Rotate board	18 mo.			
Places 2 ⊙ and 2 ▣ in Bayley Blue Board		19 mo.			
Places ▣ in formboard		20 mo.			
Completes formboard		22–24 mo.			
Bayley Pink Board, Rotated 180°	Remove pieces, Rotate board	25 mo.			
Two-piece puzzle (half of picture)	◖ ◗	42 mo.			
Three-piece puzzle, interlocking pieces, Timed	No frame	48–53 mo.			
Four-piece puzzle, interlocking pieces	No frame	48–53 mo.			
Two-piece rectangle	◺◹ makes ▱	60 mo.			

Blocks

Task	Specific Criteria	Age	Notes	P	F
Puts 1 block in cup	After demonstration	9–12 mo.			
Tower of 2 blocks (i)		15 mo.			
Puts 10 cubes in cup	After demonstration	18 mo.			
Tower of 3 blocks (i)		18 mo.			
Tower of 6 blocks (i)		24 mo.			
Train of 2 or more (i)		24 mo.			
Train of 3 or more (i)		27 mo.			
Tower of 8 blocks (i)		30 mo.			
Train of 3 w/ Chimney (i)		30 mo.			
Tower of 9 blocks (i)		36 mo.			
Bridge (i)		36 mo.			
Bridge (m)		42 mo.			
Gate (i)		48 mo.			
Simple 3–4 cube block designs	On card, 1–3 colors	48 mo.			
Gate (m)		54 mo.			

Drawing – Writing

Task	Specific Criteria	Age	Notes	P	F
Scribbles (i)		13 mo.			
Scribbles (s)		16 mo.			
Draws line – any direction (i)	After demonstration of vertical lines	17 mo.			
Draws vertical line	or within 30°	22 mo.			
V stroke (i)		24 mo.			
"Round and Round" (i)		24 mo.			
Draws horizontal line (i)		24–30 mo.			
Draws 2 or more strokes for cross (i)		30 mo.			
Copies (c)		36 mo.			
Cross (i)		36 mo.			

Drawing — Writing (cont'd.)

Task	Specific Criteria	Age	Notes	P	F
Copy cross (c)		42–48 mo.			
Traces diamond ◇	Child draws on lines of diamond model	42 mo.			
Draws a man — 3 pts.	Any 3 parts (pairs of pts. = 1 pt.)	49 mo.			
Draws ⊡ (i)	With 4 corners, lines may extend past corners, not rounded	50 mo.			
Copy ⊡ (c)		54–57 mo.			
Draws a man — 6 pts.	As above	58 mo.			
Copies tri-angle △ (c)		60 mo.			
Copies ⊠ (c)	Rectangle with diagonals	60 mo.			
Copy star ✳ (c)	3 or more lines, cross mainly at center	60–65 mo.			
Copy diamond ◇		72 mo.			

Concepts — General

Task	Specific Criteria	Age	Notes	P	F
Follows simple one-step directions	"Put it on chair" "Give it to me" etc.	18–24 mo.			
Identifies — gives — objects by name	"Point to the ball" or "Give me the ball"	18–24 mo.			
Names objects	1 object–18 mo.; 3 objects–24 mo., 5 objects–30 mo.	18+ mo.			
Identifies — gives — pictures by name	1 picture–18 mo., 5 pictures–21–24 mo., 7 pictures–30 mo.	18+ mo.			
Names pictures	1 picture–18–21 mo.; 5 pictures–30 mo.; 14 pictures–48 mo.	18+ mo.			
Obeys prepositions	2 prepositions–30 mo.; 3 prepositions–42 mo.; 4 prepositions–48 mo.	30+ mo.			
Identifies "what do you hear with?"	Verbal Response not required	30 mo.			

Concepts — General (cont'd.)

Task	Specific Criteria	Age	Notes	P	F
Gives use of common objects	"What is a pencil for" etc.	30 mo.			
Identifies objects by use	Gives object ". . . .we drink out of" etc.	30 mo.			
Identifies action in pictures	"Give me the picture of the boy running" etc.	30–35 mo.			
Understands cold/tired/hungry	"What do you do if you're cold/tired/hungry?"	34–42 mo.			
Tells action in pictures		36 mo.			
Gives heavier block	Two blocks same size, different weights	42 mo.			
Identifies big/little objects		42 mo.			
Identifies longer/shorter lines		42 mo.			
Identifies pictures by use		48–54 mo.			
Opposite Analogies	"Brother is a boy, sister is a _____"	48–54 mo.			
Can pick which of 3 pictures is *not* same (i.e. different)		54 mo.			
Can tell if two pictures are same or not same (i.e. different)		60 mo.			

Concepts — Colors

Task	Specific Criteria	Age	Notes	P	F
Matches colors	Red, blue, green, yellow	30–35 mo.			
Recognizes–points to–3 colors	Points to 3 of 4–red, blue, yellow, green	36 mo.			
Labels one color–usually red–expressively		48 mo.			
Names 4 colors	Red, yellow, blue, green	60 mo.			

Concepts — Numbers

Task	Specific Criteria	Age	Notes	P	F
Concept of "one"	Gives 1 block	30 mo.			
Counting 2 blocks	Give 2 ask "How many?"	35 mo.			
Counts 2 circles	Answers "how many?"	45 mo.			
Counts 3 circles	Answers "how many?"	48 mo.			
Counts 4 objects	Answers "how many?"	54 mo.			
Counts 5 circles	Answers "how many?"	57 mo.			
Counts 10 objects	Answers "how many?"	60 mo.			
Names penny, nickle, dime		60 mo.			
"What comes after 8?"		66 mo.			
Counts 12 objects correctly	Answers "how many?"	66 mo.			
Adds and subtracts within 5	Total of numbers less than 5	72 mo.			

Body Image

Task	Specific Criteria	Age	Notes	P	F
Pats doll in imitation		12 mo.			
Points to body parts	"Show me your ___" 1 pt. = 18 mo. 3 pts. = 20 mo.	18+ mo.			
Points to body parts on doll	"Show me dolls ___" 1 pt. = 18 mo. 3 pts. = 20 mo. 5 pts. = 22 mo.	18+ mo.			
Follow directions w/doll	Put in chair, give drink, wipe nose 2 of 3 = 20 mo. 3 of 3 = 22 mo.	20+ mo.			
Identifies — points to — paper doll parts	4 pts. = 24 mo. 6 pts. = 30 mo.	24+ mo.			
Identifies self in mirror	Definite statement or overt action	24–29 mo.			
"What do you hear with?"		29 mo.			
Knows own sex	"Are you a boy or girl?"	36 mo.			

Body Image (cont'd.)

Task	Specific Criteria	Age	Notes	P	F
Draws a man	2–3 parts = 48 mo. 6 pts. = 58 mo. pairs of pts. = 1 pt.	48+ mo.			
"What do you do with your eyes/ears?"		54 mo.			
Draws missing parts on incomplete man		60 mo.			
Knows right/left on self	Hand, ear, eye	60 mo.			
Completes manikin – arms or legs may be reversed		69 mo.			
Knows left/right on others		72 mo.			

Matching Skills

Task	Specific Criteria	Age	Notes	P	F
Matches colors	Red, yellow, blue, green	30–35 mo.			
Matches shape to shape (1 of 5)	Lotto style, solid colored shapes	30 mo.			
Matches shape to shape (3 of 5)	Lotto style, solid colored shapes	36 mo.			
Matches—points to— outlined shapes (6 of 10)	Points to shape on large card which matches sm. indiv. card – may not match as in lotto	42 mo.			
Matches—points to— pictures of animals	Points to animal on large card which matches indiv. card – not lotto	42 mo.			
Matches silhouetted shapes – Decroly – 3 or more	Lotto style	42–47 mo.			
Matches outlined shapes – as above (8 of 10)		48 mo.			

Matching Skills (cont'd.)

Task	Specific Criteria	Age	Notes	P	F
Matches outlined shapes — as above (9 of 10)		54 mo.			
Matches silhouetted shapes — Decroly — 12 or more	Lotto style	54–59 mo.			

Visual Memory — Object Constancy

Task	Specific Criteria	Age	Notes	P	F
Looks for fallen spoon	Drop spoon while child watching child turns and looks at floor	6 mo.			
Uncovers toy from cloth	Place small cloth over toy, child uncovers toy	8 mo.			
Lifts cup to secure cube	Place cube on table, cover with cup	9 mo.			
Unwraps cube	Wrap cube in paper, child unwraps	12 mo.			
Finds 1 of 2 hidden objects	Hide two objects, 1 under each of 2 cups, have child find 1. 3-second delay	19 mo.			
Finds toy hidden under one of 3 boxes, all same color	10-sec. delay, correct 2 of 3 trials	22 mo.			
Finds picture of animal from memory	Show small picture of animal, remove, child finds picture of animal he saw on large card with several animals	36 mo.			
Identifies "what's missing" (one of three objects)	Show 3 objects, child close eyes covers 1, "what's missing?"	48 mo.			

Auditory Memory

Task	Specific Criteria	Age	Notes	P	F
Repeats single words (2 of 4)	Recognizable, not necessarily well articulated	22 mo.			
Repeats single words (4 of 4)		24 mo.			
Repeats 2 digits (1 of 3 trials)	In order	30 mo.			
Repeats 3 digits (1 of 3 trials)	In order	36 mo.			
Repeats up to 6 word sentences	"Baby sleeps in a little bed" etc.	41 mo.			
Repeats 3 digits (2 of 3 trials)	In order	42 mo.			
Repeats up to 10-word sentences	"We are going to buy some candy for mother"	48 mo.			
Repeats 4 digits (1 of 3 trials)	In order	54 mo.			
Follows 3-step directions	In order	54 mo.			
Repeats 4 digits (2 of 3 trials)	In order	72 mo.			
Repeats 5 digits (1 of 3 trials)	In order	84 mo.			
Repeats 3 digits reversed (1 of 3 trials)		84 mo.			

Expressive Language

Task	Specific Criteria	Age	Notes	P	F
Vocalizes 2 different sounds	2 distinct separate sounds	2 mo.			
Two-syllable repetition of same sound	Such as "baba," "dada," "mama"	8 mo.			
One "word"–(By report if necessary)	Other than "dada" or "mama" word or syllable for definite object or situation	11 mo.			
Jabbers expressively	Vocal inflections resembling conversational intonation	12 mo.			

Expressive Language (cont'd.)

Task	Specific Criteria	Age	Notes	P	F
Imitates words	Recognizable, may consist of vowels only	13 mo.			
Uses gestures to make wants known	Refusing toy, pushing away, reaching out, etc.	15 mo.			
Names objects	1 object 18 mo.; 3 objects 24 mo.; 5 objects 30 mo.	18+ mo.			
Uses words to make wants known	Asks for at least two things by name	18 mo.			
Names pictures	1 picture 18–21 mo.; 5 pictures 30 mo.; 14 pictures 48 mo.	18+ mo.			
Combines two words	2 different concepts such as "Daddy gone" "Shut door" etc.	22 mo.			
Uses plurals	Regulars plurals which add "s" to form plural	30–42 mo.			
(For more items see Concepts–General)					

Receptive Language

Task	Specific Criteria	Age	Notes	P	F
Responds to verbal request	Any one, consistantly	9 mo.			
Inhibits on command	Stops or changes activity on command	10 mo.			
Follows simple 1-step directions	"Put it on chair," etc.	18 mo.			
Identifies–gives–objects by name	"Point to the ball" "give me the ball"	18–24 mo.			
Identifies–gives–pictures by name	1 picture 18 mo.; 5 pictures 21–24 mo.; 7 pictures 30 mo.	18+ mo.			
Obeys prepositions	2 prepositions 30 mo. 3 prepositions 42 mo. 4 prepositions 48 mo.	30+ mo.			
(For more items see Concepts–General)					

Play and Socialization

Task	Specific Criteria	Age	Notes	P	F
Discriminates strangers	Any discriminative behavior to strangers, staring, frowning, crying, etc.	4–5 mo.			
Plays peek-a-boo or other cooperative game with examiner	After demonstration looks for examiner to repeat procedure	6–8 mo.			
Repeats performance laughed at		11 mo.			
Solitary or onlooker play predominates		18–23 mo.			
Parallel play predominates		24–42 mo.			
Dramatization and imaginative play begins		36+ mo.			
Associative group play taking place of parallel play		42 mo.			
Plays cooperatively with other children		48 mo.			

Gross Motor

Task	Specific Criteria	Age	Notes	P	F
Walks without help and without falling		15 mo.			
Walks backwards	2 or more steps	15 mo.			
Stands on 1 foot w/help		16 mo.			
Walks upstairs w/help		16–21 mo.			
Walks upstairs w/1 hand held		18 mo.			
Runs		18 mo.			
Crosses feet at ankles, while sitting	Imitates	18–23 mo.			
Holds cup well while drinking		20 mo.			
Throws ball	Must go forward	20 mo.			
Kicks ball	Must go forward	20 mo.			
Walks downstairs, 1 hand held		21 mo.			

Gross Motor (cont'd.)

Task	Specific Criteria	Age	Notes	P	F
Jumps in place		22 mo.			
Stands on 1 foot, momentarily		23 mo.			
Pedal trike	10 ft. or more	24 mo.			
Walking board, stands w/2 feet	No support	25 mo.			
Jumps from bottom step		25 mo.			
Walks up stairs alone, both feet on ea. step		25 mo.			
Walks downstairs, both feet on ea. step		26 mo.			
Walks on tip-toe, few steps		26 mo.			
Walks backwards, 10 feet		27.8 mo.			
Walks up and down-stairs alternating feet		30 mo.			
Walks on tip-toe, 10 feet		30 mo.			
Walks on line, 10 feet		30 mo.			
Jumps over string 2" high (1 of 3 trials)		30 mo.			
Balance on 1 foot, 1 second		30 mo.			
Walking board, alter-nates steps part way	2 or more steps	30 mo.			
Hops on 1 foot	2 or more hops	30 mo.			
Broad jump (at least 8½")	Jumps over 8½ x 11 paper (1 of 3 trials)	34 mo.			
Balance on 1 foot, 5 sec.	2 or 3 trials	38 mo.			
Catches bounced ball	with hands, not arms	46 mo.			
Skips on 1 foot	Alternate foot, takes a walking step	48 mo.			
Balance on 1 foot, 10 sec.	2 of 3 trials	54 mo.			
Skips alternating feet		60 mo.			

REFERENCES FOR EPEC SCALES

Bayley, N. *Manual for Beyley Scales of Infant Development* New York: The Psychological Corporation.

Cattell, P. (1940) *The Measurement of Intelligence of Infants and Young Children.* 1960 revision, New York: The Psychological Corporation.

Doll, E. (1953). *The Measurement of Social Competence. (A Manual for the Vineland Social Maturity Scale).* Washington, D.C.: Educational Testing Bureau.

Frankenburg, W. and Dodds, J.B. (1968). *Denver Developmental Screening Test* Ladoca Project and Publishing Foundation, Inc.

Gessell, A. *The first five years of life* New York: Harper and Row. 1940.

——— and Amatruda, C. (1947). *Developmental Diagnosis: Normal and Abnormal Child Development* New York: Hoeber Medical Division, Harper and Row.

Ilg, F. and Ames, L. (1965). *School Readiness* New York: Harper and Row.

Mecham, M.J. (1958). *Verbal Language Development Scale* Circle Pines: American Guidance Service, Inc.

Slosson, R.L. (1963). *Slosson Intelligence Test for Children and Adults* New York: Rev. Slosson Educational Publications.

Stutsman, R. (1948). Merrill Palmer Scale of Mental Tests in *Mental Measurements of Preschool Children* New York: Harcourt, Brace, and World, Inc.

Terman, L.M. and Merrill, M.A. (1960). *Stanford Binet Intelligence Scale. Manual for the Third Revision, Form L-M,* Boston: Houghton Mifflin Company.

CHAPTER FIVE

Audiological Assessment

MARILYN LOWELL

The evaluation of hearing is an important aspect of the identification and differential diagnosis of the autistic child. The absence of language development or the inability to follow verbal instructions may be due to an auditory impairment. This chapter is designed to acquaint the professional with the use of audiologic assessment in the overall evaluation of the autistic child. It will provide a basic understanding of the procedures an audiologist might use when a difficult-to-test individual such as the autistic child is referred.

WHAT CAN A NON-AUDIOLOGIST DO TO ASSESS HEARING?

Case History

The case history is the first step in the assessment because it can yield important information about the child. If the professional works in a large clinical setting, much of the case history may already be available. However, if not, it will be necessary to obtain sufficient information for an adequate assessment of the child.

In approaching the assessment of any child, one gathers together as much information as possible through use of a carefully obtained medical and developmental history. A review of such data may suggest particular features to be stressed during an interview with the child or family. The mere presence of autism does not exclude the existence of other diseases; thus, it is most important to document prenatal, paranatal and postnatal events. Unusual occurrences during pregnancy may have been overlooked by the family but can surface during a diagnostic interview. Any accidents or illnesses which occurred during the first trimester may be causative factors for a hearing impairment. Be alert for possible occurrences of maternal rubella, Rh incompatibility, toxemia, or other maternal illnesses during pregnancy and for any medications given to the mother.

If the family cannot provide information regarding the delivery and hospital stay, the medical records are usually available upon request. Make note of any complications during or following delivery which could harm the infant such as excessively long or hard labor, abrupt presentation, breech birth, caesarian section, anoxia, or jaundice. While jaundice may not be immediately present at birth, hospital records will reveal whether the bilirubin count ever reached significantly high enough levels that such measures as blood transfusion were ever contemplated or undertaken.

Postnatal trauma may affect the child at any age. Inquiry about any and all childhood diseases such as measles, mumps, or other viral infections may be important. Sometimes measles or mumps leads to a more complex illness such as meningitis or encephalitis. Even if the parents do not report that a hospitalization was required, other indices such as sudden loss of balance or falling may indicate that VIIIth nerve mechanisms were affected by the illness. A considerable number of students in schools for the deaf suffered spinal meningitis postnatally. High fevers may also account for some degree of hearing loss.

Sometimes medications given for treatment in life-threatening illnesses can be ototoxic. Drugs known to cause deafness or severe hearing impairment are dihydrostreptomycin, Kanamycin, ethacrynic acid, and, in some individuals, large doses of aspirin. This pertains to the normal as well as the autistic child.

The mother's recall of the child's developmental milestones or a review of the baby book is also useful. If there is a large lag in communication, in contrast to motor development (such as crawling, sitting, standing, or walking), one can rule out the presence of a hearing impairment as the basis for a language delay. The autistic child may develop some speech and then stop using it at approximately two years of age.

Ideally, all children who are referred for diagnosis should have a hearing evaluation. Certainly if any of the above pre-, para-, or postnatal difficulties apply, those children should be automatically referred for audiological assessment.

Observation

Observation of the child's spontaneous reactions to auditory stimuli which occur during any diagnostic evaluation should be recorded. Since many autistic children tend to ignore auditory signals, keeping record of any responses to auditory stimuli is necessary and can be very helpful. He may not be responsive to verbal commands but may cease activity if a noise occurs in an adjoining office. Perhaps the hum of a tape recorder, or a digital clock, or the noise created by scratching his nails on a metallic surface will interest him. These children may be attracted to minimal auditory stimuli and yet ignore very loud noises. Watch for the child's response to *other* than verbal stimuli. If you have a question about the child's ability to hear, a referral for an audiologic evaluation is appropriate.

WHAT TECHNIQUES ARE AVAILABLE TO THE AUDIOLOGIST?

Many of the audiologic techniques utilized in a clinic setting will not apply. The autistic child who cannot participate in cooperative play cannot be expected to give voluntary responses to test stimuli. Autistic behavior will exclude the use of many formal measures routinely used in a hearing clinic. The basic paradigm of audiometric techniques is one of presenting controlled stimuli and recording observable responses which are elicited. There is a whole hierarchy of measures available for the understanding, cooperative individual who can do the traditional pure tone tests on the one hand, to *observation* of the non-cooperative child on the other hand. The audiologist must assess the child's ability to function and "plug" him in at the appropriate level.

The clinical assessment battery normally used in a hearing and speech center can be divided into two categories—subjective or objective. Some tests are called "subjective" because a subjective judgment must be made about interpretation of test data. Others are called "objective" tests because the audiologist relies more on the instrument for interpretation of hearing status.

Subjective Procedures

Pure Tone Audiometry

This test requires total cooperation of the child. Calibrated audiometric equipment is normally utilized for formal assessment. The child is asked to indicate by pressing a button or raising his hand that he hears a test signal. The report of voluntary thresholds for the right and for the left ears is recorded on a form called the "audiogram." This graph tells the examiner not only about presence or absence of hearing impairment, but helps to delineate where the disturbance in the auditory pathway may be, and how much difficulty the individual might have in understanding speech. The test involves presentation of pure tone signals which are within the speech frequencies via earphones, a room speaker, or a bone conduction receiver. The audiologist is concerned with determining how *intense* or how *loud* a signal must become before the individual is able to "hear" it. Since the person is asked to indicate when a signal is heard at minimum levels, a great deal of cooperation is required. The pure tones generated from a wave generator within the audiometer allows presentation of different frequencies within the speech range. The lower frequencies carry mostly vowel information while the higher frequencies help us to make fine discriminations between consonants.

Use of earphones or room speakers test the entire auditory pathway via air conduction. Use of a bone conduction receiver (a small vibrator placed on the mastoid bone) enables the audiologist to test the nerve of hearing directly and by-pass the middle ear. If a difference between air conduction and bone conduction results occurs, one gains information about the site of the lesion, if it exists.

Modified Speech Audiometry

Other tests involving the reception of speech and the use of discrimination tasks also require an interaction between the testee and the examiner. If the child has some speech skills, one can obtain a check on behavioral pure tone thresholds by utilizing a modified speech reception threshold. The examiner may name objects placed in front of the child and ask him to "find the kitty" or "find the baby," etc. Speech can be presented either via earphones, a room speaker or a bone conduction receiver. If the child has little or no speech, he may cease activity or in some way alter his play, thus providing a "speech awareness" threshold. These tests are not usually feasible with the autistic population due to their lack of cooperation, lack of social interaction, and their limited speech skills.

Play Audiometry

This test requires cooperation but not to the extent of the formal audiogram. The young child who is not able to press a button or tell the examiner that he hears the tone, or repeat back words can sometimes be taught a "conditional" task. This is usually successful with children whose mental age is two years or above. The child is taught to drop a block in a box or put a ring on a peg each time he sees a drum being beaten (Lowell, 1956). If the child learns this association, the drum is removed from the child's visual field and the same procedure is followed. The "conditioned" task is then transferred from requiring a response to an auditory stimuli without any visual cues. The next step of the procedure requires that the child manipulate a toy in response to a pure tone signal emitted from either a room speaker or an earphone. If the child accepts the headset, voluntary responses can be obtained for each ear. Even if the child is unwilling to accept the headset, an individual earphone can be held tightly to either the right or the left ear. By utilizing a "conditioning" technique, an accurate, pure tone audiogram can be obtained from the young child; however, many autistic children will not be able to perform such an activity.

Troca

This technique requires less cooperation. The operant conditioning equipment for testing severely retarded children has been described by Lloyd (1968). The technique called TROCA (Tangible Reinforcement Operant Conditioning Audiometry) utilizes positive reinforcement for appropriate responses to auditory stimuli. The child is taught to press a response button when he perceives a sound. Candy, cereal or other food reinforcement are dispensed from the machine if the response occurs within an appropriate time delay of stimulus presentation.

This technique can be very useful in testing the autistic child as many are intrigued with mechanical objects and avoid interpersonal contact. The TROCA equipment establishes a working relationship with the child while the examiner remains out of view.

COR

Conditioned Orienting Response Audiometry is still another technique which does not require total cooperation. The child is placed in a test room between and facing two speakers. A tone is emitted from one of the speakers. If the child looks in the direction of the speaker, a light on top of the speaker flashes; the child may find this to be reinforcing. If the child does not look in the direction of the speaker, no light reinforcement is provided. Observations of the child's turning in the direction of the sound source then allows assessment of hearing acuity.

BOA

For the child who is not able to interact with the examiner in a cooperative manner, BOA or Behavioral Observation Audiometry is utilized. Observation of the young child's gross responses to sounds presented in the test room serves as another "subjective" test. Calibrated sounds such as warbled tones, pure tones within the speech frequencies, voice, music, toy noisemakers are presented either from earphones or room speakers. The pure tone stimuli used in more formal tests are not meaningful to the young infant and, as a result, do not elicit observable responses. The baby becomes accustomed to his mother's voice and has learned to associate mother with pleasurable happenings such as food, love, and dry diapers. As a result, the infant is much more responsive to voice or music as a test signal than to standard pure tones. Similarly, he is responsive to noisemakers as he is often entertained by these toys during his waking hours. The examiner records the child's response or lack of response to the various test signals and the loudness of each. Young children and babies may give a wide variety of overt responses some of which are very subtle. The examiner will be alert for and record:

Startle
Cessation of activity
Alteration of activity
Widening of the eyes
Shutting the eyes
Covering the ears
Movement of all or part of the body
Facial grimaces
Crying
Cessation of crying
Shifting the eyes in the direction of the sound source
Change in breathing rate
Change in sucking pattern
Turning the head in the direction of the sound source
Walking over to the speaker from which the sound is emitted

Dr. Kevin Murphy (1962) of Reading, England, studied the orienting responses of infants from birth to two years of age. He has provided us with detailed observations of motor responses which infants make at specific developmental levels. He also suggests that the failure to inhibit a startle response after six weeks of age may be indicative of a lowered intelligence level. Typically, the infant in the newborn nursery will elicit a Moro response to a hand clap. In effect, there is a generalized movement of the body with arms flailing outward. According to Murphy, the premature infant will exhibit this response for a longer time than the full-term infant and the anencephalic child never does inhibit this "hyperkinetic" response.

The autistic child is often very subtle in his response to sound. The evaluator must be particularly cautious in reporting behavior he "thinks" is a response, for these children tend to ignore even extremely loud sounds and may not startle to very intense stimuli which may also be tactile. When low frequency pure tones such as 250 and 500 Hertz are presented via a room speaker at maximum intensity levels, there is an accompanying vibration; thus, it is difficult to determine whether the sound was heard or felt. A deaf child with little or no residual hearing may respond to very loud, low frequency stimuli because of its tactile quality. The autistic child, however, may ignore even these stimuli.

Regardless of the technique utilized, a knowledge of behavior modification techniques and operant conditioning is essential in utilizing some of these measures with the autistic child.

Objective Procedures

Other methods available to the audiologist are said to be "objective." The judgment of a response occurring is removed from the examiner and designated to electronic equipment. Based on various criteria, the audiologist interprets test results for determination of hearing status. Some of the "objective measures" are essential to the formal clinical battery and add important information about the pathology of the ear but may not yield "threshold level" responses.

Impedance Audiometry

This technique was recently added to the audiologic battery. Briefly, this technique allows evaluation of middle-ear pathology, the presence of recruitment, and determination about hearing sensitivity by measuring acoustic impedance and the aural reflex (Lilly, 1973). Unfortunately, the individual must remain very still for reliable results. Since the autistic child is not likely to sit quietly, let alone allow probe tubes to be placed in his ear canal, sedation may be required. Some hospital settings (Jerger, 1974) have a cooperative staff and available operating rooms to perform such tests under anesthesia but this is not the general rule. If the autistic child resides in a clinical setting where behavior modification techniques are utilized, cooperation may be elicited without the use of sedation.

Cribogram

This technique may be used as a screening device for early detection of hearing impairment (Simmons 1974b). At Stanford University this technique is being utilized in the nursery to test the newborn babies' hearing before they go home. Each crib is attached to a very sensitive transducer which measures movement or activity following stimulus presentation. The examiners found that the very early morning hours were the best time for testing as most cribs were then occupied. Although the yield is very low in a normal newborn nursery, the test has been very useful in the intensive care unit.

Evoked Response Audiometry

This is thought to be particularly useful as an "objective" hearing instrument. This technique yields "threshold" determination by averaging brain waves in response to various auditory stimuli through the use of a special purpose computer. Small disks or electrodes are taped to the infant's head. The computer averages the random activity of the EEG (electro-encephalogram) and adds together the minute responses which are time-locked to a stimulus presentation—if the person is hearing the stimulus. The resultant wave-form, which is readout on a strip chart, represents the individual's "evoked" response to that stimulus.

Most of the research with young children reveals that this test may provide variable results and requires additional expensive equipment not normally available in a speech and hearing center. The practice of using sedation with this technique varies from test center to test center. Some examiners routinely utilize sedation while others prefer to test in the awake state. The results of a longitudinal study with high-risk infants (Lowell, 1968) show that this technique can be of assistance in assessing hearing without requiring use of sedation. During the four-year study only two infants were untestable on one occasion. In 80 percent of the cases, evoked response results agreed within 20 decibels of later voluntary thresholds. Many of the infants were the result of maternal rubella infection and exhibited autistic behavior. Again, the use of sedation may be necessary for those autistic children not able to sit quietly or allow electrodes to be taped to their heads for testing. A recent study of vestibular nystagmus with these children shows that they can be taught to sit quietly for testing using positive reinforcement and no sedation (Ornitz, 1974). Certainly skilled technicians accustomed to working with these very difficult children are essential to testing in the waking state.

ECO

Another variation of this technique involves the use of similar procedures and is called Electrocochleography (ECO) or Far Field testing. There are presently two schools of thought on the placement of the electrodes for testing and as a result "threshold" determination varies. Some otologists (Simmons, 1974b; Brachman, 1973) prefer to go through the ear drum and place the electrodes on the promontory. The advantage of piercing the ear drum allows the investigator to obtain responses closer to "threshold." Others (Jewett, 1971; Jerger, 1974; and Ornitz and Walter, in press) prefer not to traumatize the ear and obtain surface electrode recordings. This test is thought to tell us about the integrity of the nerve of hearing and auditory brain stem function. Unless sedation is utilized, this test may not be practical for use with the autistic child, although Ornitz and Walter (in press) were able to record from some autistic children without sedation.

PGSR

Another of the "objective" techniques which may yield a "threshold" determination is called Psychogalvanic Skin Response or PGSR. This test involves pairing a tone with a shock. The individual soon learns that a tone will be followed by an electric shock on his finger tip or palm of his hand. Sometimes the pure tone is not paired with the shock, yet having learned to expect a shock, the patient gives an autonomic response which manifests itself in changes of the moisture content of the skin. This change is detected by sensitive electrodes and electronic equipment. PGSR is useful in cases of adult malingerers who may hope to gain remuneration for having developed a hearing impairment. However, it is not particularly desirable for use with children; one reason is the discomfort involved. None of us like to harm or irritate the young child. Certainly if he begins crying, test results will not be accurate. Also, young children have a tendency to be somewhat active and this extra movement makes interpretation of small amplitude changes in the strip chart readout highly unreliable (Grings, 1961). Not only is the test unfavorable for testing infants and children, it can be even more variable with the non-cooperative, autistic child.

Other techniques were developed in the hope that they would lead to an "objective" hearing test. Such tests were plethysmography, which measured changes in blood flow in the finger, or conditioning of eye blinks. These techniques were discarded.

Respiration Audiometry

Of recent interest is a technique which records changes in breathing rate in response to an auditory signal. Bradford (1974) utilizes this technique with both adults and children and he feels that it has promise. Subjects must be completely relaxed and quiet, thus all are given sedation before testing. The use of sedation precludes the utilization of this technique as a routine audiometric technique. Most audiologic centers do not have the facilities for sedating patients nor do they have time and space available to wait for the sedative to take effect. With an autistic child, this is further complicated by the variance in response of these children to sedation or stimulants.

PECULIARITIES OF AUTISTIC RESPONSES

In addition to the routine clinical audiometric tests there may be other indications of hearing function. Some of these children show hyper-sensitivity to sounds. As mentioned before, many will cry or cover up their ears to the whirring of a blender or the flushing of a toilet. These children seem to ignore most auditory sounds but will alert to one specific signal. One child, particularly fond of soda pop to the point that he would gorge himself on it, would come running from another room in the house if he heard a pop-top can opened. Another child ignored most household sounds, as well as speech stimuli, but would awaken from sleep if the water was run anywhere in the house.

Peculiar overreaction to auditory stimuli may work to a disadvantage in that the autistic child excludes all other sensory input. Some children are so attracted to non-verbal auditory stimuli that it interferes with other play behavior. One child was very interested in the minute buzzing of appliance motors. Any attempt to record samples of speech and play behavior would be precluded once the child became aware of the tape recorder hum. He spent his time at home listening to the refrigerator, washer, dryer or dish-washer. The mother reports the child would open the refrigerator door only to make the motor turn on. The fact that this type of activity may last for only a few months illustrates the importance of obtaining a careful case history.

Another teenage autistic boy did not react to verbal communication but was alert to the sound of his father's car. He loved to go for a ride in the car and would sit for hours in one of the family's two cars waiting for some-one to take him for a drive. In order to get to work, the father would take whichever car the boy was not sitting in. The boy would awaken from sleep if he heard the motor of the car start up. The family reported that he would even awaken if the father pushed the car out of the garage across the gravel driveway. As a result, the father kept his car parked down the block.

If the child is echolalic, or tends to echo speech, a further test of hearing acuity involves monitoring echolalic responses with modified speech reception techniques. Some children may appear mute, but tape recorders left in the child's sleeping room have recorded surprising language samples. Although the autistic child may not utilize speech during the day when others are around, he may practice and play with speech in a darkened room just before falling asleep and just after awakening.

Some autistic children react unusually to particular sounds or fre-quencies (Ornitz, 1968). No specific frequency has been determined as being unique to all autistic children. Some of them will begin self-stimulation, hand-flapping, or finger-flicking in response to a 3000 Hz tone. When a different frequency is presented, such activity ceases but can be reinstituted with a return of the 3000Hz stimulus.

Some of the children who ignore sound and verbal communication will press a level or a bar for a reward of given musical passages. Others may respond by dancing or rocking to music but ignore single frequency presentations of pure tone represented in the music.

MANAGEMENT OF THE HEARING IMPAIRED AUTISTIC CHILD

As stated earlier, autism does not preclude or insure that a child will not also have a hearing impairment. Once a hearing loss in the autistic child is detected, several factors must be considered: (1) degree of loss, (2) type of loss, (3) if medical treatment cannot improve the hearing, would use of amplification be of benefit, (4) selection of the appropriate instrument, and (5) educational management.

Degree of loss

Hearing loss is not an all-or-none phenomenon. The autistic child with a *mild* loss may not receive special attention for his hearing impairment and educational management will focus on his autism. The child will usually develop language normally. If the hearing impairment is *moderate*, language development may be slow and speech will be defective. He will be able to hear loud speech from a short distance. The child with either *severe* or *profound* hearing impairment will not develop speech and language without special assistance and may hear some loud sounds near his ear.

Type of loss

Review of the hearing impairment by an otologist is very important as medical treatment might well be indicated. If the child has chronic ear infections and a conductive hearing loss, medical and surgical intervention may well reverse the impairment. However, if the hearing loss is sensorineural or due to "nerve deafness," the otologist can still be of assistance in establishing a preventive program to protect residual hearing.

The otologist may also be of assistance to the family in explaining the hearing loss and answering any questions they may have about possible "cures" for the child's hearing impairment. One present technique which has stirred much interest is "acupuncture." Aber (1974) conducted a carefully controlled study of the use of acupuncture as a possible treatment for hearing impairment. Several studies thus far conducted in the United States

(Katinsky, 1974) show that there is no significant "improvement" in hearing following a series of acupuncture treatments.

Use of amplification

Not all children or adults with hearing impairment can successfully utilize a hearing aid. Some individuals have "recruitment" which is a heightened sensitivity to small increments in loudness. These individuals often find use of a hearing aid uncomfortable or intolerable. The audiologist will record any suggestion of the possibility of recruitment during the assessment as it will play an important part in the use of a hearing aid or in the selection of the instrument.

A very important consideration in recommending use of amplification with the autistic child is his behavior. If the child's behavior is negative or inconsistent from day to day, he might well destroy all or part of the hearing aid. Careful observation of the hearing-impaired autistic child with an amplification unit may give meaningful information as to whether the child will initially accept or reject amplification.

Selection of appropriate instrument

No gross generalization can be made about whether autistic children can and should use hearing aids. Rather, selection of such should be made on an individual basis. Although the body model hearing aid is sturdy and able to withstand more abuse than the smaller behind-the-ear models, this choice should also be made on an individual basis. Utilizing his or her own experience in "fitting" hearing aids for children, the audiologist will apply the same principles to the autistic hearing-impaired child.

A hearing aid will not "cure" the hearing impairment, but it can be of some assistance to the child in building language skills. Once the child is enrolled and established in an educational program, another type of amplification unit, the auditory trainer, may be used. These units are larger and are not portable but they provide greater fidelity, more volume control, and independent volume control systems for either ear should there be a vast difference in the hearing levels.

Educational Management

Educational placement for the deaf autistic child may be a forbidding and complex problem. Many school districts are not able to provide the necessary education for a child with more than one handicap, especially small school districts which may have minimal numbers of handicapped children. The difficulty with the multi-handicapped arises when one must make a decision as to which is the *most* handicapping condition. To illustrate this problem a national committee recently met to write guidelines about how to provide proper education for the hearing-impaired, mentally retarded child. Who is responsible for providing these youngsters an education—the school for the deaf or the institution for the retarded? Neither really wants the assignment nor do they feel qualified to do an adequate job.

The deaf-autistic child is not necessarily retarded, but who is responsible for his education? Many school districts do not have classes for autistic children and schools for the deaf may feel their educational approach is not appropriate for the deaf-autistic child. The audiologist or educational consultant may need to serve as the advocate for these special children to insure they receive the same educational opportunities provided other children. Recent court decisions in suits throughout the United States on behalf of retarded children will set a precedent for the autistic child's education.

At present the schools for the deaf may provide the best classroom placement because of their techniques for establishing communication skills. Manual communication has been successfully introduced in TMR (Trainable Mentally Retarded) classrooms in California with children who have hearing. The use of sign or gesture system seems to relieve the frustration of not being able to communicate. For the deaf-autistic child, development of communication is even more complex and use of manual communication may be the most useful symbol system provided for the child with multi-sensory deficits.

To illustrate the complexity of accurately testing the autistic, take the example of two autistic children who presented such a complex diagnostic picture that their hearing losses were overlooked. Both children had severe to profound hearing impairments but never had proper audiologic assessment (see audiograms). Neither child established good eye contact, and both flapped their hands or occupied themselves with self-stimulatory behavior. The seven-year-old-boy had been placed in an Educationally Handicapped classroom and the seven-year-old girl was placed in a Trainable Mentally Retarded classroom. Neither had developed communication skills although the boy had developed some sight reading skills. Neither of these children had been provided with an educational setting which would accommodate their hearing impairments. With minimal training both of these children were able to do the task necessary for play audiometry and showed their delight when sounds were heard. The introduction of supra-threshold auditory signals caused the children to vocalize and show excitement. Within a very short period of time and with food reinforcement, we were able to teach the girl to "sign" for candy.

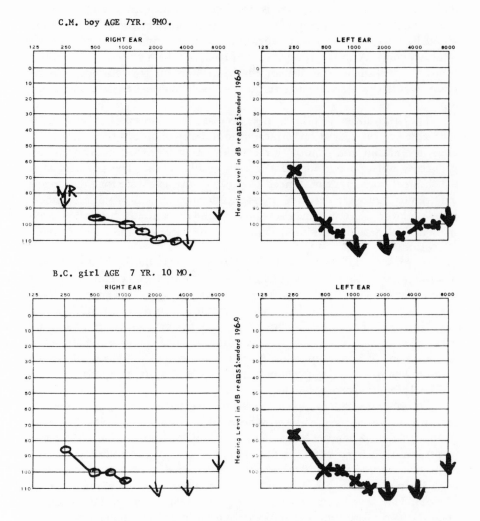

C.M. boy AGE 7YR. 9MO.

B.C. girl AGE 7 YR. 10 MO.

Following a staffing of these children and a review of their educational needs, the school administrators will now enroll these children in a multi-handicapped, deaf program which should assist them in developing communication skills. Although neither of these children have much residual hearing, as is reflected in their audiograms, amplification will be attempted on a trial basis. The hearing aid may be of some assistance in helping them monitor whatever speech they may develop. It should also serve as an alerting system that someone is talking to them and they should attend. Perhaps even more important, it will serve as a warning system for danger—a car is approaching and they should get out of the way.

SUMMARY

The autistic child presents a unique challenge and problem for the audiologist. Because of the child's behavior, accurate assessment of hearing status is a highly complicated task—imagination and creativity are necessary in applying the techniques available and interpreting their results.

REFERENCES

Aber, W. (1974). Letter to editor—acupuncture. *Archives of Otolaryngology* 100:246-247.

Brackman, D.E. (1973). Personal communication.

Bradford, L.J. (1974). Paper read at American Speech and Hearing Association Convention, Las Vegas.

Grings, W.W., Lowell, E.L., and Honnard, R.R. (1961). GSR conditioning with preschool deaf children. *Journal of Comparative and Physiological Psychology* 54:143-48.

Jerger, J. (1974). Personal communication.

Jewett, D.L. and Williston, J.S. (1971). Auditory evoked far fields averaged from the scalp of humans. *Brain* 94:681-96.

Katinsky, S. and Durrant, J. (1974). Results of audiometric study of sensorineurally impaired subjects treated with acupuncture. Paper read at American Speech and Hearing Association, pp. 411-414.

Lilly, D.J. (1973). Acoustic impedance at the tympanic membrane. *Handbook of Clinical Audiology*, pp. 434-469.

Lloyd, L., Spradlin, J., and Reid, M. An operant audiometric procedure for difficult to test patients. *Journal of Speech and Hearing Disorder* 33:236-245.

Lowell, E.L., Lowell, M.O., and Goodhill, V.G. (1968). Evaluation of averaged evoked auditory response testing of young children. Paper read at American Speech and Hearing Association Convention, Denver, Colo.

—— Rushford, R.G., Hoversten, G., and Stoner, M. (1956). Evaluation of pure tone audiometry with preschool age children, *Journal of Speech and Hearing Disorder* 21:292-303.

Murphy, K.P. Ascertainment of deafness in children. *Panorama* 1962, 3.

Ornitz, E.R. (1974). Personal communication.

—— and Ritvo, E.R. (1968). Perceptual inconstancy in early infantile autism. *Archives of General Psychiatry* 18:76-98.

—— and Walter, D. (in preparation). The effect of sound pressure waveform on human brain stem auditory evoked response.

Simmons, F.B. and Russ, F.N. (1974). Automated newborn hearing screening, the cribogram. *Archives of Otolaryngology* 100:1-7a.

—— (1974b). Personal communication.

PART III

Current Research

CHAPTER SIX

Clinical and
Electrophysiological Research

PETER E. TANGUAY

Within the past decade there has been a radical, even revolutionary change in our understanding of the nature of early infantile autism. This change in attitude has had many benefits, not the least of which has been to stimulate a considerable amount of research into the nature, etiology and treatment of the syndrome. This chapter will take a look at some of this research, especially as it pertains to clinical and electrophysiological studies published within the past five years.

DIFFERENTIAL DIAGNOSIS

We recognize that progress in medical science is always based upon a "splitting-off" of new syndromes from the mass of undifferentiated illness, leading ultimately to an understanding of the nature and treatment of the syndrome in question.

In regard to early infantile autism we know that the "splitting" process is far from complete. For one, we have yet to resolve the question of the relationship between the "classical" form of the illness as originally described by Kanner (1943), and autistic-like syndromes in which some, but not all, of the classical symptoms are present. Additionally, there is the question of the relationship between early infantile autism and what is called "childhood schizophrenia." To most experts early infantile autism is an early and severe form of psychotic development, but "childhood schizophrenia" may mean either an entirely different type of illness whose onset is usually in middle or later childhood, or it may be used as a generic term to cover most psychosis of childhood including autism. The lack of agreement among expert child psychiatrists is indication enough that we are far from solving this question. I think, however, that one may find the recent work of Kolvin (1971; Kolvin et. al., 1971) to be of particular interest on the subject. His work replicated and extended the previous work of Rutter on the subject (Rutter and Lockyer, 1967).

Kolvin and his colleagues examined a cohort of eighty psychotic children and divided them into two groups by age of onset. (This decision made sense in that almost all cases had their onset either before two years of age or after seven years of age.) He found several marked differences between the two groups. They were, of course, rather different in symptomatology, which might be expected solely on the basis of their differing ages of onset. The infantile psychotic group was clearly autistic. The late onset psychotic group differed in that 81 percent hallucinated and many showed clear evidence of an overt thought disorder. Among the autistic children who could talk, none had definite evidence of hallucinations and the incidence of overt thought disorder (i.e. blocking, loosening of associations, etc.) was fairly low.

The two groups differed in two other characteristics. The infantile group came predominantly from a higher socioeconomic strata, and the incidence of adult schizophrenia among their parents was no higher than that found in the general population. The late onset group came predominantly from lower socioeconomic strata, and the incidence of schizophrenia in their parents was quite high.

Not all investigators agree with the above findings, of course. Ritvo (Ritvo et al., 1971) has produced data which suggests that autistic children do not come from a higher socioeconomic group, while Bender and Faretra (1972) have reported a high incidence of schizophrenia in the relatives of both autistic and late onset psychotic subjects.

Nonetheless, having weighed the evidence from Kolvin's study, and compared it with previous work, I personally believe that a reasonable case can be made for the following statements: Early infantile autism and childhood schizophrenia are distinctly different illnesses. Early infantile autism is a syndrome which occurs quite early in life and is related to that spectrum of illnesses termed the "developmental disabilities." Childhood schizophrenia is the downward extension of adult schizophrenia into childhood.

THEORIES REGARDING THE ETIOLOGY
OF EARLY INFANTILE AUTISM

A number of interesting hypotheses have been advanced to explain the etiology of early infantile autism. These may be grouped into three categories:

(1) Theory of perceptual inconstancy

(2) Theory of a defect in cross-modal associations

(3) Theory of a central cognitive defect

The theory of perceptual inconstancy was put forward by Ornitz and Ritvo (1968). It is based upon clinical observations which suggest that autistic children suffer from a defect in the homeostatic regulation of sensory input and motor output. As a result of this defect the child fails to gain a stable inner representation of his environment, and hence, he cannot learn to interact normally with others or to use communicative speech. Within the past few years a number of electrophysiological studies have been interpreted as supporting this hypothesis. The most pertinent studies are those of Ornitz, Ritvo and their colleagues (Ritvo et al., 1969; Ornitz et al., 1973; 1974). The focus of their electrophysiological work has been upon phenomena whose occurrence is mediated by the vestibular nuclei in the brainstem. Their findings may be summarized as follows:

(1) When waking autistic children are subjected to vestibular stimulation by whirling in a Baronay chair in a lighted room, their vestibular reactivity as measured by the duration of ocular nystagmus is markedly diminished in comparison with normal subjects. This reduction in vestibular reactivity is *not* seen when autistic children are whirled in the dark. More recent work by Ornitz et al. (1974) has suggested that the reduction in duration of ocular nystagmus in autistic children is not a result of their fixating on objects in the lighted room, but is a result of abnormal interaction between the light and vestibular stimuli.

(2) The second finding concerns the occurrence of rapid eye movements during "dreaming" sleep. It should be noted that such rapid eye movements are themselves mediated by the medial and descending vestibular nuclei. Higher centers may of course also play a role in the modulation of activity within these nuclei, and hence may influence the occurrence of the rapid eye movements. In autistic children, there is a significant reduction in the tendency of the rapid eye movements of REM sleep to cluster into bursts (Ornitz et al., 1969). In this regard, two- to five-year-old autistic children resemble normal six- to twelve-month-old babies. These latter findings have recently been replicated in my own laboratory (Tanguay et al., in preparation). Additionally, Ornitz et al. (1973) have shown that the increase in eye movement burst duration seen as a result of mild vestibular stimulation during sleep in normal subjects is deficient in autistic children.

Two additional groups of investigators have presented data relating to the theory of perceptual inconstancy. Their studies do not pertain to vestibular reactivity, but they do suggest an impairment in the operation of homeostatic brain stem reflexes—an impairment which Ornitz and Ritvo have suggested may underlie perceptual inconstancy. Both studies pertain to cardiovascular regulation. In a study by Piggott et al. (1973) "psychotic" children were noted to have less well-coordinated mechanisms for the regulation of sinus arrhythmia. MacCulloch and Williams (1971) have noted that autistic children appear to have a defect in the homeostatic mechanisms which regulate heart rate.

A second theory which purports to explain the symptoms of early infantile autism is that which postulates that autistic children suffer from a defect in cross-modal associations. Normally, children become quite adept at receiving information in one mode (auditory, visual, tactile, etc.) and responding in another. The central connections which underlie such cross-modal associations must be very complex and are not at all understood at present. Evidence supportive of a theory that autistic children suffer from a defect in cross-modal association has been presented by several investigators. Lovaas et al. (1971) have noted that when normal children are reinforced for responding to a complex stimulus involving auditory, visual and tactile cues, all three cues soon "take command" of the responses in question, so that on later presentation of *any one* of the cues, the response will occur. In contrast, while autistic children could be conditioned to respond to all three cues given at once, when the cues were presented singly no more than one of the three cues was found to control this response. In another experiment, Bryson (1970) has shown that when presented with stimuli delivered in one mode (either visual or vocal), autistic children have great difficulty in responding in a different mode from that in which the stimulus was presented.

The work of Lelord et. al. (1973) may be interpreted as providing some electrophysiological substantiation of the above observations. Lelord employed averaged, evoked responses recorded using standard computer techniques. He noted that when normal subjects received auditory stimuli, their evoked response measured from the occipital region was small and variable. When each auditory stimulus was followed 300 msec later by a strong flash stimulus, the auditory evoked responses were considerably enhanced. This enhancement could not be produced in autistic children, suggesting that the interaction between auditory and visual pathways in autistic subjects was defective.

Based on the autistic child's inability to comprehend or to use communicative speech, a third theory has been proposed to explain the etiology of early infantile autism. Rutter et. al. (1971) has postulated that autistic children suffer from a central cognitive defect which presumably prevents them from using language. There is little doubt that autistic children may have a great deal of difficulty with encoding or decoding in the auditory, and to a lesser extent, in the visual mode. Frith (1970) has shown that when speaking autistic children are presented with short sentences made up solely of random words, their recall may be as good as that of normal children matched for mental age. When presented with sentences in which the same words have been rearranged into a meaningful message, the recall rate of autistic children does not increase, while that of normal children does so markedly. Investigations by Shapiro et al. (1972; 1974) have suggested that when autistic children do learn speech, their morphological competence is often in advance of their communicative competence. One need not speak only of the autistic child's inability to encode or decode language. Tubbs (1966) has found that autistic children have difficulty encoding information in both the auditory and visual modes. Two studies have been published which suggest that autistic children may have special difficulty in processing material whose information is encoded as a "sequential" or "linear" pattern. One, by Hermelin (1972), showed autistic children to be quite insensitive to temporally-patterned visual material, while the other, by DeMyer et al. (1972), showed that autistic children are unable to reproduce a sequence of bodily movements.

In relation to the above, it is well to bear in mind that some autistic children may retain certain "islands of function" amidst their handicaps. Autistic children may score comparatively well on certain subtests of the WISC: namely, digit span, block design and object assembly (Lockyer and Rutter, 1970). They may develop remarkable ability to perceive, store and reproduce "meaningless" phrases or "useless" information, seemingly doing so by rote. Hermelin (1972) has demonstrated that autistic children may do relatively well in organizing material within a spatial frame of reference. To some, these observations may suggest that autistic children are better able to process information in a *holistic* fashion without regard to any sequential code of information which may be present in the material.

To anyone who has been following the growing literature on the subject of hemispheric specialization, these observations may appear especially interesting. Specifically, the handicaps of the autistic child (i.e. his language deficits, his inability to process information in a linear fashion) involve functions whose gradient is predominantly in the *left hemisphere*. In contrast, the abilities of the autistic child involve functions whose gradients are predominantly in the *right hemisphere*. This does not imply that autistic children have a lesion or lesions which affect the left hemisphere. We know, however, that differentiation of function between the two hemispheres develops within the first few years of life, and that at first, both hemispheres may function in a more-or-less similar manner. It appears possible that this function involves a holistic rather than a linear mode of processing information. Based on the above, it may be suggested that autistic children fail to develop hemispheric specialization in the normal manner; they are

Table I.
Mean Right/Left Amplitude Ratios

	Normals $n = 7$	Autistics $n = 10$
anterior (Fp_2T_4/Fp_1T_3)	1.35 —————.01—————	0.98
posterior (P_4O_2/P_3O_1)	1.19 —————.01—————	0.86

Right/left amplitude ratio of auditory evoked responses recorded in seven autistic and ten normal children aged two to five years. Recordings were carried out while the children were in REM sleep.

left with two sides of the brain which remain relatively immature and plastic, able at best to process information in a relatively holistic and spatially-oriented manner.

Recent electrophysiological studies carried out in my laboratory are of interest in regard to this hypothesis. Auditory evoked responses were recorded over the right and left sides of the scalp in ten two- to five-year-old autistic children, and in ten four-month to five-year-old normal children. The studies were carried out while the children were asleep. All ten normal children showed larger evoked responses over the right hemisphere during REM sleep—an observation which parallels that made previously in adult subjects in the waking state (Ruhm, 1971). As can be seen in Table I, no consistent hemispheric differences were found in the autistic children. The right/left ratios were significantly greater in normal as compared to autistic children at $p < .01$.

TREATMENT OF EARLY INFANTILE AUTISM

Pharmacotherapy

Occasional studies have claimed that various medications are of use in treating early infantile autism, but such studies are rare. A recent double-blind study by Engelhardt et al. (1973) suggested that both haloperidol and fluphenazine produced beneficial effects in relieving some of the symptoms of autism, and a previous study by Campbell et al. (1970) reported that thiothixene could be effective in lessening withdrawal, psychotic speech and stereotyped behaviors in some young "schizophrenic" children. In view of the number of studies reporting negative results and based upon my own clinical experience and that of my colleagues, there is pessimism regarding the effectiveness of any drug in ameliorating the specific symptoms of early infantile autism.

Educational and Experential Treatments

A number of emminently practical treatment programs for early infantile autism have been described in the literature within the past few years (Rutter and Sussenwein, 1971; Schopler and Reichler, 1971; Fenichel, 1974). These programs have largely grown out of years of trial-and-error searching by various experts, though some aspects of these programs are the result of careful experimental work.

Two major points have been strongly emphasized in all of the above literature:

(1) In treating an autistic child it is essential that a working partnership exist between the *professional* and the *parent*. Mutual respect must exist between both parties in this partnership. The professional provides his expertise to encourage and guide the parents, but the treatment itself must eventually be effected largely by the parents in the home. For the most part, such therapies rely heavily on principles of social learning theory.

The experience of Lovaas et al. (1973) emphasizes the need for parental involvement. While autistic children treated solely by professionals improved in the hospital, the improvement did not last when the children returned home unless the parents were involved in actively continuing the treatment. Additional study by Rutter and Bartak (1973) has shown that advances made by autistic children in a school setting will not necessarily generalize to the home; involvement of the parents in implementing the treatment is essential.

The practical details of treatment are eloquently described by Rutter and Sussenwein (1971) and by Schopler and Reichler (1971). To paraphrase Schopler, the advantages of parental involvement include:

(a) Avoiding the mystique and unfounded authority of the therapist who reports only to the parents regarding his private observation of the child. When parents and professionals work together they are more likely to agree on details and interpretations of the child's behavior.

(b) It affords a realistic opportunity for the parents to see the therapist modeling therapeutic interventions.

(c) When parents are permitted to see the therapist's struggles, frustrations, and occasional mistakes, they are likely to become less critical of themselves and more confident in dealing with their child.

If the parents are found to be suffering from a reactive depression as a result of their experiences with their autistic child, or if serious family problems have already developed, treatment of the depression or the family situation—using traditional methods—will be necessary.

(2) Any treatment program for autistic children must possess structure. This structure should be designed with the individual child's handicaps in mind. It should be aimed at minimizing his stereotyped and isolating behavior while maximizing his opportunity to learn more adaptive ways of dealing with people and objects. The need for structure was particularly well demonstrated in published studies by Bartak and Rutter (1973) and Rutter and Bartak (1973). Autistic children attending some three schools were involved in the study. One school employed a warm, permissive atmosphere and largely non-directive approach, a second school employed a more highly structured and didactic approach, while a third school was an amalgamation of the two approaches. Follow-up over a three-and-a-half- to four-year-period demonstrated that children at all three schools had made considerable progress in achieving a better educational, cognitive, linguistic and behavioral status. Nonetheless, comparison of the results among schools indicated that large amounts of specific teaching in a well-controlled classroom situation was likely to produce the greatest benefits in terms of scholastic progress. Schopler et al.'s (1971) findings are in agreement with this latter observation. Given a structured versus an unstructured situation, autistic children reacted much more favorably to the *structured one*. Structure appears to be especially important for lower-functioning autistic children.

Although experts agree that as much as possible autistic children should remain outside of an institution, two recent publications have emphasized that proper treatment may be carried out even under institutional auspices. Bowness (1972) describes what appears to be a model unit for autistic children at Balderton Hospital in Nottinghamshire, England. The success of the latter program appears to depend upon a high staff/ patient ratio, and considerable psychological and psychiatric back-up for the nurse-therapists. Rieger (1972) has recommended moving acutely disturbed children from the state hospital ward to "satellite homes" in the community. These homes would be staffed by expert therapists acting as surrogate parents, and no home would have more than four disturbed children. While the homes would be governmentally funded, Rieger emphasizes that they should be under the administration of a citizen's group which would be advised by sophisticated and experienced professionals. At least one such home is currently in operation in Ventura County, California, and others are scheduled to begin.

REFERENCES

Bartak, L. and Rutter, M. (1973). Special education treatment of autistic children: A comparative study—1. Design of study and characteristics of units. *Journal of Child Psychology and Psychiatry* 14:161-179.

Bender, L. and Faretra, G. (1972). The relationship between childhood schizophrenia and adult schizophrenia. In Kaplan, A.R., ed., *Genetic Factors in Schizophrenia* Springfield, Ill.: Charles C. Thomas.

Bowness, S. (1972). The autistic child. *Nursing Times* 68:1021-25.

Bryson, C.Q. (1970). Systematic identification of perceptual disabilities in autistic children. *Perceptual and Motor Skills* 31:239-46.

Campbell, M., Fish, B., Shapiro, T., and Floyd, A. (1970). Thiothixene in young disturbed children. *Archives of General Psychiatry* 23:20-72.

DeMyer, M.K., Alpern, G.D., Barton, S., DeMyer, W.E., Churchill, D.W., Hintgen, J.N., Bryson, D.Q., Pontius, W., and Kimberlin, C. (1972). Imitation in autistic, early schizophrenic, and non-psychotic subnormal children. *Journal of Autism and Childhood Schizophrenia* 2:264-287.

Engelhardt, D.M., Polizos, P., Waizer, J., and Hoffman, S.P. (1973). A double-blind comparison of fluphenazine and haloperidol in outpatient schizophrenic children. *Journal of Autism and Childhood Schizophrenia* 3:128-37.

Fenichel, C. (1974). Special education as the basic therapeutic tool in the treatment of severely disturbed children. *Journal of Autism and Childhood Schizophrenia* 4:177-86.

Frith, U. (1970). Studies in pattern detection in normal and autistic children. *Journal of Experimental Child Psychology* 10:120-35.

Hermelin, B. (1972). Locating events in time and space: experiments with autistic, blind and deaf children. *Journal of Autism and Childhood Schizophrenia* 2:288-98.

Kanner, L. (1943). Autistic disturbances of affective contact. *Nervous Child* 2:217-50.

Kolvin, I. (1971). Six studies in childhood psychoses: III. The family and social background in childhood psychoses. *British Journal of Psychiatry* 118:396-402.

———, Ounsted, C., Humphrey, M., and McNay, A. (1971). Studies in childhood psychoses: II. The phenomenology of childhood psychoses. *British Journal of Psychiatry* 118:385-95.

Lelord, G., Laffant, F., Jusseaume, P., and Stephant, J.L. (1973). Comparative study of conditioning of averaged evoked responses by coupling sound and light in normal and autistic children. *Psychophysiology* 10:415-25.

Lockyer, L. and Rutter, M. (1970). A five- to fifteen-year follow-up study of infantile psychosis: IV. Patterns of cognitive ability. *British Journal of Social and Clinical Psychology* 9:152-63.

Lovaas, O.I., Schreibman, L., Koegel, R., and Rehm, R. (1971). Selective responding by autistic children to multiple sensory input. *Journal of Abnormal Psychology* 77:211-222.

———, Koegel, R., Simmons, J.Q., and Long, J.S. (1973). Some generalization and follow-up measures on autistic children in behavior therapy. *Journal of Applied Behavioral Analysis* 6:131-66.

MacCulloch, M.J. and Williams, C. (1971). On the nature of infantile autism. *Acta Psychiatrica Scandinavia* 47:295-314.

Ornitz, E.M. and Ritvo, E.R. (1968). Perceptual inconstancy in early infantile autism. *Archives of General Psychiatry* 18:76-98.

———, Brown, M.B., Mason, A., and Putnam, N.H. (1974). Effect of visual input on vestibular nystagmus in autistic children. *Archives of General Psychiatry* 31:369-375.

——, Forsythe, A.B., and de la Pena, A. (1973). The effect of vestibular and auditory stimulation on the rapid eye movements of REM sleep in autistic children. *Archives of General Psychiatry* 29:786-91.

——, Ritvo, E.R., Brown, M.B., LaFranchi, S. Parmelee, T., and Walter, R.D. (1969). The EEG and rapid eye movements during REM sleep in normal and autistic children. *Electroencephalography and Clinical Neurophysiology* 26:167-75.

Piggott, L.R., Ax, A.F., Bamford, J.L., and Fetzner, J.M. (1973). Respiration sinus arrhythmia in psychotic children. *Psychophysiology* 10:401-414.

Rieger, N.I. (1972). From state hospital to satellite home. *Exchange* pp. 34-46.

Ritvo, E.R., Cantwell, D., Johnson, E., Clements, M., Benbrook, F., Slagle, P., Kelly, P., and Ritz, M. (1971). Social class factors in autism. *Journal of Autism and Childhood Schizophrenia* 1:297-310.

——, Ornitz, E.M., Eviatar, A., Markham, C.H., Brown, M.B., and Mason, A. (1969). Decreased postrotatory nystagmus in early infantile autism. *Neurology* 19:653-658.

Ruhm, H.B. (1971). Lateral specificity of acoustically-evoked EEG responses: I. Non-verbal, non-meaningful stimuli. *Journal of Research* 11:1-8.

Rutter, M. and Bartak, L. (1973). Special education treatment of autistic children: A comparative study—II. Follow-up findings and implication for services. *Journal of Child Psychology and Psychiatry* 14:241-70.

—— and Lockyer, L. (1967). A five- to fifteen-year follow-up study of infantile psychosis. I. Description of sample. *British Journal of Psychiatry* 113:1169-82.

—— and Sussenwein, F. (1971). A developmental and behavioral approach to the treatment of preschool autistic children. *Journal of Autism and Childhood Schizophrenia* 1:376-97.

——, Bartak, L., and Newman, S. (1971). Autism: A central disorder of cognition and language? In Rutter, M., ed. *Infantile Autism: Concepts, Characteristics and Treatment*. London: Churchill Livingston, 148-71.

Schopler, E. and Reichler, R.J. (1971). Parents as cotherapists in the treatment of psychotic children. *Journal of Autism and Childhood Schizophrenia* 1:87-102.

Schopler, E., Brehm, S.S., Kinsbourne, M., and Reichler, R.J. (1971). Effect of treatment structure on development in autistic children. *Archives of General Psychiatry* 24:415-21.

Shapiro, T., Chiarandine, I., and Fish, B. (1974). Thirty severely disturbed children—evaluation of their language development for classification and prognosis. *Archives of General Psychiatry* 30:819-25.

Shapiro, T., Fish, B., and Ginsberg, G.L. (1972). The speech of a schizophrenic child from two to six. *American Journal of Psychiatry* 128:1408-14.

Tubbs, V.K. (1966). Types of linquistic disability in psychotic children. *Journal of Mental Deficiency Research* 10:230-40.

CHAPTER SEVEN

Neurobiochemical Research

ARTHUR YUWILER
EDWARD GELLER
EDWARD R. RITVO

In 1968, we established a collaborative research venture between clinicians at the Neuropsychiatric Institute and neurobiochemists at the Brentwood Veterans Administration Hospital. Before describing the results of our research, we would like to illustrate the general problems of neurobiology by recounting a fable.

Some time ago, a large space ship landed in the middle of the UCLA campus. It contained a multidisciplinary group of scientists from Jupiter sent to determine if there was intelligent life on earth. It was a Sunday and the campus was largely deserted except for the chemistry building which smelled bad and which they avoided. As they strolled along, however, they came upon the central computer facility. Noting that it carried out activities resembling low level intelligence, they decided to determine how it worked.

One of the Jupiterians was a neuroanatomist and he cut off one-inch slabs to examine the physical wiring. One was a physiologist and he put electrodes in here and there to examine the functional wiring. One was a neurologist who mounted an antenna on the roof and monitored the total electrical output. The pharmacologist injected glue and solder at different locations, the biochemist ground up pieces and analyzed for glass and metals, the psychologist talked to it, and the psychiatrist listened. From their separate bits of information they hoped to determine its operating principles.

The brain is infinitely more complex than the simple computer. It contains over ten billion nerve cells, and some 100 billion other cells which are involved in the brain's function in still undefined ways. Each nerve cell may have as many as 200,000 connections, and none are connected in an identical manner. Some have argued that this may be why nerve cells do not regenerate when injured or destroyed, since it is unlikely that a replacement cell would be able to make an identical set of connections. Misconnections could cause greater confusion than no connections at all.

Neurons and their interconnections are organized into structural groups and clusters subserving different functions and are cross-linked to still other clusters. This allows for mutual interchange of information. For example, in the rat hypothalmus, a region about the size of the head of a match, there are twenty-seven clusters of cells which control different actions such as hormone production, physiological response to stress, emotional reactions, eating, drinking, and sex.

Such complexity accounts for the brain's capacity to conduct many functions at the same time. For example, a driver on the freeway not only carries out continuous complex calculations as to the trajectory of adjacent cars and minutely adjusts his muscles to match the curve of the road and changes of speed, but also listens to the radio, sings, mulls over the events of the day, listens to the news, decides what to do tomorrow, anticipates dinner, and worries about the stock market—all at the same time. This unbelievable complexity of functions derives from the intricacy of the brain.

CHEMICAL MESSENGERS

It has been clearly established that nerve cells communicate by means of chemical messengers called "neurotransmitters." These chemicals are released from the tip of one nerve and alter the permeability of an adjacent nerve. There are a number of chemical compounds which have been identified as neurotransmitters in the human brain (Eiduson et al., 1964). We have been particularly interested in studying the group of transmitters called "monoamines." These consist of dopamine, norephinephrine and serotonin. Anatomical studies indicate monoamines are found in areas of the brain which control emotions and behavior. Biochemical and pharmacological evidence indicates that they are involved in the therapeutic activity of psychoactive drugs.

During the course of our studies, we have developed ways of measuring serotonin in the peripheral bloodstream where it is carried in platelets (Yuwiler et al., 1970). The amount of serotonin in the blood is very small, on the order of 0.2 micrograms per milliliter (μg/ml). To illustrate how small that is, remember that a raisin weighs about one gram. If you chop a raisin into a thousand pieces, each piece would weigh one milligram. If a one-milligram piece is then chopped into a thousand bits, each will weigh one microgram (μg). One-fifth of that represents the amount of serotonin in one cubic milliliter of human blood.

SEROTONIN AND AUTISM

In 1968, Dr. Ritvo was conducting neurophysiological sleep studies in autistic children. It had been previously reported in the literature that serotonin controlled one of the phases of sleep and that certain autistic children might have elevated blood serotonin levels (Jouvet, 1969; Schain and Freedman, 1961). To explore the implications of these reports, he initiated the collaboration with Drs. Yuwiler and Geller.

When we began, there was little data on blood serotonin in normal or autistic children in the literature, and methods for assaying blood serotonin were unreliable and inadequate. Thus, one of our first tasks was to perfect an assay technique (Yuwiler et al., 1970). Next we studied a small population of autistic children. The results indicated that some of them had extremely elevated levels of blood serotonin when compared to normals. This presented us with a problem; we had to decide whether it was worthwhile to pursue this observation since we knew it would take years of effort and considerable expense to simply determine if the differences were real, and if they were important.

Let us explain this dilemma by looking into the mirror of scientific history. In the 1930s, a Norwegian physician, Følling, was told by a mother that her retarded child's urine had a peculiar odor. Dr. Følling was quite intrigued. After much diligent and imaginative research, he reported in 1934 (Følling, 1934) that ten retarded patients—some of them siblings—excreted an abnormal amount of phenylpyruvic acid. Since not all mentally retarded children excrete high levels of phenylpyruvic acid, this left the question, Is it worthwhile to find out whether this is a *real* finding, i.e., directly related to the retardation, or is it an artifact that has no connection with retardation?

Five years later, Jervis (1939) demonstrated that the combination of high phenylketone excretion and mental retardation was inherited via an autosomal recessive gene. In 1953, Jervis further reported that the basic metabolic error was an inability to convert one amino acid, phenylalanine to tyrosine, leading to the accumulation of phenylaline and the excretion of its metabolic product, phenylpyruvic acid. (The current rationale for dietary therapy is based upon this finding.)

All this illustrates the complexities of such studies. Demonstrating a difference between normal and abnormal children does not necessarily mean that the difference reflects a key factor in the disease. What is directly related to a disease and what is a secondary reflection of a disease process, must be determined by careful research. In our own case, we recognize that the blood is not the brain. While our data suggests that some autistic children have above-normal blood serotonin concentrations we do not know if this reflects a basic abnormality, if it is due to some secondary process of the disease, or if it is unrelated to the disease itself but rather to some general phenomenon in some children.

BIOCHEMISTRY OF SEROTONIN

Serotonin is derived from the amino acid tryptophan. Tryptophan is an *essential* amino acid because it cannot be manufactured by the body and must be supplied in the diet. Serotonin is formed *both* in the brain and in peripheral organs by enzymes which are not necessarily the same in these two areas of the body.

To form serotonin in the brain, tryptophan must first cross the blood brain barrier and enter nerve cells. There it is converted to serotonin and stored in vesicles within the cell until it is released when the cell is activated.

Blood serotonin is formed in peripheral tissues, primarily the intestine and liver. It is carried in the blood by platelets where it is stored in vesicles which have properties similar to those of nerve cells (Pletscher, 1968). Blood platelets can be studied easily by obtaining samples of blood drawn from a child's arm. Despite similarities in the pharmacological responses of neuronal and platelet storage vesicles, there are obvious difficulties in drawing a parallel between blood and brain serotonin because of marked differences in the formation, regulation, and even the function of serotonin in the two different systems. Thus, what we see in the blood may or may not represent what occurs in the brain or even in the rest of the body.

When we began our studies, no reliable normative data was available in the literature regarding serotonin levels in children. Thus, we first examined a large number of "normal children" and plotted curves of their values (Ritvo et al., 1971). These studies showed that infants had high levels of serotonin which rapidly decreased during the first two years and then slowly decreased to adult levels by age thirteen or fourteen. From that age, the adult levels remained stable. (See Figure 1.) This indicated two things: first, in order to compare normals with autistics, careful age matching of groups would be necessary; second, we would have to take into account the large variance noted within each age group. Figure 2 shows the results obtained from our first study (Ritvo et al., 1970) with autistic children in which we compared serotonin levels in different age groups with normals.

As discussed previously, serotonin is transported in platelets in the peripheral blood stream. Figure 3 shows that platelet counts have a similar

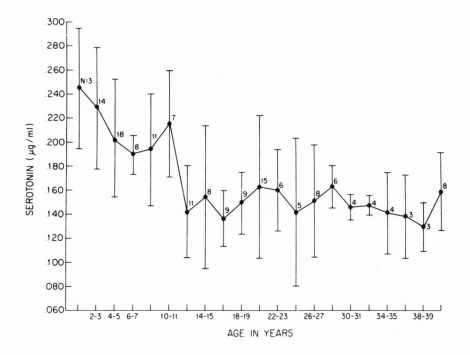

FIG. 1. Maturational changes in blood serotonin levels. Normal subjects were divided in groups according to age at time of testing. Each point represents the mean value for the number of individuals indicated by the numeral above the point. The vertical lines extend for 1 SD above and below each point.

maturational shift as serotonin levels, being higher in infants and decreasing with age until adult levels are reached by age thirteen to fifteen. Figure 4 shows a comparison of autistics' and normals' platelet counts. In this figure, as before, the heavy line represents the values for autistic children and the lighter line that for normals.

The findings that both platelet counts and serotonin levels were elevated in the autistic children raised the old "chicken and egg" question. We had no way of knowing whether one caused the other, or whether they were independent phenomena. The evidence to date tends to suggest that serotonin elevation is more closely related to autism since the average serotonin content per platelet is also elevated in autistic children.

FACTORS WHICH COULD EFFECT SEROTONIN LEVELS

One of our first efforts was to determine if serotonin and platelet differences were due merely to artifacts which plague all clinical-biological

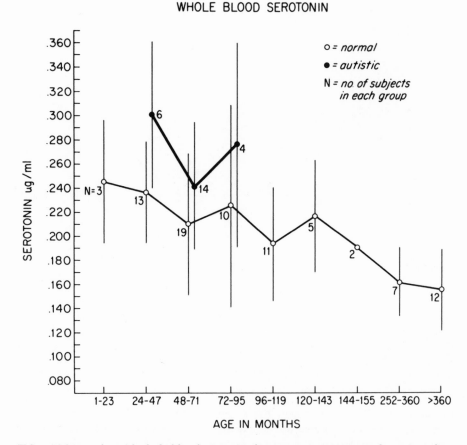

FIG. 2. Mean values of whole blood serotonin for two-year age groups shown together with number of subject in each group. Standard deviation of each group (vertical lines).

studies. The first one we assessed was diet. We took serial samples from ourselves after we had eaten peculiar diets rich in serotonin. For example, Dr. Ritvo ate eight bananas one morning. This produced no rise in his blood level of serotonin or platelets. Obviously, however, a more careful study in children is still required before dietary artifacts can be completely ruled out.

Effects of drugs and other medications also had to be controlled systematically. Thus, we established strict criteria for the autistic and comparison cases used in our studies. Only children free of medication for two months prior to being studied were included in our samples. A further restriction was that no psychoactive drugs such as Thorazine or Stelazine could ever have been taken by the patients. Furthermore, we generally used

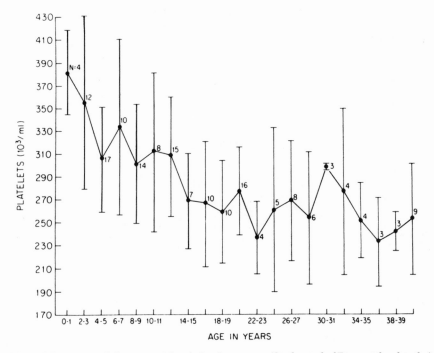

FIG. 3. Maturational changes in blood platelet counts. (See legend of Figure 1 for details.)

children hospitalized on the same ward with the autistic patients as comparison cases. This assured that both groups received the same general diet over a prolonged period of time and had been exposed to similar living environments. The exact consumed diet, however, has not yet been controlled.

Activity patterns may not have been the same for our autistic and comparison populations, so we had to examine this factor separately. It was also important to examine circadian rhythmicity because many biological substances and processes, such as temperature and hormone release, are known to undergo daily cyclic changes (Sollberger, 1965). To minimize circadian variation we first standardized the time of the blood-drawing procedure by taking samples only in the morning before breakfast. We then conducted a separate study (Yuwiler et al., 1971) with two autistic and three non-autistic children as well as with normal adults to determine if groups differed in circadian phasing. Blood samples were taken every four hours over a twenty-four-hour period, once a week for three weeks. The results of this circadian rhythm study are shown in Figures 5, 6, 7, and 8. Serotonin and platelet changes in these groups were normalized to individual means so

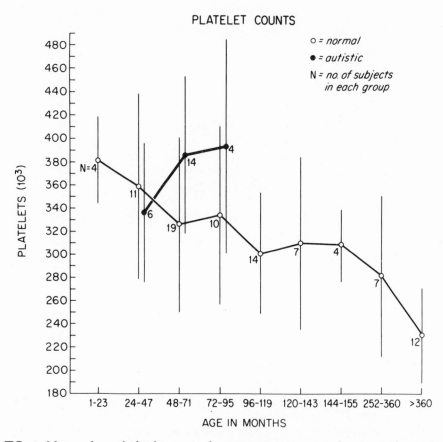

FIG. 4. Mean values of platelet counts for two-year age groups shown together with number of subjects in each group. Standard deviation of each group (vertical lines).

as to clearly bring out any circadian variation. As can be seen, circadian variation was small and did not differ between the two groups. We also examined the data by constructing Aschoff plots which use the peaks across each day's circadian curve to determine the mean periodicity of each individual cycle. As shown in Figures 9 and 10, this analysis failed to suggest that the groups differed in circadian periodicity of these variables. On these bases we concluded it unlikely that altered circadian rhythmicity could account for our previous results.

AN ATTEMPT TO LOWER BLOOD SEROTONIN LEVELS

One method to test whether blood serotonin was related to the clinical state of autism would be to see if they changed in concert. For a variety of

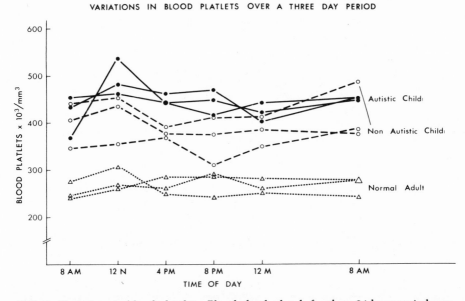

FIG. 5. Variations in blood platelets. Blood platelet levels for three 24-hour periods are shown for one autistic child, one non-autistic child, and one normal. Samples were taken every four hours between 8 A.M. and midnight and at 8 A.M. the following day. Each point is the average of two duplicate samples.

reasons, this sort of test is *not* definitive (whether positive or negative results are obtained) but we thought it might be informative. L-dopa had recently been introduced as treatment for Parkinson's Disease; one of its unwanted side effects was to lower blood serotonin levels. We hoped to make use of this side effect in our studies (Ritvo et al., 1971). Following a seventeen-day-placebo period, four hospitalized autistic boys (three, four, nine and thirteen years old) were given L-dopa for six months. They remained in the hospital throughout the study and careful monitoring of many parameters was undertaken. The results of administering L-dopa on serotonin are shown in Figure 11. As indicated in the Figure, the blood serotonin level of two of the patients and two controls were lowered slightly. The results of administering L-dopa on platelets are shown in Figure 12. These data indicated that L-dopa had little effect on platelet counts.

Global clinical ratings of the children over the six-months' observation period failed to indicate changes in clinical state, while serotonin changes were minimal. The results of the study are therefore ambiguous. On the one hand, we may not have been able to lower serotonin levels sufficiently to lead to clinical changes and on the other, we may have missed a critical phase in the development of the illness. If a critical phase were missed or if

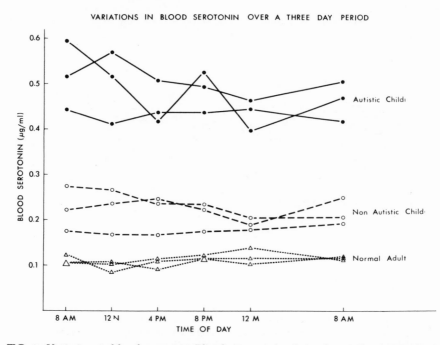

FIG. 6. Variations in blood serotonin. Blood serotonin levels for three 24-hour periods are shown for one autistic child, one non-autistic child, and one normal. Samples were taken every four hours between 8 A.M. and midnight and at 8 A.M. the following day. Each point is the average of two duplicate samples.

irreversible damage had already occurred, then changing serotonin levels would of course have no effect on the clinical picture. (Removal of a bullet from the brain will not restore life although the bullet may have been the cause of death.) Our next obvious step is to try to lower the serotonin levels of very young autistic children by *dietary* means. We have not yet begun such studies.

TEST-TUBE STUDIES OF SEROTONIN AND PLATELETS

As we described previously, serotonin in the blood is actively picked up and transported by blood platelets. It is possible to study the rate of uptake of serotonin by platelets in the test-tube. This is usually done by using radioactive serotonin to determine the radioactivity in platelets after a set time of exposure. Platelets are placed in a solution with a known amount of radioactive serotonin and incubated for different lengths of time. Samples are extracted at these time points, the platelets isolated and the radioactivity in the platelets and that remaining in the solution measured. The serotonin-

PLATELET

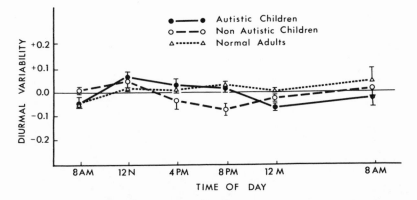

FIG. 7. Daily variations in blood platelet counts. The lines represent the average blood platelet counts during the course of three 24-hour periods for three autistic children, two non-autistic children and three normal adults. Values obtained over each 24-hour period for each individual were converted to Z-scores by dividing each value by the 24-hour mean. Daily Z-score values were averaged for each individual and the individual averages were re-averaged for all subjects in the designated diagnostic groups. The points represent these Z-score averages and the bars represent the standard errors.

SEROTONIN

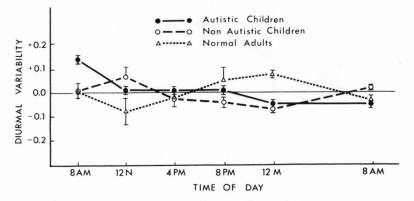

FIG. 8. Daily variations in blood serotonin concentrations. The lines represent the average serotonin concentrations during the course of three 24-hour periods for three autistic children, 2 non-autistic children, and three normal adults. Values obtained over 24 hours for each individual were converted to Z-scores by dividing each value by the 24-hour mean. Daily Z-scores were averaged for each individual and the individual averages re-averaged for all subjects in the designated diagnostic groups. The points represent these group Z-score averages and the bars represent the standard error.

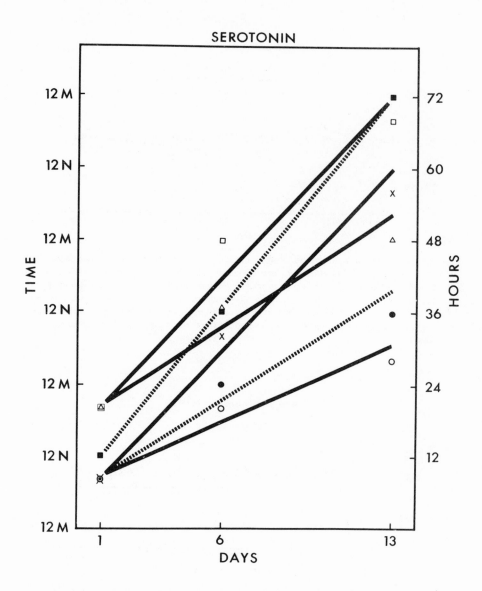

FIG. 9. Time of peak serotonin concentrations during three 24-hour periods. The ordinate represents the time of day at which peak serotonin concentrations were observed. The axis indicates the day of testing. The lines (dotted: autistic children; solid line: non-autistic subjects) represent the best line fit of the peak serotonin times on the three days of testing. The slope of the line can be used to calculate ultradian periodicities. The extreme values of the data yield calculated periodicities of 25.2 hours and 27.5 hours.

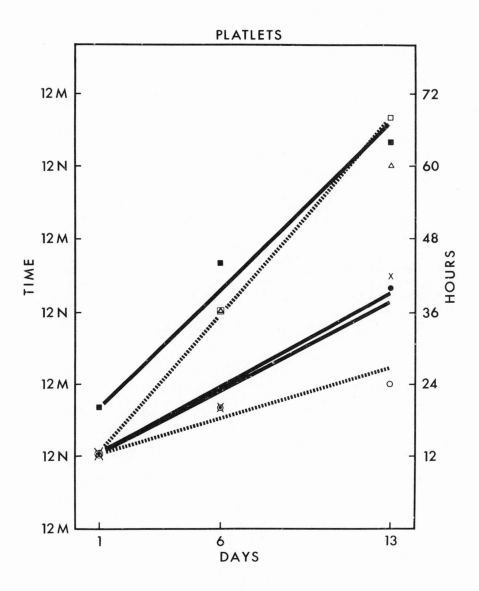

FIG. 10. Time of peak platelet counts during three 24-hour periods. The ordinate represents the time of day at which peak platelet counts were observed. The axis indicates the day of testing. The lines (dotted line: autistic children, solid line: non-autistic subjects) represent the best line fit of the peak times. The slope of the lines can be used to calculate ultradian periodicities. Such calculations based upon the extreme values presented yield periodicities of 25.2 hours and 28.6 hours.

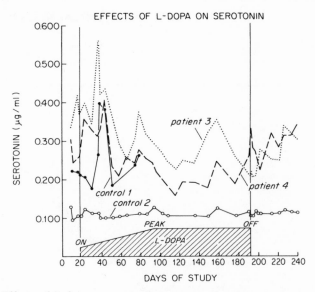

FIG. 11. Effects of L-dopa on serotonin concentration in two younger patients. (The older patients are omitted to simplify the drawing.) *Control 1* refers to a 4-year-old non-autistic boy, *control 2*, to a normal adult. L-dopa administration began on the 17th day of the study (ON) and was discontinued on the 191st day (OFF).

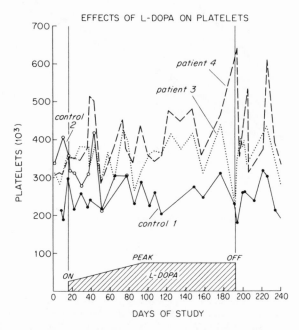

FIG. 12. Effects of L-dopa on platelet counts in two younger patients. *Control 1* refers to a 4-year-old non-autistic boy; *control 2*, to a normal adult. L-dopa administration began on the 17th day of the study (ON) and was discontinued on the 191st day (OFF).

98

loaded platelets can then be resuspended in media free of serotonin and after a given time period, the platelets and media sampled to see how much serotonin came out or leaked from the platelet (efflux). Recent reports in the literature indicate that platelets from autistic children may have different uptake and efflux rates for serotonin than do platelets from normals (Boullin et al., 1970).

We undertook a series of studies to replicate these findings (Yuwiler et al., 1975). In Figure 13 the experimental schema is diagramed. Half of the method is a replication of that used by other investigators who reported finding differences in serotonin efflux from platelets of autistic and non-autistic children. This is labeled Procedure B. This procedure involves incubating the platelet-rich plasma with serotonin in a carbon dioxide-oxygen atmosphere. At the end of the incubation period, the platelets are centrifuged to separate them from plasma and are resuspended in platelet-free plasma to measure the loss of serotonin from the platelets. This procedure, which involves centrifugation and resuspension of platelets, has a number of technical complications because platelets are fragile and can be destroyed by centrifugation. Platelet destruction obviously would lead to serotonin escaping into the platelet-free plasma in which they were resuspended and would appear as "leakage." To circumvent this we devised a second alternate procedure labeled—Procedure A—which involves placing the serotonin-loaded platelets in a special container with a semipermeable membrane. This membrane allows radioactive serotonin to leak out without manipulating the platelet. In both of the procedures, we sampled the serotonin content of the platelets and the media in which they were suspended (the supernatant) before and after incubation periods. The results of these studies are shown in Figure 14. The left side of the Figure shows the uptake data and the right side shows the efflux. It can be seen that serotonin in the plasma declines with time while the radioactivity in the platelets increases. Thus, the platelets are accumulating the radioactive serotonin. The accumulation is concentration-dependent in this range.

When platelet-serotonin content reached the plateau level, at about ninety minutes in our system, the platelets and plasma are placed in a dialysis frame and the serotonin in the external plasma diffuses away. The open circles on the right side of Figure 14 show that the platelets lose a little serotonin and then level off. The small loss presumably represents serotonin in the platelet cytoplasm while the serotonin in the vesicles remains constant until the platelets die and disintegrate.

Table I summarizes the results of our uptake and efflux studies. As shown, we were not able to find statistically significant differences in uptake or efflux among platelets of autistics, hospitalized comparison groups, or normals.

Table I.
Basal Serotonin, Serotonin Uptake and Efflux by Platelets

A

Group	Age (months)	Basal		
		Serotonin μg/ml	Platelets $10^3/mm^3$	5HT μmoles/10^{11} Platelet
	mean±S.D.	mean±S.D.(N)	mean±S.D.(N)	mean±S.D.(N)
Normal	95.5±25	0.205±0.17(12)	310±12(14)	0.369±0.027(12)
Autistic	60.2±13	0.273±0.030(12)[a]	333±23(12)	0.516±0.060(12)[a]
Hospital Controls	69.4±20	0.240±0.014(14)	324±21(12)	0.436±0.033(12)

B

Group	Procedure A		Procedure B	
	Uptake μmoles 5HT/10^{11} plat.	Efflux % change	Uptake μmoles 5HT/10^{11} plat.	Efflux % change
	mean±S.D.(N)	mean±S.D.(N)	mean±S.D.(N)	mean±S.D.(N)
Normal	1.452±0.070(11)	−22.8±3.3(11)[b]	1.482±0.016(11)[b]	2.01±2.8(12)[b] 0.49±0.8(12)[c]
Autistic	1.221±0.092(11)	−22.3±3.1(11)[b]	1.400±0.050(11)	−0.56±3.5(12)[b] 0.52±1.1(12)[c]
Hospital Controls	1.309±0.020(13)	−23.7±3.6(13)[b]	—	—

Values are mean and standard error. The number of patients within each group is indicated within parentheses.

[a]Significantly different from normals, p < 0.05.

[b]Calculated from difference in platelet radioactivity between beginning and end of *efflux* period.

[c]Calculated from differences in supernatant radioactivity between beginning and end of *efflux* period.

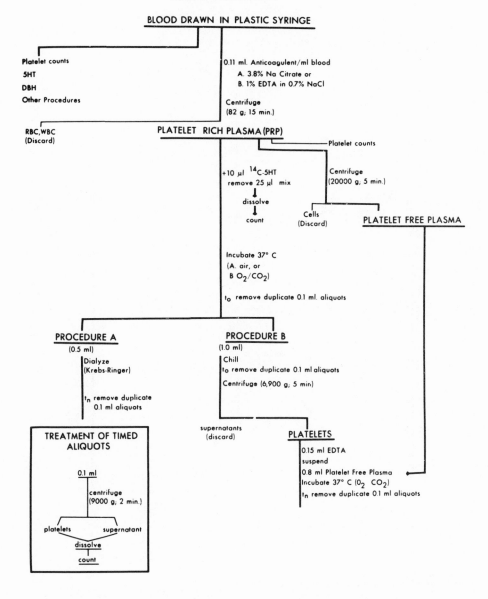

OUTLINE OF PROCEDURE

BLOOD DRAWN IN PLASTIC SYRINGE

Platelet counts
5HT
DBH
Other Procedures

0.11 ml. Anticoagulent/ml blood
A. 3.8% Na Citrate or
B. 1% EDTA in 0.7% NaCl

Centrifuge
(82 g; 15 min.)

RBC, WBC
(Discard)

PLATELET RICH PLASMA (PRP)

Platelet counts

+10 μl ^{14}C-5HT
remove 25 μl mix

dissolve

count

Centrifuge
(20000 g; 5 min.)

Cells
(Discard)

PLATELET FREE PLASMA

Incubate 37° C
(A. air, or
B O_2/CO_2)

t_0 remove duplicate 0.1 ml. aliquots

PROCEDURE A
(0.5 ml)

Dialyze
(Krebs-Ringer)

t_n remove duplicate
0.1 ml aliquots

PROCEDURE B
(1.0 ml)

Chill
t_0 remove duplicate 0.1 ml aliquots

Centrifuge (6,900 g; 5 min)

TREATMENT OF TIMED
ALIQUOTS

0.1 ml

centrifuge
(9000 g; 2 min.)

platelets   supernatant

dissolve

count

supernatants
(discard)

PLATELETS

0.15 ml EDTA
suspend
0.8 ml Platelet Free Plasma
Incubate 37° C (O_2 CO_2)
t_n remove duplicate 0.1 ml aliquots

Figure 13

101

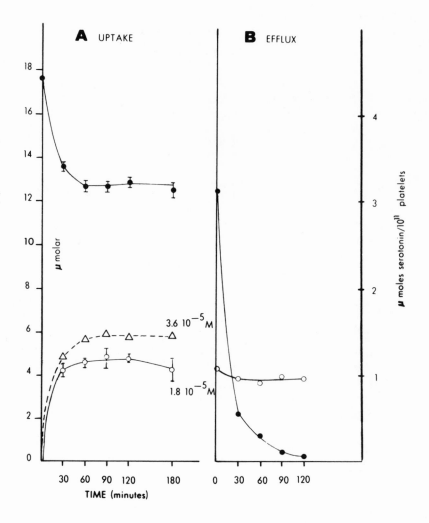

FIG. 14. Platelet serotonin uptake and efflux.

(A) The uptake of exogenous ^{14}C-serotonin into platelets (lower curves) and the concomitant loss of serotonin from the plasma (upper curve). Uptake curves for two concentrations of serotonin are shown. The curve for serotonin loss from the plasma is that obtained using a serotonin concentration of 2×10^{-5}M.

(B) The loss of serotonin from platelets (open circles) and supernatant solution (closed circles) in the dialysis tube during the efflux procedure.

REVIEW OF OUR RESULTS TO DATE

Our results to date suggest that autistics have higher blood serotonin, higher platelet counts, and somewhat higher serotonin per platelet than age-matched non-autistic children. These differences have occurred in each subset of our studies and in the total population of our gradually enlarging sample which now contains over seventy autistic patients. These differences do not appear to be artifactual (due to drugs, hospitalization, hematologic abnormalities, circadian variation, or age). We have not, however, systematically studied other variables, such as activity or chronic dietary intake. Thus, we are not yet certain that the differences are directly related to autism. Indeed, some autistic children do not have "abnormal values," and some non-autistic children do. Furthermore, we do not know whether the serotonin differences or the platelet differences are more important. Either may be directly related to fundamental processes involved in the disease or may be secondary and due to non-specific factors associated with it.

Our cumulative data to date suggests that serotonin has a bimodal distribution. This could indicate that there are "two kinds" of autistics or that some secondary influence causes a bimodal distribution. The wide differences between autistics' and non-autistics' platelet counts have diminished over the course of our studies. Initial data were obtained by hand counting platelets, and later data were obtained by automated counting. Thus, we do not know if the change is due to differences in population or methodology, or whether it reflects a greater association between autism and serotonin than between autism and platelet counts.

FUTURE PLANS

Our future plans fall along these lines: first, we wish to determine if our neurobiochemical findings are primarily or secondarily related to the disease. There are several ways to examine this. We can see if we can change behavior by manipulating serotonin, we can correlate changes in clinical state with changes in biological variables, and we can examine environmental artifacts which might account for our observations.

The amino acid, tryptophan, is the precursor of serotonin and it may be possible to lower serotonin by using a low-tryptophan diet. If this is possible, we could then see if the behavioral syndrome is correspondingly altered. This procedure has a number of complications. Obviously, it is necessary to demonstrate that a low-tryptophan diet does indeed alter blood serotonin in the human child as it is known to do in the rat. It is also necessary to devise a behavioral rating system capable of detecting subtle clinical change. Since tryptophan is an essential amino acid necessary for normal growth and development, the experimental diet would have to be individually adjusted for each age group and sufficiently palatable to allow complete consumption. Also, nitrogen balance studies would have to be done on each child to assure that the dietary restriction is not deleterious to growth. Such a study could have two clear outcomes—behavior would be altered as serotonin was lowered or behavior could be unaffected. In the first case, if behavior improved, the results would be compatible with the view that serotonin is related to behavior. However, the relationship could still be indirect. If symptomatology was not altered, then the serotonin changes may be unrelated to the disease, or sufficient damage may have already occurred so that reversal is no longer possible.

Another approach would be to correlate clinical change with biological variables. Two experimental paradigms can be considered. The first consists of objectively rating various aspects of the clinical state of our subjects (both controls and patients) and assessing any correlations between these clinical measures and biological variables. Because of individual variance among subjects on the biological measures and the developmental factors involved in both clinical and biological variables, this approach is somewhat limited.

An additional approach would be to longitudinally follow patients and attempt to correlate changes in clinical state with changes in biological variables. Again, a quantitative rating scale is required and variables must be adjusted for normal maturational changes. We could anticipate that a large number of children would have to be studied in this manner since clinical improvement is unfortunately neither frequent nor dramatic. Positive results would be encouraging but not definitive. A negative result would also be ambiguous since clinical change could result from the development of secondary compensatory processes rather than simply a reversal of the initiating biological impairment.

In any event, it is essential to attempt to control environmental variables which might account for the apparent relationship between autism and serotonin. This of course is a Herculean task since the number of such variables is infinite. Two of the more likely variables we have yet to examine are activity and diet. Both are difficult to control. Within a hospital setting, a constant diet can be provided but considerable nursing personnel is required to assure that what is available is also consumed. Control of the diets of outpatients and normal controls is more difficult and would require parental cooperation and support. Activity levels cannot be controlled but only monitored and then correlated with the biological variables. These are only two of many possible variables.

Finally, there is another indirect approach to the general problem of assessing the meaning of our current observations. We could examine more fundamental biological factors controlling serotonin per platelet and platelet numbers. While this approach would not directly address itself to the relevance of these variables in autism, it could expose more fundamental variables or processes. For example, elevated serotonin may be due to excessive hydroxylation and this would point to a peripheral and/or central defect in the control of the enzyme, tryptophan-5-hydroxylase. Or, perhaps platelet differences reflect differences in age distribution of platelets. This in turn may be due to a more fundamental difference in the control of tissue aging.

In summary, studies of serotonin differences between populations involve evaluation of free, bound and total blood tryptophan, tryptophan metabolism in peripheral tissues, examination of serotonin uptake and storage in platelets, estimation of serotonin formation in peripheral tissues, and examination of serotonin-degrading enzymes. Some can be directly assessed and some cannot. Similarly, studies of platelet differences would involve estimations of platelet age via ATP content, platelet morphology, platelet half-life, platelet vesicle content, platelet fragility, and vesicular membrane properties.

CONCLUSIONS

Our present plans are to continue to study serotonin metabolism and other biochemical factors in autistic and comparison cases. We accept the challenge posed both by inconsistent results and the as yet unanswered question, "So what?" The future will test the wisdom of this decision. Our obvious hope is that such research will identify specific pathological factors in autism and lead to the development of a rational therapy.

REFERENCES

Boullin, E.J., Coleman, M., and O'Brien, R.A. (1970). Abnormalities in platelet 5-hydroxytryptamine efflux in patients with infantile autism. *Nature* 226:371-372.

Eiduson, S., Geller, E., Yuwiler, A., and Eiduson, B.T. (1964) *Biochemistry and Behavior.* D. Van Nostrand Co. Princeton, New Jersey.

Følling, A. (1934). Über ausscheidung von Phenylbrenztraubensaüre in den Harn als Stoffwechselanomalie in Verbindung mit Imbezillität. *Zeitschrift für Physiologische Chemie* 227:169-176.

Jervis, G.A. (1939). The genetics of phenylpyruvic oligophrenia. *Journal of Mental Science* 85:719.

——— (1953). Phenylpyruvic oligophrenia: deficiency of phenylalanine oxidizing system. *Proceedings of Society for Experimental Biology and Medicine* 82:514-515.

Jouvet, M. (1969). Biogenic amines and the states of sleep. *Science* 163:32-41.

Pletscher, A. (1968). Metabolism, transfer and storage of 5-hydroxytryptamine in blood platelets. *British Journal of Pharmacology and Chemotherapy* 32:1-16.

Ritvo, E.R., Yuwiler, A., Geller, E., Ornitz, E.M., Saeger, K., and Plotkin, S. (1970). Increased blood serotonin and platelets in early infantile autism. *Archives of General Psychiatry* 23:566-572.

——, Yuwiler, A., Geller, E., Kales, A., Rashkis, S., Schicor, A., Plotkin, S., Axelrod, R., and Howard, C. (1971). Effects of L-dopa on autism. *Journal of Autism and Childhood Schizophrenia* 1:190-205.

Schain, R.J. and Freedman, D. (1961). Studies on 5-hydroxyindole metabolism in autistic and other mentally retarded children. *Journal of Pediatrics* 58:315-20.

Sollberger, A. (1965). *Biological Rhythm Research.* Elsevier, Amsterdam.

Yuwiler, A., Plotkin, S., Geller, E., and Ritvo, E.R. (1970). Rapid accurate procedure for the determination of serotonin in whole human blood. *Biochemical Medicine* 3:426-36.

——, Ritvo, E.R., Bald, D., Kipper, D., and Koper, A. (1971). Examination of circadian rhythmicity of blood serotonin and platelets in autistic and non-autistic children. *Journal of Autism and Childhood Schizophrenia* 1:421-35.

——, Ritvo, E.R., Geller, E., Glousman, R., Schneiderman, G., and Matsumo, D. (1975). Uptake and efflux of serotonin from platelets of autistic and non-autistic children. *Journal of Autism and Childhood Schizophrenia* 5:83-98.

CHAPTER EIGHT

Pharmacotherapy for Autistic and Schizophrenic Children

BARBARA FISH

Drug treatment for autistic and schizophrenic children cannot be discussed apart from the other aspects of their treatment; therefore, I shall first review general issues of treatment before discussing the part played by specific medications.

Autism is a disorder for which we do not as yet have any "cure." There is no specific antidote which can reverse the underlying pathology. Whenever a new treatment comes along that offers even a slight chance of improving a few children, it immediately releases a tremendous flood of enthusiasm and hope; there tends to be too extreme a swing in the new direction. This is understandable emotionally, but it is not a realistic expectation. Current treatments of autism are *symptomatic*. This doesn't denigrate any of the treatments, because in much of medicine our treatments are *only symptomatic*. If one could significantly improve most of a child's symptoms we would be very happy—even if this didn't reverse the *underlying* biological disorder.

PLANNING TREATMENT

To plan treatment for a child one first evaluates how he is functioning in every major area of development. Then one outlines a program of treatments directed at each one of the deficits, insofar as treatments are available. In this sense, treatment must always be *individualized*. No one treatment takes care of everything that is wrong with these children.

Frequently, autistic children have disturbances of their physiological patterns of eating and sleeping, allergies, and varying sensitivities to illness. A high proportion of autistic children have celiac disease. We do not know if these are non-specific associations in children who have poor homeostasis or if when we find the biochemical mechanism in autism if it will explain these associations.

We also must evaluate the child's state of attention—whether he seems under or over aroused, whether his attention is fragmented, or whether he appears dreamy and preoccupied. We also have to examine his mode of affective response and assess whether he is overexcited and/or very under-responsive. Many of these children will fluctuate rather erratically between these two states and this lability has to be taken into account. Similarly, motor behavior may be hyperkinetic or hypokinetic, or a child may have combinations of the two—remaining almost rooted to one spot and then suddenly darting off.

In addition, one must evaluate the more specific developmental disorders of visual-motor, perceptual, language and social functioning. All of these constitute the gamut of target symptoms to which treatment should be directed.

Basically, there are two major modalities of treatment; one is biological and the other is social-educational. At the moment, drug treatment is the major biological modality. I believe that any child with a disorder as serious as autism deserves a trial of drug treatment. Only in much milder psychiatric conditions can social and educational measures completely resolve the symptoms and return the patient to normal functioning. But in autistic children, unfortunately, this is not the case. Some biological adjunct is required to improve a child's receptivity to social and educational modalities.

Aside from drugs, the only other biological treatment that has been used is electroshock treatment (ECT). In this country, Dr. Lauretta Bender has been the only major advocate of this form of treatment. I trained with her in the 1950s before any of the major neuroleptics were available. ECT was capable of stimulating some of the children to respond to the educational program when nothing else worked. The minor tranquilizers available at that time did not help these children at all. While I was Director of Child Psychiatry at Bellevue Hospital, we only tried shock treatment for a few autistic children who failed to respond to all the drugs which were then available. If they had failed to respond to drugs, they also did not respond to ECT or inulin shock. I therefore am skeptical that these treatments are more efficacious than medication, but some children might respond to them.

The social and educational therapies should be planned on a long-term basis, beginning as soon as the child is diagnosed and continuing throughout his life. They should include early stimulation of development, speech therapy, social stimulation and milieu treatment. Behavior therapy is a scientific approach to develop patterned behavior. In the therapeutic program at Bellevue, many of these goals were reached in a freer and more flexible way, with such positive reinforcers as food, affection or other kinds of attention. Aversive conditioning was limited to a sharp "No!" or removal to a chair at the edge of the nursery. These methods were equally effective as the more "scientific" methods for shaping more mature, organized behaviors. Our goal was to prepare the child for all the special educational measures and vocational training which are discussed in other chapters.

I also include psychotherapy under the educational modalities. This is only appropriate when a child is not severely withdrawn and can play or verbalize some of his feelings. Some of these children then express feelings of depression, of feeling different, or feeling quite isolated. At that stage, as with other children who have such feelings, they can be helped to understand that they are not the only ones in the world who have increased sensitivity.

AN APPROACH TO PHARMACOTHERAPY

For a rational approach to drug treatment, one first has to recognize what medication is able to do. Basically, one is attempting to modify the disturbances of physiological patterning of attention, affect, and of motor behavior. It is easier to find agents which inhibit and decrease behavior—or improve the organization and control of behavior—than it is to find agents which can stimulate new behaviors and more initiative. The latter is the main problem with the autistic child who needs to have his development stimulated.

Our most effective drugs do much more than sedate. There is considerable evidence to show that effective major neuroleptics can reduce and nearly eliminate major psychotic symptoms, including disorganized, noncommunicative speech and loosening of associations. Such improvement can only occur in children who are not so stereotyped or so impaired cognitively that they cannot respond to any kind of therapy.

What drugs do, when they are effective, is to make a child more receptive to educational and social therapies. They do not replace other therapies which must go on all the time for the child's development to be promoted and his improvement to continue. Drugs are limited in their ability to reverse fixed deficits in development. There must be some innate capacity for growth, and the drug response will depend on the age of the child when he is treated.

EFFECTIVENESS OF SPECIFIC MEDICATIONS

One can categorize psychotropic drugs in four groups. The stimulants and antidepressive agents have primarily *excitatory effects*, and the minor tranquilizers and the neuroleptics have predominantly *sedative effects*.

The *stimulants* are *amphetamines* and *methylphenidate*. In general, these drugs make autistic children worse. It is important to emphasize this, because many physicians lump all hyperactive children together without recognizing the importance of the different diagnostic groups (Fish, 1971). Unfortunately, I have seen many autistic and schizophrenic children given amphetamines or methylphenidate (Ritalin), with resultant exaggeration of their psychosis (Fish, 1971). Too often, when this happens, more potent drugs are not tried; it is assumed that if stimulants do not work on the hyperactivity, nothing will. However, there are rare exceptions, and I have seen a couple of children who responded slightly to amphetamine and did not respond to major neuroleptics.

Of the *anti-depressant* drugs, the only one studied so far in autistic children is *imipramine* (Tofranil). We tried this in our psychopharmacology research program at Bellevue, New York University Medical Center. Imipramine had some stimulating and some sedative effects, but on the whole, it was a poor drug for the autistic children (Campbell et al., 1971b). However, it was better than amphetamine, and about 20 percent of the children showed marked improvement—less psychotic speech, an increase in speech, increase in responsivity, and an increase in all their play patterns. This tended to occur at the two extremes of the autistic/schizophrenic spectrum. There were children who initially were less severely psychotic by the time they were treated with imipramine, although one had been very severe earlier. There were also children who were completely mute; one was extremely hyperactive, another was very apathetic, but these two also improved. But over three-quarters of the children on imipramine became worse. They were the more severely and floridly psychotic children—some with speech and some without. These results are similar to the findings in severe adult schizophrenics who are given antidepressant medication.

In our search for other drugs which might stimulate autistic children, (in this series of controlled trials with various medications) we tried *methysergide* (Sansert), which is used for migraine. Bender and Faretra (1963) reported that LSD and methysergide had a marked stimulating and therapeutic effect on severely schizophrenic children they treated at Creedmore State Hospital. Bender's reasoning was that both drugs are in the same chemical class. They have a marked anti-serotonin effect which might be useful, since there was a suggestion that serotonin was elevated in the autistic child (Ritvo et al., 1970). We found, as they had, that the children did show an initial stimulation with methysergide (Fish et al., 1969b). There was a brightening of affect, an increased responsivity, increased alertness and eye-to-eye contact. These effects only lasted for three days. After this, when the children were maintained on the drug, they seemed to adapt to the positive, stimulating effects, but they gradually showed increasing irritability, somnolence and disorganized activity. These effects counteracted any previous improvement they had shown. Again, there were a couple of exceptions; these were the most retarded children in the group. One was initially very apathetic, another extremely hyperactive. These two did not completely adapt to the therapeutic effect of methysergide, even though it was continued for about two months. Although they did not show as much improvement at the end of the treatment as they had in the first few days, it indicated to us that there might be a subgroup of autistic children who could respond to this drug.

A comparison of these two studies shows how little we know about the mechanisms underlying the action of these drugs and the disturbances in the children. Imipramine is thought to potentiate serotonin, and methysergide to inhibit it. Yet both drugs showed very much the same kinds of behavioral effects in the children.

Under the *mild sedative drugs*, we include the tranquilizers and hypnotics or sleeping pills. These are generally not effective for autistic children. Sometimes *chloral hydrate* or *barbiturates* may be needed for bedtime sedation. Even then they may not help, and may only serve to excite the child. We have found that *diphenhydramine* (Benadryl), which is an antihistamine, was the most effective of the mild sedatives (Fish, 1960). It is less effective than chlorpromazine (Fish and Shapiro, 1965).

The *major neuroleptics* are, in general, the most effective drugs available for autistic children. *Chlorpromazine* (Thorazine) is the classic example of this group; the oldest and most familiar one. In my very early clinical work, when these drugs were first available, it appeared to me that the most retarded, autistic children, especially the underactive, "dreamy" ones, seemed to be very sensitive to the sedative effect of chlorpromazine (Fish, 1960). By the time the dose had reached a level which had an organizing, antipsychotic effect, what little babbling or speech had been present was often suppressed. Thus, chlorpromazine is still the major drug for older schizophrenic children who have more advanced speech and development in other areas—it is not as effective for young autistic patients.

Of the earlier major tranquilizers, *trifluperazine* (Stelazine), which has less prominent sedative effects than chlorpromazine, is more effective for the very retarded, severely autistic children with verbal IQs below 70 (Fish, 1960). Therefore, when we began to study the newer drugs, we looked for medications which had still less sedative effects.

Of the *butyrophenones*, haloperidol (Haldol) is most frequently used. We did not test this drug, but studied a more "stimulating" member of that group, *trifluperidol*. This drug was not marketed commercially, although we found it effective in autistic children (Fish et al., 1969a). It had a narrow therapeutic margin and was difficult to regulate.

Of the *thioxanthenes*, we studied *thiothixene* (Navane). This acted somewhat like trifluperazine. It had less of a sedative effect and more of a stimulating effect on the young, preschool, autistic children (Campbell et al., 1970). We were often able to compare two drugs, since children stayed in the therapeutic nursery for many months. Thus, the same child could have a series of drugs in a crossover study.

We learned that many autistic children react differently to drugs as they grow older. Some who need stimulating drugs when young may react poorly when older. By eight or nine, they may need a drug like chlorpromazine, which had not helped when they were younger.

Molindone has effects similar to thiothixene, but it was more difficult to regulate. Even children who improved often had brief periods of inexplicable crying (Campbell et al., 1971a).

Recently, we compared *lithium* to chlorpromazine. Neither was very effective for these children. Lithium acted somewhat like chlorpromazine, but it had less antipsychotic properties (Campbell et al., 1972). It had a sedative action, and was more difficult to regulate than chlorpromazine. One had to take blood levels frequently. Furthermore, the more evidence there was of mental retardation, the more sensitive were the children to very low doses of lithium. Toxicity developed at low blood levels (0.3-0.8 mEq/1). Thus, there was a very narrow therapeutic margin. I do not consider lithium to be one of the more promising drugs available for these children.

The last class of agents might be called "physiological." I would put treatment for hypoglycemia in this category, as well as the megavitamin regime. We have not done a controlled study of either of these therapies and none have been reported (American Psychiatric Association, 1973). Anecdotal reports that particular children respond may be due to spontaneous fluctuations in their illness. One needs adequately controlled, large-scale studies to assess whether changes are related to a treatment.

We most recently completed a controlled study of *tri-iodothyronine* (T3) in twenty autistic children (Campbell et al., 1973). We tried this drug because of its potentially stimulating effect. In the 1950s, Sherwin had treated two six-year-old autistic children with T3 who showed some improvement. Theoretically, T3 enhances noradrenergic activity and produces effects similar to dextroamphetamine. We therefore did a crossover study of both drugs, expecting that the autistic children might become agitated on T3 as they did on amphetamine; however, this did not occur. Frequently what happened was that each time we increased the dose, they showed some increased hyperactivity or excitability, but then they quickly adapted and lost these symptoms. All but three of the twenty children improved. This included not only the underactive children, whom we expected to improve, but also those who were the most hyperactive, excitable and agitated. Only the nonpsychotic hyperactive children became worse. There was no relationship between the improvements on T3 and dextroamphetamine. It is therefore unlikely that the adrenergic effects of T3 were responsible for the improvement observed in the autistic children. T3 was as effective as the best major neuroleptics. These children were not clinically hypothyroid before treatment and the mechanism of T3's therapeutic action needs to be studied further. It may provide some clues as to the CNS disorder in schizophrenia. A word of caution is necessary. We only kept children on T3 for three months. Before thyroid treatment is given for longer periods, precautions would have to be taken to prevent eventual retardation of growth. Schapiro (1966) demonstrated that thyroid accelerated development in immature rats but they reached their growth ceiling sooner, and, in the long run, they were more retarded than the untreated rats.

DETERMINING OPTIMAL DRUG AND DOSE FOR A PATIENT

To determine which medication will be beneficial for a child, one has to try a series of drugs and see which is the most effective. With each drug, one must titrate the dose very carefully up to the most effective level, assess clinical change and then try another drug. We helped many children who had been referred by doctors saying, "I tried everything and nothing worked." We used the same drugs; but it was necessary to be meticulous in regulating dosage. We regularly increased the dose of a particular drug, recording in detail what the therapeutic effects were and weighing these with whatever toxic or deleterious effects occurred at each step. One increases dosage until *toxic effects outweigh benefits*. Only in this way does one know that one has gone through the entire useful dose range for a drug in a child, and has determined the full extent of possible effectiveness. We found as much as a twenty-fold difference between the effective dose for one child and that for another, using the same drug. Anyone who only gives a dosage level recommended by the package insert may completely miss the effective range.

Even after one finds the optimal dosage level, it does not always remain the same for a child. Changes are often required after infections and with increasing age. One should frequently try and see if a child can maintain his improvement if the dose is dropped. Once a child's development has been stimulated by using medication, and his speech or other performance has become established, these gains may continue without further medication. One does not want to introduce foreign substances into the system unless they are really necessary. Any medication may have toxic effects.

ULTIMATE EFFECTIVENESS OF TREATMENT

The critical question which one needs to ask is, how far can a child progress given the optimal drug for him and a total therapeutic program? The answer will depend on how impaired he was initially. Follow-up studies indicated that *language* is the critical prognostic variable (Eisenberg, 1956). If there was useful speech by age five, more children improved and adjusted moderately well. If they didn't have useful speech by five, then the prognosis was poor. In Bender's (1972) long-term series, an initial verbal IQ over 70 was the best single indicator of whether the child would adjust outside of an institution as an adult.

In our Bellevue studies of preschool autistic and schizophrenic children, we used various rating scales in order to objectively define initial severity and any improvement in the children. We also wished to see if it would be possible to predict which children would improve. Our scales were therefore based on the following data and used language as the critical variable (Fish, 1964, 1968). Language was assessed in a semistructured examination which varied depending on what the child could or could not do. It included an attempt to elicit speech, social interaction, performance on the Gesell, motor behavior and response to frustration. The children were then divided (Fish et al., 1968) into those with and without speech. Those classified having "no speech" had unformed sounds, incomprehensible babbling, jargon, and no words. The children without speech were subdivided into those "with comprehension" (group "C") and "without comprehension" (groups "A" and "B"). Comprehension was defined as at least one definite response to symbolic language. Those without comprehension were subdivided into those with "no adaptive skills" (group "A") and those with "minimal adaptive skills" (group "B"). Generally, the minimum adaptive skill was the ability to place the round block in the round hole of the Gesell form-board. (Often, autistic children can pass such tests of form perception almost at age level but not do anything else.) If they did pass, they then were in the next to the lowest group ("B"), but not the very lowest group ("A").

The "speaking group" was subdivided into those with language abilities under or over 33 percent of that expected for their age. Since these were preschoolers, those "under 33 percent" (group "D") spoke in single words. If

Table I.
**Number of Children Whose Language Improved on
Trifluoperazine or Trifluperidol[a], by Groups**

Degree	(N)	A (4)	B (4)	C (4)	D (3)	E (6)
No improvement		4	3	3	2	1
Moderate improvement[b]		0	0	1	1	3
Marked improvement[c]		0	1	0	0	2

[a]No children in C' and D' groups received these drugs.

[b]Language improved in amount or in communicativeness, but remained predominantly psychotic.

[c]Language became predominantly communicative.

they used two-word phrases, that is, if they functioned at a twenty-one-month level, they were in the group "with over 33 percent" (group "E"). This included echoing or spontaneous speech. Thus, it didn't take very much speech to get them into this group. The differentiation within group "E" depended on how severe the rating for stereotyped behavior was.

Only one child in group "E" responded to a placebo and the total program (in the absence of medication) with "marked improvement." This meant not only an *increase* in speech, but a shift to *communicative* speech on our rating scales. If speech increased in amount, but not in its communicative function, this was rated as only a "moderate improvement." If there was an improvement only in social or affective responses, motor symptoms, or attention, but no language improvement, this was rated as only "slight improvement," since we considered communicative speech to be critical. The only child who improved without medication appeared to have had some specific environmental factors which precipitated his autistic withdrawal at three years.

In 1968, we reported on the first thirty-two of the preschool schizophrenic children treated in the research program with a series of drugs (Fish et al., 1968). One analysis compared their responses to the two most potent drugs we had tested by then, trifluperazine and trifluperidol (Table I). The only child in the low group "B" who responded was treated before

Tables I, II and III reprinted with permission from Fish et al, 1968. Copyright 1968, The American Psychiatric Association.

Table II.
Distribution of Verbal IQs at Follow-Up by Groups

IQ	(N)	Psychotic					Nonpsychotic	
		A (7)	B (6)	C (4)	D (5)	E (6)	C′ (2)	D′ (2)
Noncommunicative language IQ								
Mute = 0		6	2	0	0	0	0	0
< 33		1	2	4	3	1	1	0
33-70		0	0	0	2	2	0	0
Communicative language IQ								
< 33		0	0	0	0	0	0	0
33-70		0	2[a]	0	0	0	0	0
71-90		0	0	0	0	2[a]	1[b]	0
> 90		0	0	0	0	1[b]	0	2[b]

[a]Had originally shown marked improvement (shifting to communicative speech) while on medication.

[b]Had originally shown marked improvement while on placebo.

age two. She succeeded on the form-board at twenty-one months. The other children treated at about two years were much more retarded. In general, the moderate and marked improvements in communicative speech occurred in the less retarded children (Table I). In group "C" there was one child who had some comprehension and began to talk while on medication, but he retained stereotyped behavior and had no further speech development after four years when he was first treated. He looks exactly the same now, at age fifteen. In the least retarded group (group "E"), the less stereotyped children who improved markedly with a potent drug, also appeared better at follow-up. They were borderline in verbal IQ and functioned in classes for normal children. From this we concluded that if the child responded well to a potent pharmacological treatment, it meant not only that the drug was effective, but that his biological disorder was capable of responding.

Table II shows the current verbal IQ at follow-up—at least five years after initial treatment. In the mute group "A", who had no comprehension and no adaptive skills, all but one were still mute in adolescence. The one who spoke did so in an occasional monosyllable. Sometimes it was com-

Table III.
School Placement at Follow-Up, by Groups[a]

		Psychotic					Nonpsychotic	
Placement	(N)	A (5)	B (6)	C (4)	D (4)	E (6)	C' (2)	D' (2)
Age range (9/67)		8-9	6-9	6-10	6-10	6-11	5-9	5-9
Classes or institution for mentally retarded		2	3	1	1	1	0	0
Classes or institution for psychotic children		3	2	3	3	2	0	0
Classes for moderately deviate[b]		0	0	0	0	0	1	0
Classes for normal children[c]		0	1	0	0	3	1	2

[a]Excluding three children (two in A, one in D), under five years.

[b]Nine-year-old in class for aphasic children.

[c]This category indicates grade placement appropriate for age. One child in each group (B, E, C' and D') is in nursery or kindergarten; remaining three are doing academic work at grade level.

municative, but only once in six months. Thus they all continued to function on a severely retarded level. In group "B," there were two children who developed communicative speech; but they never developed beyond retarded verbal IQs. In this group was the little girl who showed a remarkable recovery at twenty-one months. The group "D" children—with speech under 33 percent—when treated before five years old sometimes reached a verbal IQ of 70, but never developed communicative speech. Only children in the mildest group "E" who initially had some two-word phrases (even if limited to echoing) eventually developed communicative speech. The outcome, in terms of *school placement*, is related to the verbal IQ as shown in Table III. The children with least function before five years went to schools for the severely retarded or special schools for psychotic children.

Our research has demonstrated that it is possible to identify some schizophrenic children in the first months of life (Fish, 1975; Fish et al., 1965b, 1973). In our future research, we shall focus on this early identification. Hopefully, if we can begin biological treatment early, it may be possible to avoid deficits that are secondary to withdrawal.

REFERENCES

American Psychiatric Association (1973). Megavitamins and orthomolecular therapy in Psychiatry. *American Psychiatric Association* Task Force Report, No. 7, Washington, D.C.

Bender, L., Faretra, G., and Cobrinik, L. (1963). LSD and UML treatment of hospitalized disturbed children. In Wortis, J., ed., *Recent Advances in Biological Psychiatry* New York: Plenum Press, 5:84-92.

———— and Faretra, G. (1972). The relationship between childhood schizophrenia and adult schizophrenia. In Kaplan, A.R. ed., *Genetic Factors in Schizophrenia* Springfield: Charles C. Thomas, pp. 28-64.

Campbell, M., Fish, B., Shapiro, T., and Floyd, A. (1970). Thiothixene in young disturbed children. A pilot study. *Archives of General Psychiatry* 23:70-72.

———— Fish, B., Shapiro, T., and Floyd, A. (1971a). Study of molindone in disturbed preschool children. *Current Therapeutic Research* 13:28-33.

———— Fish, B., Shapiro, T., and Floyd, A. (1971b). Imipramine in preschool autistic and schizophrenic children. *Journal of Autism and Childhood Schizophrenia* 3:267-282.

————, Fish, B., Korein, J., Shapiro, T., Collins, P., and Koh, C. (1972). Lithium and chlorpromazine: A controlled crossover study of hyperactive severely disturbed young children. *Journal of Autism and Childhood Schizophrenia* 2:234-263.

————, Fish, B., David, R., Shapiro, T., Collins, P., and Koh, C. (1973). Liothyronine treatment in psychotic and nonpsychotic children under 6 years. *Archives of General Psychiatry* 29:602-608.

Eisenberg, L. (1956). The autistic child in adolescence. *American Journal of Psychiatry* 112:607-612.

Fish, B. (1960). Drug therapy in child psychiatry: pharmacological aspects. *Comprehensive Psychiatry* 1:212-227.

———— (1964). Evaluation of psychiatric therapies in children. In Hoch, P., and Zubin, J., eds., *The Evaluation of Psychiatric Treatment* New York: Grune and Stratton, pp. 202-220.

———— (1968). Methodology in child psychopharmacology. In Efron, D.H., and Cole, J.O., eds, *Psychopharmacology, Review of Progress, 1957-67* Washington, D.C.: Public Health Publication, No. 1836, pp. 989-1001.

———— (1971). The "one child, one drug" myth of stimulants in hyperkinesis. Importance of diagnostic categories in evaluating treatment. *Archives of General Psychiatry* 25:193-203.

———— (1975). Biologic antecedents of psychosis in children. In Freedman, D.X. ed., *The Biology of the Major Psychoses: A Comparative Analysis*. Association for Research in Nervous and Mental Disease, Publication No. 54, New York: Raven Press. pp. 49-80.

———— and Hagin, R. (1973). Visual-motor disorders in infants at risk for schizophrenia. *Archives of General Psychiatry* 28:900-904.

———— and Shapiro, T. (1965). A typology of children's psychiatric disorders: I. Its application to a controlled evaluation of treatment. *Journal of the American Academy of Child Psychiatry* 4:32-52.

————, Campbell, M., Shapiro, T., and Floyd, A. (1969a). Comparison of trifluperidol, trifluoperazine, and chlorpromazine in preschool schizophrenic children: The value of less sedative antipsychotic agents. *Current Therapeutic Research* 11:589-595.

————, Campbell, M., Shapiro, T., and Floyd, A. (1969b). Schizophrenic children treated with methysergide (Sansert). *Diseases of the Nervous System* 30:534-540.

————, Shapiro, T., Campbell, M., and Wile, R. (1968). A classification of schizophrenic children under five years. *American Journal of Psychiatry* 124:1415-23.

————, Shapiro, T., Halpern, F., and Wile, R. (1965b). The prediction of schizophrenia in infancy: III. A ten-year follow-up report of neurological and psychological development. *American Journal of Psychiatry* 121:768-775.

Ritvo, E., Yuwiler, A., Geller, E., Ornitz, E., Saeger, K., and Plotkin, S. (1970). Increased blood serotonin and platelets in early infantile autism. *Archives of General Psychiatry* 23:566-572.

Schapiro, S. (1966). Effects of thyroxine on maturation and development of the infant rat. *Endocrinology* 78:527-532.

CHAPTER NINE

Language and Autism

LORIAN BAKER
DENNIS P. CANTWELL
MICHAEL RUTTER
LAWRENCE BARTAK

It is generally agreed that a cardinal symptom of the syndrome of infantile autism is a disturbance of language (Kanner, 1943; Creak, 1961; Rimland, 1964; Rutter, 1968). Nevertheless, it is often asked what insights the study of language can bring to an understanding of the syndrome. In this chapter we wish to delineate three areas in which language studies can provide insights: *diagnosis, prognosis, and etiology.*

First, it is suggested that a precise characterization of "autistic language" may be an aid in establishing a clinical diagnosis. As it now stands, some autistic children have such grossly retarded speech that they present an initial problem in differential diagnosis between autism and such conditions as: mental retardation, congenital deafness, and developmental aphasia.

A second area in which language studies may be useful is that of prognosis. It has been suggested (Rutter et al., 1967) that there is an important correlation between general language level and outcome in the autistic child. Various authors (Shapiro et al., 1970; Wolff and Chess, 1965; Fay, 1967) have proposed that particular features of language are relevant to prognosis.

Finally, language studies can provide clues to the basic nature of autism. It has been proposed (Goldfarb et al., 1966a, 1966b, 1972a) that deviant maternal communication and inadequate maternal language may be causes of infantile autism. A rigorous linguistic examination of maternal language—particularly in comparison with the language of mothers of other language-disturbed children—can clarify this issue.

A modern grammatical analysis of the child's language can reveal the extent of the underlying linguistic "competence." Quasi-linguistic studies (of perception, association, etc.)) will reveal which linguistic skills are deficient and whether these deficiencies extend beyond language to other cognitive skills.

THE CLINICAL SIGNIFICANCE OF LANGUAGE STUDIES OF AUTISTIC CHILDREN

Rutter (1966a) notes that speech abnormalities are very early symptoms of autism, and indeed, are often the first symptoms to be observed. Since a language disturbance is often the motivating factor for parents bringing the child to professional attention, it is often the primary presenting complaint, and, as such, is of great importance to the diagnostician.

Although it is generally agreed that an abnormality of language is a criterion symptom of autism, diagnosis is generally made on the presence of a behavioral picture with the language disturbance being considered as but one of a cluster of symptoms (Creak, 1961; Cunningham, 1968; DeMyer et al., 1971; Ornitz and Ritvo, 1968; Weiland and Legg, 1964). Yet it is possible that diagnosis could be made solely or primarily on the basis of language behavior. Systematic study of the language of autistic children might lead to a detailed and specific profile of the linguistic abilities and disabilities of autism, and this linguistic profile could provide a basis for diagnosis. Such a specific profile would prove particularly valuable, for example, in making a differential diagnosis between autism, and developmental receptive aphasia, developmental expressive aphasia, mental retardation, elective mutism, partial blindness or partial deafness, environmental deprivation, Down's Syndrome, and other disorders in which an impairment of language is apparent.

Characteristics of Autistic Language

Much has been written about the characteristics of autistic language. However, the bulk of the literature is in the form of case reports or impressionistic statements. Systematic studies of the language of autistic children are few, and a reliable and specific profile of autistic language does not yet exist.

Kanner's early (1946) description of the autistic child included the first detailed (but impressionistic) characterization of autistic language. Kanner noted that the language of the autistic child was typified by a parroting of not-understood words and stored phrases (labeled immediate or delayed echolalia), a reversing of the pronouns *you* and *I*, a metaphorical or bizarre quality resulting from words being used with their own special references for the child, an extreme literalness, an absence of original remarks and a frequent use of verbal negations.

Recent review articles have been able to add only a few details to Kanner's original description. Savage (1968) states that echolalia, pronoun reversals, comprehension difficulties, diminished vocabulary, inappropriate and non-communicative language, mutism, neologisms and articulation difficulties are common in autistic children. Hingtgen and Bryson (1972) describe a frequent failure to develop speech, frequent immediate and delayed echoes, impaired communicative function, frequent mutism, lack of questions and informative statements, few personal pronouns, frequent use of imperatives, limited output, little comprehension or use of gestures, and deviations in articulation, pitch, rhythm, and inflection.

The first attempt to systematically study the language of a group of autistic children was made by Wolff and Chess (1965). They compared the language of fourteen autistic children under eight years of age with regard to total number of words, number of different words, average length of utterance, number of non-verbal utterances, number of immediate and delayed non-communicative repetitions, number of communicative repetitions, and number of original communicative utterances in a language sample. Although no formal comparisons were made with normal or non-autistic children, Wolff and Chess concluded that the "most striking abnormalities in the language of the children studied were stereotyped repetition of utterances . . . (and) lack of normal expressions of curiosity and of responsiveness to changing environmental cues."

There are four studies (Weiland and Legg, 1964; Rutter, 1966a; Cunningham, 1968; Goldfarb et al., 1972b) in which the language of autistic children has been formally compared with language of normals or non-psychotic controls in an attempt to delineate the unique characteristics of autistic language. Weiland and Legg (1964) compared the language of autistics and non-psychotic controls aged seven to sixteen years obtained during a "snack session" in which the children were "encouraged to talk, but asked no questions." For each of the thirty-four autistic and sixty control children, the first 750 utterances were analyzed. The method of analysis was a simplistic tallying of the "parts of speech" produced. The findings were that the autistic children used significantly more nouns, proper nouns, verbs, and imperative verbs, and significantly fewer conjunctions and personal pronouns—particularly the pronoun "we"—than controls. It was also noted that the autistic children exhibited greater variability than the control children.

Rutter (1966a) compared sixty-three Maudsley Hospital autistic children with sixty-three children matched for sex and with similar ages and IQs who were in the same department of the hospital at the same time. He found no speech at five years of age in thirty-one of the autistics (versus seven of the controls), pronoun reversal in nineteen of the autistics (versus eight of the controls), echolalia in twenty-nine of the autistics (versus nineteen of the controls) and excessive responses to sounds in twelve of the autistics (versus two of the controls). In addition, he found six of the autistics invented their own words frequently and ten talked in a strange voice, either a whisper or singsong.

Cunningham (1968) compared thirteen autistic children aged five to thirteen years with thirteen age- and intelligence-matched non-psychotics. Speech was recorded on tape during a play session with an adult and the first fifty utterances were analyzed for comprehensibility, length, and function. Functionally, utterances were analyzed as being either egocentric (repetitions, inappropriate remarks, thinking aloud, or action accompaniments) or socialized language (questions, statements, answers, or requests). Cunningham found significantly more incomprehensible and egocentric utterances among the autistic children. In particular, echoes of the interviewer, delayed repetitions, self-repetitions, thinking aloud and inappropriate remarks were more frequent in autistic children. There were no differences between the autistic children and controls for number of questions, answers, or complete sentences used, or for the use of first and second person pronouns.

Goldfarb et al. (1972b) compared language samples from twenty-five autistic and twenty-five normal children matched for age, sex, race and religious background. Volume, pitch, voice quality, rate, phrasing, fluency, stress, intonation, articulation, gestures, and expression of meaning were evaluated. While the autistic children had significantly more language and speech faults than the normals, there was considerable variation among the autistics and no specific clustering of faults could be found to uniquely characterize autistic language.

Thus, despite considerable work on the topic of characterizing autistic language, no consensus on a specific, unique profile of "autistic language" has yet been reached. Both Weiland and Legg (1964) and Goldbarb et al. (1972b) have commented on the variability of language found in the different subjects of their studies. And, there is less of a consensus across studies. Weiland and Legg (1964) have noted that *few personal pronouns* are used by autistic children, and that the pronoun "we" is particularly avoided. Cunningham (1968), however, found *no differences* in the use of first and second person pronouns between autistics and controls. Goldfarb et al. (1972b) mention an avoidance of the first person pronouns, whereas Bartak et al. (1972) suggest that when regarded in terms of sentence position, there is no difference in the use of various pronouns. Hingtgen and Bryson (1972) and Wolff and Chess (1965) mention a *lack of questions* as characteristic of the language of the autistic child, whereas Cunningham (1968) notes *no* difference between autistics and controls in amount of questioning, and Rutter et al. (1967) state that "communication is primarily by a series of obsessive questions" in the autistic adolescent.

Two explanations are possible for this lack of agreement in findings. One is that a non-homogeneous group has been chosen for study. Diagnostic problems create serious complications, and even now different investigators approach the problem of diagnosis from different viewpoints (Creak, 1961; Ornitz and Ritvo, 1968; Rutter, 1971; DeMyer, 1971). Even in cases where strict diagnostic criteria have been adhered to, children of different ages and performance IQs have been lumped together for study, possibly obscuring differences in language behavior dependent upon age or IQ. Rutter et al. (1967) have indicated, for example, that language of the adolescent autistic is very different from that of the young autistic child in as much as echolalia tends to be *outgrown*.

Other possible explanations for the diversity of findings are faults in the collection of language samples or a faulty method of language analysis. Goldfarb et al. (1972b) state that a particular language characteristic (such as echolalia or repetitiveness) may be stressed and then even regarded as characteristic, simply because it is the most dramatic and obvious to the listener. Despite this perceptive remark, Goldfarb's method itself is not free from fault. In this analysis, language is often categorized in an impression-istic manner as belonging to such ill-defined categories as *excessive questioning, confused, limited, too weak, too loud,* or *non-fluent*.

Apart from the language analysis, the data collection itself is an area in which questionable methods have often been used. Samples in which the experimenter has a free hand to "encourage conversation" (as in Weiland and Legg, 1964) are particularly subject to experimenter bias in which the experimenter may be leading the child with subtle verbal or non-verbal cues to produce the expected echolalic or repetitive behavior.

Throughout this chapter reference will be made to a comparative study of autistic and aphasic children which was undertaken to test the hypothesis that a *specific language deficit* may underlie the development of infantile autism. The initial forty-two boys in the study were selected on the basis of having a current disorder of language comprehension which had been present from infancy and which was not due to overt neurological disorder or peripheral deafness. All children also had a non-verbal IQ of at least 70. Nineteen of these children were classified as showing a syndrome of in-fantile autism using the criteria outlined by Rutter (1971). The other twenty-three children were not clearly autistic. They were diagnosed as showing an uncomplicated developmental language disorder which included an impair-ment in comprehension as well as in the production of language. At the time that they were initially seen, the mean age of the autistic children was 7 years and 0 months and of the aphasic children was 8 years and 2 months.

Initially the parents of both groups of children were interviewed and the children were tested psychometrically for intelligence, language, reading, and social behavior. Details of the initial evaluation of the children have already been published (Bartak et al., 1975). One to two years after the initial evaluation, twenty-six of the subjects, thirteen in each group, were re-evaluated. The parents were again interviewed concerning the language and behavior of the children. Also, a one-hour language sample was taped during a routine interaction between each child and his mother in the home. From this one-hour sample, the middle half-hour's data, which was found to be the most representative sample (Howlin et al., 1973), was subjected to analysis.

The first analysis consisted of a functional and linguistic analysis of the speech of both the autistic and aphasic children. The functional analysis consisted of the categorization of each of the utterances into one of the following functional categories of language:

(1) Immediate repetition of self (including prompted, appropriate and inappropriate)

(2) Immediate repetitions of others (including prompted, appropriate, inappropriate, exact, reduced, expanded, and mitigated)

(3) Delayed echoes (including both communicative and purposeless)

(4) Thinking aloud and action accompaniments ("talking to self")

(5) Metaphorical or "personalized" use of language

(6) Questions

(7) Answers

(8) Spontaneous remarks

(9) Directions (demands and requests)

(10) Automatic language (hello, please, thank you, names)

The results of the analysis are presented in Table I. For each child, the percentage of total utterances falling into each functional category was computed, and the mean percentages for the whole autistic group is reported.

Note that, in contrast to earlier characterizations of autistic language, there are actually more *communicative* or *socialized utterances* (categories 6-10) than *egocentric* or *non-communicative utterances* (categories 1-5). *Echolalia* and *repetitive language* is present (categories 1-3), but in considerably less amount than one might expect from reading earlier characterizations of autistic language. Similarly, the amount of *metaphorical language* is lower than might be expected. There are few *questions*—in agreement with Wolff and Chess's (1965) finding and in opposition to Cunningham's (1968) report. Also, there is opposition to Cunningham's finding that autistic language is characterized by few *answers* and few *spontaneous remarks*. The small number of demands found in these data is in opposition to Weiland and Legg's (1964) finding that imperative verbs are common. It

Table I.
Autistic Language Profile

Utterance Types	Mean % of Utterances
1. Immediate repetition of self	8.0
2. Immediate repetition of other	7.9
3. Delayed Echoes	5.2
4. Action Accompaniments and Thinking Aloud	6.3
5. Metaphorical Language	1.0
6. Questions	2.6
7. Answers	34.7
8. Spontaneous Remarks	20.7
9. Directions, demands	2.5
10. Automatic Language	7.1

must be remembered that these contradictory findings may be explained by the particular subjects studied (older, normal IQ children selected on strict diagnostic criteria) or by the methods of data collection and analysis.

It is possible, for example, that the fact that the language samples were of free speech obtained during normal routine in the home may explain the relatively low degree of stereotyped echolalic language and the high degree of socialized language. Hutt and Hutt (1968) found that the amount of stereotyped behavior measured in a complex social situation was double the amount found in a self-play situation, suggesting the importance of immediate environmental factors.

Among the autistic children under study, there was considerable variation in the use of language. For example, while some of the children showed no delayed echoing, one showed 52% delayed echoing. Thus, while there was no *specific* pattern by which autistic language could be defined, it has been suggested by Michael Rutter that there may be a set of *"autistic language characteristics"* of which different children may exhibit different subsets.

The Language of Autistic and Aphasic Children

It is generally thought (Rutter, 1968; DeHirsch, 1967; Wing, 1966) that the abnormality of language found in the autistic child is closely similar to that found in the child with developmental receptive aphasia (henceforth, aphasia). Thus, from both the practical standpoint of making a differential diagnosis, and from the theoretical standpoint (where questions of a unitary etiology for the two disorders arise), a precise characterization of the differences and similarities between autistic and aphasic language is needed.

Wing (1966) notes that characteristics of both autistic language and aphasic language are: imperfect grammar and articulation, confusion of the different meanings of a word, confusion of semantically related words (e.g., comb and brush) when the objects themselves are not confused, circumlocutions (e.g., calling a kettle "to make a cup of tea"), adaptations of unfamiliar words (e.g., hospital becomes "horse-a-petal") and reduction of words and sentences to syllables or words.

DeHirsch (1967) states that high auditory thresholds for speech, inferior auditory discrimination, feedback distortions, echolalia, limited verbal output, and conceptual deficits are characteristic to both autism and aphasia. But she notes that there are differences in the language behavior of the two groups. Aphasic language is often normal in pitch, stress, and inflection, while autistic language is frequently deviant in these features. Echolalia is more common in autistic language as is the idiosyncratic use of words and a "looseness of associations."

Rutter et al. (1971) agree that delayed acquisition of speech, use of jargon, inconsistent responses to sounds, made-up words, and echolalia are common to both autism and aphasia, but that echolalia is more frequent in autism than in aphasia. Other differences between autistic language and aphasic language include the presence of gestures in most aphasics but not autistics, pronoun reversals in most autistics but few aphasics, and the probable presence of "inner language" (as assessed by creative play) in aphasics but not autistics.

In the initial evaluation of the autistic and aphasic children described, similar performance scores on psychometric tests, rates of language acquisition, comprehension of speech and gestures, and acquisition of words were found for the two groups of children. However, the *use* of language was different for the two groups with the autistic group using fewer spontaneous utterances and more echoes and stereotyped remarks. This data was based on interviews obtained from the parents of the children.

A comparison of taped language samples of the twelve autistic and twelve aphasic children described provided first-hand data about the characteristics of autistic and aphasic language. From the half-hour conversations between the mothers and children, the percentage of utterances of each type was computed for each of the aphasic children. The mean results for the aphasic group are presented in Table II.

By comparing Tables I and II, surprising similarities and differences be-

Table II.
Aphasic Language Profile

Utterance Types	Mean % of Utterances
1. Immediate repetition of self	3.8
2. Immediate repetition of other	10.9
3. Delayed Echoes	0.1
4. Action Accompaniments and Thinking Aloud	0.2
5. Metaphorical	0.2
6. Questions	6.2
7. Answers	24.5
8. Spontaneous Remarks	45.2
9. Directions, demands	3.1
10. Automatic	3.3

tween the autistic and aphasic language profiles may be seen. It will be noted, for example, that the two most common categories of language usage for *both* the autistic and the aphasic groups are *answers* and *spontaneous remarks*.* Although it is true that the aphasic group had many more spontaneous remarks than the autistic group, the finding that spontaneous remarks are so common in the autistic group throws some question upon Bartak et al.'s (1972) conclusion (based on interview data) that this is a distinguishing element between the two groups. The relatively high number of repetitions in the aphasic language, particularly of repetitions of "others," suggests that the typical characterization of autistic language as having more repetitions and echoes than aphasic language may be too simplistic. It is true that there are significantly more *delayed echoes* in the autistic language, but this is the only type of repetition that is significantly different. As might be expected from the typical descriptions of autistic and aphasic language, fewer *metaphorical utterances* in the aphasic language and fewer *questions* in the autistic language were found. But again, the difference was not significantly different. In fact, when the data were sub-

*It has been suggested by Michael Rutter that while spontaneous remarks are common in autistic children, they may be of a different type than the spontaneous remarks of aphasic children. This possibility will be examined in greater detail in Cantwell et al. (in preparation a); however, an initial examination of the data did not indicate any substantive differences in the types of remarks made.

jected to a statistical analysis,* the only significantly different categories were found to be *delayed echoes* and *thinking aloud*. For both of these categories, the autistic group had more utterances.

Thus these findings show trends in the direction of earlier reported "differences" between autistic and aphasic language. But the fact that the only statistically significant differences obtained were in *delayed echoes* and *thinking aloud* suggests that these earlier trends may be based upon impressionistic statements and thus may be invalid.

Although they provide no specific data on aphasia, Shapiro, Roberts and Fish (1970) propose that a detailed analysis of imitations and echoes may distinguish autistic language from other types of language. In order to explore this possibility, a more detailed analysis of the imitations and echoes of the aphasic and autistic language samples was undertaken. Imitations and echoes were further subcategorized into the ten categories listed below:

(1) Immediate repetitions of self-prompted or appropriate
(2) Immediate repetitions of self-unprompted or inappropriate
(3) Immediate repetitions of others—prompted or appropriate
(4) Immediate repetitions of others—inappropriate
(5) Immediate repetitions of others—exact
(6) Immediate repetitions of others—reduced
(7) Immediate repetitions of others—expanded
(8) Immediate repetitions of others—mitigated
(9) Delayed echo-communicative
(10) Delayed echo-uncommunicative

The imitative and echoed utterances of the autistic and aphasic children were tallied for each of the ten categories and the results (in terms of mean percentage of utterances for each category) are presented in Table III.

A statistical analysis indicates a significant difference between the imitative behavior for the two groups with regard to three types of imitations: *appropriate repetitions* of *self*, *appropriate repetitions* of *others*, and *inappropriate delayed repetitions*. The aphasics did more of the first two types of imitating, and the autistics did more of the third type. There were also three trends in the data (autistics did more *inappropriate repeating* of *self*, aphasics did more *expanded echoing*, and autistics had more *imitative language* in general) but these did not reach the statistically significant level. Thus, Shapiro et al.'s (1970) claim that autistic language could be distinguished by a prevalence of *exact* and *reduced echoes* (termed "rigidly congruent" by them) was not confirmed.

*Computing assistance was obtained from the Health Sciences Computing Facility, UCLA, supported by NIH Special Research Resources Grant RR-3. Due to a skewed distribution in the language sample of the children, a z-test of *weighted* estimates of means along with a logistic transformation was employed.

Table III.
Autistic and Aphasic Echoes and Imitations
Mean Percentage of Total Utterances

Imitation Types	Mean % for Autistic	Mean % for Aphasic
Immediate repetition of self (appropriate)	0.8	1.8
Immediate repetition of self (inappropriate)	4.8	0.8
Repetitions of others (appropriate)	2.2	6.7
Repetitions of others (inappropriate)	1.2	1.6
Repetition of others – exact	4.5	7.5
Repetitions of others – reduced	3.8	2.1
Repetitions of others – expanded	0.4	1.3
Repetitions of others – mitigated	8.5	0.0
Delayed Echo	2.5	0.1
Delayed Echo (inappropriate)	2.8	0.0

PROGNOSTIC SIGNIFICANCE OF LANGUAGE IN INFANTILE AUTISM

A second area in which language studies are of relevance to the study of autism is the area of prognosis. The language disturbance of autistic children is not an isolated symptom, but is intimately related to other features of the syndrome and to eventual outcome. Ruttenberg and Wolf (1967) state that progress in language acquisition is correlated with progress in establishing relationships with people. Fish et al. (1968) suggest that level of language may be correlated with eventual progress on drug or placebo treatment. Rimland (1964) notes that the non-speaking autistic child was less alert to sounds in infancy and shows more autistic behavior in later life. Davis (1967) states that the level of language acquired is correlated with the "pervasive concreteness of all behavior."

Eisenberg (1956) states that children who have not acquired "useful speech" by age five will uniformly follow a course of gross retardation and disturbed behavior in later life. But Rutter et al. (1967), in a follow-up study of thirty-two children without speech at five years, noted that seven of the children later gained speech. This later improvement was thought to be the result of high IQ, and it was further proposed that IQ may be more relevant than language as a predictor of long-term prognosis.

If the "language by five" hypothesis is to have any real prognostic value, the separate roles of linguistic achievement and measured intelligence must be teased out. A precise and reliable definition of *how much* language and *what quality* of language is necessary by five must be formulated. The suggestion that there be "useful" language is too vague. A more reliable definition would be in terms of mean utterance length, scores on standardized language tests, or some other objective and repeatable measure.

Language studies of autistic children generally have been both subjective and impressionistic, and hence could not be reliably carried out by more than one investigator. Davis (1967), for example, describes a method of appraisal of language behavior in which inner language is evaluated by "degree of sophistication" in fantasy play and expressive language is evaluated by ability to imitate sounds. But there is bound to be some disagreement across examiners as to what constitutes sophisticated play and what constitutes an accurate imitation of sounds. Fish et al. (1968) describe a method of classification of language abilities which also does not seem very reliable. They distinguish, for example, between the child with no comprehension and the child with minimal comprehension by the presence of "one appropriate response." Similarly, the child with no language and the child with sparse uncommunicative language is distinguished by the presence of "one recognizable word." Admittedly, these distinctions are precisely defined. However, one is reminded of the story of setting the chimps to the typewriters. Eventually, in the course of a chimp typing or an autistic child babbling, one recognizable word will be produced. It is questionable whether this really should be taken as evidence of a certain level of linguistic ability.

Thus, while it has been generally recognized that there is a relationship between language and prognosis, this relationship has typically been stated in terms of the expected progress for the child with *some* language as opposed to the expected progress for the child with *no* language. A precise characterization of the prognosis that may be expected for children with different levels of language acuisition at different ages has not been made.

There have been several attempts to explain the use of a particular type of language in terms of a certain level of development of "ego organization." Although there have been no studies aiming to correlate level of ego organization (as revealed through language) with prognosis, this is a logical next step if these ego models are to be taken seriously. Such models include the work of Griffith and Ritvo (1967) who state that the use of negative echolalia is indicative of disturbed object relationships. Ekstein (1964) claims delayed echoing during psychotherapy is indicative of "primitive incorporation." Weiland and Legg (1964) suggest that the frequent use of imperative verbs among autistic children is probably the result of "an attempt to control impulsivity that cannot adequately be contained because of the immature ego." However, these phenomena can be explained by a purely linguistic model. Echolalia has been explained as the natural result of a failure to comprehend (Mykelbust, 1957; Rutter, 1968). Reversals of the pronouns *you* and *I*—once thought to be the result of inadequate ego strength—are now generally accepted as the apparent result of the echolalia itself. Bartak and Rutter (1974) have shown that if such linguistic factors as position of occurrence in the sentence are controlled for, there is in fact, no avoidance of the pronoun *I* by autistic children. The predominance of imperative verbs in Weiland and Legg's (1964) data may be due to the fact that the imperative is one of the linguistically simplest forms to produce.

Thus, most of the ego models that have been put forth as hypotheses are subject to alternative explanations. The only such model based upon systematic study is that of Shapiro et al. (1970). They examined the basic hypothesis that "degrees of flexibility in imitative speech could be used as an index of ego flexibility and adaptive capacity." They suggest, in particular, that a certain type of echo called "rigidly congruent echoes" (in which the echo is an exact or exact-reduced repetition of the original utterance) is characteristic of "ego inflexibility." Their study involved the comparison of eight autistic children and eighteen normal children. Ten-minute speech samples were collected and all imitations were categorized. The categories of analysis were: (1) rigidly congruent echoes, (2) non-grammatic echoes (a non-grammatical expression containing some of the words of the original utterance), (3) jargon additions (in which jargon or nonsense has been added to the original utterance), (4) telegraphic echoes (in which omissions of small words and changes in inflectional endings from the original utterance occur), (5) mitigated echoes (in which grammatical restructuring of the original utterance occurs).

It was found by Shapiro and his colleagues that the autistic children had a significantly greater number of rigidly congruent echoes than the control group. Further, among the control group of normals, the number of congruent echoes decreased with age and the number of mitigated echoes increased with age. It was concluded that congruent echoing was indicative of poor ego organization; whereas mitigated echoing was indicative of increased ego organization.

Even ignoring the interpretation of ego organization, these results are particularly significant because, if repeatable, they will provide a relatively simple and easy classification of autistic children according to severity of disorder and probable outcome. Hence, it was decided to try to replicate the results using the data from the autistic-aphasic study described.

The three children with the best language (*high group*) and the three children with the worst language (*low group*) were selected from the group of autistic children described above. The imitations and echoes found in the language samples of these children were analyzed by using the categories discussed. For purposes of direct comparison with the results obtained by Shapiro et al. (1970), the category of "rigidly congruent echoes" was added to categorization.

Three hypotheses about the predictive value of echolalic language were investigated:

(1) Wolff and Chess (1965) and Fay and Butler (1968) claim that the amount of echoing is negatively correlated with total linguistic ability.

(2) Shapiro et al. (1970) claim that the amount of rigidly congruent echoes is negatively correlated with linguistic ability.

(3) Shapiro et al. (1970) and Fay (1967) claim that amount of mitigated echoing is correlated with linguistic ability.

The results are presented in Table IV.

These findings do not support hypothesis one. The total amount of echolalic language was higher for the *high* language group than for the *low* language group. There is some support for hypothesis two—that the amount of congruent echoing is negatively correlated with language skills. The data further indicate that hypothesis two may be simplified: exact echoes (of which congruent echoes are partially made up) alone seem to distinguish between the two groups of autistic children. Although these data indicate that more mitigated echoes do occur in the *high* language group than in the *low* language group, there is insufficient difference to provide support for hypothesis three.

LANGUAGE AND THE ETIOLOGY OF INFANTILE AUTISM

Autism as a Disorder of Psychogenic Origin

There has been considerable controversy over the etiology of autism (Rutter, 1971; Rutter et al., 1973). Various hypotheses have been proposed concerning the roles of organic versus psychosocial factors. Kanner's original (1946) hypothesis regarding the "emotional refrigeration" of the parents is now generally being replaced by Rutter's (1968) hypothesis that a cognitive defect involving language comprehension lies at the basis of autism. However, the role of psychosocial factors cannot be entirely dismissed, as it may be necessary for certain environmental circumstances to occur in order for the syndrome of autism to develop in children who have the necessary (but not sufficient) cognitive defect.

Rutter and his colleagues carried out a systematic evaluation of this possibility in the comparative study of autistic and aphasic children (Cox et al., 1975). They devised specific measures to assess those parental

Table IV.
Echolalic Profiles for "High" and "Low"
Autistic Children

Types of Echoes	Mean % of Use for "High" Group	Mean % of Use for "Low" Group
Exact Echoes	2.0	10.0
Reduced Echoes	3.0	3.3
Congruent Echoes	2.3	7.0
Expanded Echoes	0.3	0.3
Mitigated Echoes	1.3	0.0
Inappropriate or Purposeless	14.3	6.6
Total Repetitions and Echoes	24.0	5.0

characteristics and stresses in the environment which have been hypothesized by other authors to play a role in the etiology of infantile autism. They assessed the social characteristics of the family, the presence of parental psychiatric disorder and family stress, the presence of parental obsessional behavior and neurotic behavior, parental warmth to the child, emotional demonstrativeness and responsiveness of the parents, and sociability of the parents. They found no significant differences between the parents of the autistic children and the parents of the aphasic children in any of these measures with the exception of the fact that more parents of the autistic children were of a higher social class. Their conclusion was that these parental personality characteristics were unlikely to play a significant role in the etiology of autism.

Some form of deviant parent-child interaction, particularly verbal communication between the mother and child, has been implicated by a number of authors (Kanner and Eisenberg, 1955; Bettelheim, 1967; Goldfarb et al., 1966a, 1966b, 1972a). It has been further hypothesized by Meyers and Goldfarb (1961) and Goldfarb et al. (1966a) that not only is the maternal pattern of communication deviant, but that the maternal language itself is deficient as a language model for the child. Studies of the linguistic interactions between mothers and their autistic children and of the actual language of mothers of autistics should shed light on these issues.

The Mother-Child Interaction

Lennard et al. (1965) have compared communications in families of autistic children with communications in families of normal children. They discovered more questions being asked by the parents of autistics and more 'intrusiveness" in general in autistic families and concluded that these families were discouraging self-motivated behavior. Goldfarb et al. (1966b) compared the communication styles of mothers of autistics with the styles of mothers of orthopedically hospitalized but otherwise normal children during a "surprise visit" by the mother to the hospital. They concluded that the mothers of autistic children were abnormal in that they did not "stimulate an interest in talking." However, this study may be criticized on methodological grounds; not only were the conclusions drawn in a highly impressionistic way, but the very experimental format of a "surprise visit" was not designed to elicit normal communication. Both the Lennard study and the Goldfarb study may be further criticized on the basis of their comparing the autistic group with a linguistically normal group, and thus failing to account for the extent to which the child's aberrant communications and behavior affected the parents. It is open to question as to whether the normal parents would not have seemed abnormal also, when faced with the task of communicating with an autistic child.

In order to account for this variable, Cantwell et all. (in preparation a) compared the interactions of autistic children and their mothers to the interactions of a group of children with a similar language defect and their mothers. The subjects were thirteen* autistic and thirteen aphasic children described above and their mothers. A sixty-minute language sample of mother-child interactions was recorded in the home during a time when the mother and child were normally together. The middle half hour of this hour sample was extracted, and the mothers' utterances were categorized according to function using a predetermined set of categories. These categories (the development of which is described in Howlin et al. [1973]) are:

(1) Questions

(2) Answers

(3) Imitations (exact repetitions of child's speech)

(4) Mitigated Echoes (of child's speech)

(5) Reductions (of child's speech)

(6) Expansions (of child's speech)

(7) Corrections (of child's syntax, semantics, pronunciation, or of facts)

(8) Directed Mimicry (in which child is instructed to say something, and exact words are provided)

(9) Prompting (mother indicates, by tone or content, what child is expected to say)

---

*The language of twenty-six mothers but only twenty-four children were compared because one child from each group was mute.

Table V.
Interaction Patterns for Mothers

Interaction Category	Autistic Children's Mothers mean % of utterances	Aphasic Children's Mothers mean % of utterances
Questions	31.0	28.0
Answers	0.8	1.7
Imitations	3.0	3.0
Mitigated Echoes	0.2	0.4
Reductions	0.2	0.4
Expansions	1.8	1.0
Corrections	1.6	5.6
Directed Mimicry	0.3	0.0
Prompting	2.6	3.6
Direct Reinforcements	2.9	3.0
Direct Reinforcements – one word	6.0	4.0
Directions	18.0	10.0
Statements	19.0	32.0
Affectionate Remarks	5.0	0.6
Critical Remarks	3.0	1.0
Total Number of utterances	178.0	160.0

(10) Direct Reinforcement (mother indicates she is listening or approves)

(11) Directions, Demands, Suggestions

(12) Statements or Observations (no response expected)

(13) Affectionate Remarks, Approving Remarks

(14) Disapprovals and Criticisms.

The results of this analysis are presented in Table V in which the mean percentage of occurrences for each utterance category is computed for the mothers of both the autistic and aphasic children. It will be noted from an examination of Table V that the same general pattern of interaction categories occurs for the two groups. *Questions, statements* and *directions* are the most frequently occurring categories for both groups of mothers. And *answers, imitations, mitigated echoes, reductions, expansions, directed mimicries, prompts, direct reinforcements* and one-word *direct reinforcements* are rarer in the two groups. The only category in which there was a statistically significant difference was the category of *affectionate remarks* in which the mothers of autistic children showed a higher mean percentage of utterances than the mothers of aphasic children.

Thus, these findings do not support earlier hypotheses that mothers of autistic children are deviant in their communication patterns. Although there were a large number of questions among the mothers of autistics (giving some support to Lennard et al. [1965]), this also occurred in the mothers of aphasic children, and hence was not felt to be deviant. The only area in which the interaction was significantly different between the two groups was the area of *affectionate remarks*, and this difference, if anything, argues in favor of the mothers of autistic children being *more* warm and responsive.

The Language Model Offered by the Mother to the Child.

Goldfarb et al. (1972a) state that the average mother of an autistic child is deficient in speech, and therefore presents a poor speech model for her child to emulate and is a poor teacher of acceptable speech patterns. These conclusions are based on a number of studies (Goldfarb et al., 1966a, 1972a; Meyers and Goldfarb, 1961) in which some evaluation of the "clarity" of the language of mothers of autistics is compared with that of mothers of normals. These conclusions are open to question due to certain methodological deficiences of the studies. Klein and Pollack (1966) have criticized the Goldfarb studies for a failure to match the mothers for age, education, IQ, social class and special interests, all of which, they claim, could have some effect on language. It can also be argued that it is inappropriate to be comparing mothers of *autistics* and mothers of age-matched *normals* in any event. There is now a considerable body of evidence (Snow, 1972; Olim, 1970) that the mother modifies her language level according to the language level of her child. Thus, one would expect that the language of mothers of normals would be considerably more sophisticated than that of mothers of children of the same age with some degree of language retardation. Thus, if normal children are used for purposes of comparison, they should be matched for *language age*, rather than for *chronological age*. Goldfarb's methods of analysis of the language are also somewhat subjective.

Howlin et al. (1973) note that no details were given of the diagnostic criteria, that speech assessments were made under unusual conditions which seemed to disturb several children, that there was no data from normals in a similar situation, that only deficits in parental speech were analyzed with positive aspects being ignored, that the categories of analysis were often rather loosely defined or applied and that the periods of interaction were extremely short (usually two minutes or less) and likely to be unrepresentative of normal mother-child interaction.

An attempt was made to replicate Goldfarb's findings using a more rigorous method of selection of subjects and analysis of language (Cantwell et al., in preparation b). The subjects were the autistic and aphasic children and their mothers described. The children were matched for age, performance IQ, and language level (as evaluated by Peabody Test scores).

Two methods of analysis were used to evaluate the mothers' speech: a tabulation of the "clarity errors" found (using the method of Goldfarb et al. [1966b]) in the half-hour long sample, and an evaluation of the linguistic sophistication and grammaticality of the mothers' speech. The "clarity" analysis was primarily concerned with the content of the mothers' utterances, whereas the linguistic evaluation was primarily concerned with the structural qualities of the mothers' speech. The *clarity errors* were: lack of denotative or connotative clarity, inconsistency, irrelevance, lack of elaboration, not responding to the child's questions or statements, reality distortion, misinterpreting the child, interrupting the child, speaking simultaneously with the child, introducing unrelated topics, giving excessive elaboration, speaking indistinctly, changing topics inappropriately, and failing to correct any lack of clarity. The linguistic evaluation consisted of computations of *mean sentence length, mean preverb length*, number of utterances that were only *phrases*, number of *adjectives*, number of *repetitions of oneself*, number of only *one-word utterances*, number of *inexplicit commands*, number of *ungrammatical utterances*, and *number of failures to correct* or *reinforcements of ungrammatical utterances* in the child. All measures, where possible, were expressed as a percentage of the total utterances.

The results are presented below in Table VI. It was found that there were significantly more *clarity errors* among the mothers of aphasics than among the mothers of autistics. When broken down according to particular error types, it was found that the total difference was due to greater aphasic *errors* of three types: lack of connotative clarity, lack of elaboration, and reality distortion. When statistical analysis was done, it was found that there was *no significant difference* between the two groups of mothers for any of the linguistic sophistication and grammaticality measures. Thus, there was no evidence of more inadequate language in the mothers of autistic children. It may be concluded from this that the mothers of autistic children have language behavior which is typical for mothers of language-disabled children.

Autism as a Variety of Mental Subnormality

The almost inevitable retardation of speech and language evident in the autistic child has led some investigators to posit that *mental subnormality is the basis of autism* (Rutter et al., 1973). This, in turn, led to a controversy

Table VI.
Mothers' Language Models

	Autistic Mean	Aphasic Mean
Total "Clarity Errors'	8.7	14.4
Mean utterance length (in words)	4.9	4.3
Mean preverb length (in words)	2.3	2.0
Phrases	16.2	14.7
Adjectives (per utterances)	15.0	8.0
Ungrammatical utterances	2.2	0.8
Reinforcements of poor grammar	0.2	0.2
Failures to correct poor grammar	2.3	1.8
Repeats self	3.3	3.8
One-word utterances	0.6	0.9
Inexplicit commands	9.5	22.5

as to whether autistic language was merely "delayed" (as in mental retardation) or was a more complex disturbance or "deviance". Studies of
the language acquisition of an autistic child over time are few (Cunningham
and Dixon, 1961; Cunningham, 1966; Shapiro et al., 1972; Ward and
Hoddinott, 1968), but the consensus of evidence suggests that the pattern of
language acquisition in these children is not a normal one. Studies comparing linguistic abilities of autistic children versus mentally retarded
children based on the Illinois Test of Psycholinguistic Abilities (Tubbs,
1966) or on originally constructed tests (Frith, 1970; Hermelin, 1971) indicate that the linguistic characteristics of the two groups are different. In
addition, it is now felt that, while a large portion of autistic children are
intellectually retarded, this is not a *necessary* characteristic of the syndrome
(Rutter et al., 1967). Rutter (1966a) suggests that some of the poor level of
intellectual attainment found in autistic children may be attributed to
specific defects in language rather than to a *global* deficiency of intellect.
Comprehensive language descriptions for autistic children of different intelligence levels should shed light on these issues. The findings discussed above
suggest that the language disturbance of autistic children with a performance IQ in the normal range may be different from that of the lower IQ
autistic children. In particular, it was found that autistic children with
normal performance IQs did not fit in with earlier characterizations of the
"typical" autistic child as having predominantly echolalic or metaphorical

language and having very little socialized language such as questions, answers, directions or spontaneous remarks.

Autism as Response to a Language Defect

It has been proposed by Rutter (1966a, 1966b, 1967, 1968, 1971; Churchill, 1972) that the primary deficit of autistic children is an abnormality in the comprehension of language similar to that found in developmental receptive aphasia. Rutter (1968) cites four pieces of evidence to support this hypothesis: (1) similarities between autistic and aphasic language (2) follow-up studies in which the prognostic value of language was seen (3) the pattern of cognitive abilities of autistic children which show deficiencies in abstraction, concept-formation and symbolization, even when speech is not required, and (4) the fact that autistics do not use *meaning* in recall (Hermelin and O'Connor, 1967). In order to account for the fact that there are aphasic children with a disorder of comprehension who do not exhibit autistic behaviors, it is hypothesized that the language disorder is "wider and deeper" in the autistic children. Rutter (1971) cites the absence of creative play or "inner language" and of gestures in autistic but not aphasic children as evidence that the disorder of language is greater in autistics.

Bartak et al. (1972), in comparing autistic children with aphasic children matched for age, sex, and performance IQ, concluded that the language defect in autism was more severe (as was shown by lower scores on the Peabody and Reynell tests) and more extensive (since autistic children used language less in social contexts).

The findings reported above on the same group of children using language samples as a data base suggest that the use of language is not all that different between autistic and aphasic children. In addition, an analysis of the level of language acquisition as evidenced by the occurrences of different structures in free speech did not support the contention that autistic language is more severely impaired than aphasic language.

The method of analysis was essentially an attempt to construct a *mini* transformational grammar from the language samples of the autistic and aphasic children. A list of five syntactic transformations, eight morphological transformations, and five base structures was composed, and the language of each child was evaluated for the acquisition, partial acquisition or non-acquisition of each rule or structure. In addition, the number of *semantic mistakes* (errors in the meaning of words, in combining words that should not be combined, or in making up words) were tallied. The linguistic rules considered are presented in Table VII.

The detailed results of this analysis will be reported elsewhere (Cant-

Table VII.
Basic Linguistic Rules

A. Syntactic Transformations

(1) Imperative (subject of the sentence is deleted, e.g., "get it")

(2) Wh-Inversion (Wh words such as who, what, when, and where are placed at the beginning of the sentence, e.g., "where is it?")

(3) Q-Inversion (the subject and verb of the sentence are inverted to form questions, e.g., "where is this", "can I?")

(4) Do support (the word 'do' is inserted to form certain expressions, e.g., questions "does Billy read?", or negatives "I do not read")

(5) Negative ("not" is inserted in the proper position in the sentence)

B. Morphological Rules

(1) *−ing* added to verbs to indicate progressive tense

(2) *−s* added to nouns to indicate plural

(3) *−ed* added to verbs to indicate past tense

(4) *'s* added to nouns to signify possession

(5) *−s* added to verbs to indicate third person singular

(6) Case for pronouns (e.g., distinction between I, me; he, him; etc.)

(7) Possessive pronouns (e.g., mine, his, yours, etc.)

(8) Adverb formation (e.g., quickly, nicely, etc.)

C. Basic Structures

(1) Noun phrase (determiner + adjective + noun, e.g., "the big boy")

(2) Verb phrase: (verb + noun, e.g., "kiss me")

(3) Prepositional phrase (preposition + determiner + noun, "in the box")

(4) Simple sentence (noun phrase + verb phrase, e.g., "I hit the dog")

(5) Complex sentence (any sentence more complex than (4) above, e.g., questions, negations, or sentences with many phrases ["I threw the ball to Jack yesterday"])

well et al., in preparation a). For the purposes of this chapter they can be briefly summarized by stating that from this manner of analysis it could be concluded that the language levels of the autistic and aphasic children in this sample were approximately the same. That these findings are in contradiction with those of Bartak et al. (1975) with the same children is not surprising in light of recent reports (Dever, 1972; Prutting et al., 1975) suggesting that performance on form language tests does not accurately reflect performance in free speech.

Social Withdrawal as the Primary Defect of Autistic Children

Although Rutter (1968) concludes that social withdrawal is not the primary defect in autism, the etiological role of a basic social handicap in autism is not known. Careful language studies in which the *use* of language is considered separately from the *structural deficits* in language can shed light on this question. The data comparing the language of autistic and aphasic children suggests that autistic children may have a greater abnormality in the use of language than in the structural acquisition of language, at least when compared with aphasic language. The finding of Bartak et al. (1975) that use of gestures was extremely rare in autistic children even though the children were able to comprehend and produce gestures on demand indicates further that the language *performance* of these children may be more impaired than is their underlying language knowledge or *competence*. Whether this abnormal use of language is due to an *unwillingness* or an *inability* to use language is not known.

Autism as a Response to a Larger Cognitive Deficit

Language is not a unitary phenomenon but is a conglomerate of skills—including the ability to segment utterances into words, the ability to understand concepts or "meaning" and symbols, the ability to recall and retrieve information, the ability to associate across different modalities such as seeing, hearing, and speaking. Thus, when it is stated that autism involves a defect in language, it is important that it is made clear which of these skills are impaired—some of them, all of them, or some necessary for more than just language.

Autistic children demonstrate a characteristic pattern of abilities and disabilities on intelligence tests. They perform well on block design, object assembly, digit span, similarities, and picture completion tasks; they perform poorly on comprehension, arithmetic, vocabulary, picture arrangement, and digit or symbol coding tasks (Simmons and Tymchuk, 1973). Although it has been stated (Rutter, 1968) that poor performance on intelligence tests by autistics occurs primarily in areas requiring language skills, it can be seen that some of the areas in which the autistic children perform *well* are also areas involving linguistic skills. The digit span test requires good auditory memory, and the similarities test requires being able to abstract and label. Both of these are skills necessary for language production and comprehension, suggesting that not all of the language skills are impaired in autism. There is also evidence that those skills which are impaired are not skills unique to language.

Linguists are now coming to the conclusion (Krashen, 1972) that the language faculty (while functionally separate), shares certain brain mechanisms with other aspects of cognition and that, in fact, there may be no mental abilities unique to language. If this is true, we would expect to find non-linguistic impairments in the autistic child which parallel the linguistic impairments found. It has been suggested, for example, that the autistic child's stereotyped behavior and insistence on sameness in his environment may reflect the same underlying deficit as is revealed in echolalia, namely an inability to segment or break down patterns.

A number of brilliant quasi-linguistic experiments attempting to delineate the precise impairments underlying the language deficit of autism have been carried out by Hermelin and O'Connor (1970) and Frith (1970). The areas examined include perception, attention, and discrimination of stimuli; the ability to make associations across modalities; the role of concepts or meaning, recall or memory; the ability to segment or to break down patterns; and the ability to generalize patterns or to construct "rules."

Hermelin and O'Connor concluded that while perception seemed normal in autistic children, attention was impaired, at least for visual stimuli. Bryson (1970), using a simple matching test, concluded that visual discrimination was unimpaired. Lovaas et al. (1971), however, found visual discrimination of autistics far below that of normals when a complex stimulus was presented. They concluded that "overselectivity" or a focusing on one part of the stimuli while ignoring other aspects might be at fault.

Hermelin and O'Connor (1970) found difficulties in dealing with ordering: although order could be recognized in simple two-step drawings, the children were unable to learn a relatively simple seriation task. Association across modalities—particularly from the auditory to the vocal modes—was also found to be impaired.

Recall experiments suggested an inability to understand concepts in that random words were remembered as well as meaningful sentences, which is not normal in recall. Further, when given a list of items to recall, normals will tend to group these into semantic categories, whereas the autistic children failed to do this. At least a partial ability to break down sequences of words was suggested by the finding that stress was significant in recall: stressed words were "picked out" of sentences and were better remembered. Additional evidence of the ability to segment is found in the telegraphic utterances or reductions of autistic children.

Frith (1970) concluded that the autistic children seemed to be able to construct "rules" similar to linguistic rules, but that they were aberrant in their application of these rules. The findings are in keeping with those reported above that the functional use of language seemed more abnormal than the structural properties of that language.

Frith also agreed with Hermelin and O'Connor that autistic memory is abnormal: a "recency" effect was found in recall experiments whereby the most recently heard items were the best recalled.

Although by no means conclusive, research to date seems to suggest that a number of the cognitive skills necessary for language are impaired in autism, and that it is to be expected that these are skills not unique to language. The fact that many of these abilities are the so-called "left hemisphere" abilities has led researchers to posit that autism may involve an abnormality in left lateralization.

SUMMARY

There are at least three important areas of inquiry in which language studies may provide important insights into the syndrome of infantile autism: diagnosis, prognosis, and etiology. This chapter reviews previous work in this area and describes linguistic analysis of free speech samples of a group of autistic children and a matched group of aphasic children. Finally, some indication is made of the implications of the available data regarding language in autistic children for diagnosis, prognosis, and etiology.

Although the "characteristics" of autistic language (including echolalia, comprehension difficulties, and inappropriate and non-communicative language) are easily described, it is not yet possible to provide a *specific* profile of autistic language which may be used as a *diagnostic* tool. The formal linguistic character of autistic language is not as distinct from that of aphasic language as has been previously suggested, and there is evidence that the patterns of language use (e.g., egocentric versus socialized speech, and different types of echoes) are not extremely dissimilar. Since the data reviewed here was obtained from autistic children with performance IQs in the normal range, further investigation is necessary to determine whether the language of the low IQ autistic child is more distinct.

Early attempts to use language as a guide to "ego organization" and hence as an indication of ultimate *prognosis* have provided only the grossest of estimates (e.g., "if some language is present, the prognosis is better than if no language is present"). It now appears that all the so-called instances of language as "ego-indicator" may also be explained on a purely linguistic basis. A precise linguistic characterization of the level of language acquisition attained may be more relevant prognostically, but thus far no firm correlations have been established. There is some evidence that types of echoing may be relevant, however.

With regard to the *etiology* of autism, language studies have shown the inadequacy of the psychogenic theory in which the language or communication style of the mother is considered to be inadequate. Systematic comparison of the linguistic complexity and of communication styles of mothers of autistic children and mothers of aphasic children has revealed no deficiency in the mothers of autistic children. The similarity between autistic and aphasic language in children further suggests a common or similar etiology. Further studies of the cognitive and linguistic skills of autistic children are necessary, as is a precise description of the nature of the linguistic abilities and impairments of the autistic child. Any adequate treatment program must be founded upon an understanding of what is lacking and how it came to be lacking.

REFERENCES

Bartak, L. and Rutter, M. (1974). The use of personal pronouns by autistic children. *Journal of Autism and Childhood Schizophrenia* 4:217-22.

———, Rutter, M., and Cox, A. (1975). A comparative study of infantile autism and specific developmental receptive language disorder: I. The Children. *British Journal of Psychiatry* 126:127-48.

———, Rutter, M., Cox, A., and Newman, S. (1972). Comparison of autism and aphasia. *Report to the SRCC*

Bettelheim, B. (1967). *The Empty Fortress—Infantile Autism and the Birth of the Self.* New York: The Free Press, Collier-MacMillan.

Bryson, C.Q. (1970). Systematic identification of perceptual disabilities in autistic children. *Perceptual and Motor Skills* 31:239-46.

Cantwell, D., Rutter, M., and Baker, L. (in preparation a). A method to study language deviation and development in autistic and aphasic children.

———, Rutter, M., and Baker, L. (in preparation b). Mother's speech to autistic and aphasic children.

Churchill, D. (1972). The relation of infantile autism and early childhood schizophrenia to developmental language disorders of childhood. *Journal of Autism and Childhood Schizophrenia* 2:182-97.

Cox, A., Rutter, M., Newman, S., and Bartak, L. (1975). A comparative study of infantile autism and specific developmental receptive language disorder: II. Parental characteristics. *British Journal of Psychiatry* 126:146-59.

Creak, M., chairman. (1961). Schizophrenic syndrome in childhood: progress report of a working party. *Cerebral Palsy Bulletin* 3:501-504.

Cunningham, M. (1966). A five year study of the language of an autistic child. *Journal of Child Psychology and Psychiatry* 7:143-54.

——— (1968). A comparison of the language of psychotic and non-psychotic children who are mentally retarded. *Journal of Child Psychology and Psychiatry* 9:229-44.

——— and Dixon, C. (1961). A study of the language of an autistic child. *Journal of Child Psychology and Psychiatry* 2:193-202.

Davis, B. (1967). A clinical method of appraisal of the language and learning behavior of young autistic children. *Journal of Communication Disorders* 1:277-96.

DeHirsch, K. (1967). Differential diagnosis between aphasic and schizophrenic language in children. *Journal of Speech and Hearing Disorders* 32:3-10.

DeMyer, M., Churchill, D., Pontius, W., and Gilkey, K. (1971). A comparison of five diagnostic systems for childhood schizophrenia and infantile autism. *Journal of Autism and Childhood Schizophrenia* 1:175-189.

Dever, R. (1972). A comparison of the results of a revised version of Berko's test of morphology with the free speech of mentally retarded children. *Journal of Speech and Hearing Research* 15:169-78.

Eisenberg, L. (1956). The autistic child in adolescence. *American Journal of Psychiatry* 112:607-12.

Ekstein, R. (1964). On the acquisition of speech in the autistic child. *Reiss-Davis Clinical Bulletin* 1:63-80.

Fay, W. (1967). Mitigated echolalia of children. *Journal of Speech and Hearing Research* 10:305-10.

——— and Butler, B. (1968). Echolalia, IQ, and the developmental dichotomy of speech and language systems. *Journal of Speech and Hearing Research* 11:365-71.

Fish, B., Shapiro, T., Campbell, M., and Wile, R. (1968). A classification of schizophrenic children under 5 years. *American Journal of Psychiatry* 124:1415-23.

Frith, U. (1970). Studies in pattern detection: I. Immediate recall of auditory sequences. *Journal of Abnormal Psychology* 76:413-20.

Goldfarb, W., Goldfarb, N., and Scholl, M. (1966a). The speech of mothers of schizophrenic children. *American Journal of Psychiatry* 122:1220-27.

———, Goldfarb, N., Braunstein, P., and Scholl, H. (1972b). Speech and language faults of schizophrenic children. *Journal of Autism and Childhood Schizophrenia* 2:219-33.

———, Levy, D., and Meyers, D. (1966b). The verbal encounter between the schizophrenic child and his mother. In Goldman, G. and Shapiro, D., eds. *Developments in Psychoanalysis at Columbia University* New York: Hafner.

———, Levy, D., and Meyers, D. (1972a). The mother speaks to her schizophrenic child: language in childhood schizophrenia. *Psychiatry* 35:217-26.

Griffith, R. and Ritvo, E. (1967). Echolalia: concerning the dynamics of the syndrome. *Journal of American Academy of Child Psychiatry* 6:184-93.

Hermelin, B. (1971). Rules and language. In Rutter, M. ed., *Infantile Autism: Concepts, Characteristics and Treatment* Great Britain: Whitefriars Press.

——— and O'Connor, N. (1967). Remembering of words by psychotic and subnormal children. *British Journal of Psychology* 58:213-318.

——— and O'Connor, N. (1970). *Psychological Experiments with Autistic Children* London: Pergamon Press.

Hingtgen, J. and Bryson, C. (1972). Recent developments in the study of early childhood psychoses: infantile autism, childhood schizophrenia and related disorders. *Schizophrenia Bulletin* 5:8-55.

Howlin, R., Cantwell, D., Marchant, R., Berger, M., and Rutter, M. (1973). Analyzing mothers' speech to young autistic children: a methodological study. *Journal of Abnormal Child Psychology* 1:317-39.

Hutt, S. and Hutt, C. (1968). Stereotype, arousal and autism. *Human Development* 11:277-86.

Kanner, L. (1943). Autistic disturbances of affective contact. *The Nervous Child* 2:217-50.

——— (1946). Irrelevant and metaphorical language in early infantile autism. *American Journal of Psychiatry* 103:242-46.

——— and Eisenberg, L. (1955). Notes on follow-up studies of autistic children. In Hoch, P. and Zubin, J. eds. *Psychopathology of Childhood* New York: Grune and Stratton.

Klein, D. and Pollack, M. (1966). Schizophrenic children and maternal speech facility. *American Journal of Psychiatry* 123:232.

Krashen, S. (1972). Language and the left hemisphere. *UCLA Working Papers in Phonetics* 24.

Lennard, H., Beaulieu, M., and Embry, M. (1965). Interaction in families with a schizophrenic child. *Archives of General Psychiatry* 12:166-83.

Lovaas, O., Schreibman, L., Koegel, R., and Rehm, R. (1971). Selective responding by autistic children to multiple sensory input. *Journal of Abnormal Psychology* 77:211-22.

Meyers, D. and Goldfarb, W. (1961). Studies of perplexity in mothers of schizophrenic children. *American Journal of Orthopsychiatry* 31:551-64.

Mykelbust, H. (1957). Babbling and echolalia in language theory. *Journal of Speech and Hearing Disorders* 22:356-60.

Olim, E. (1970). Maternal language styles and children's cognitive behavior. *Journal of Special Education* 4:53-67.

Ornitz, E.M. and Ritvo, E.R. (1968). Perceptual inconstancy in the syndrome of early infantile autism and its varients. *Archives of General Psychiatry* 18:76-98.

Prutting, C. Gallagher, T., and Mulac, A. (1975). The expressive portion of the NSST compared to a spontaneous language sample. *Journal of Speech and Hearing Disorders* 40:40-48.

Rimland, B. (1964). *Infantile Autism*. New York: Appleton-Century Crofts.

Ruttenberg, B. and Wolf, E. Evaluating the communication of the autistic child. *Journal of Speech and Hearing Disorders* 32:314-24.

Rutter, M. (1966a). Behavioural and cognitive characteristics of a series of psychotic children. In Wing, J. ed. *Early Childhood Autism: Clinical Educational and Social Aspects* London: Pergamon Press.

———— (1966b). Prognosis: Psychotic children in adolescence and early adult life. In Wing, J. ed. *Early Childhood Autism: Clinical, Educational and Social Aspects* London: Pergamon Press.

———— (1967). A five to fifteen year follow-up study of infantile psychosis. *British Journal of Psychiatry* 113:1169-82. and 1183-99.

———— (1968). Concepts of autism: a review of research. *Journal of Child Psychology and Psychiatry* 9:1-25.

———— (1971). The description and classification of infantile autism. In Churchill, D., Alpern, G. and DeMyer, M. ed. *Infantile Autism Proceedings of the Indiana University Colloquium* Springfield, Ill.: C. Thomas Publisher.

————, Bartak, L., and Newman, S. (1971). Autism—a central disorder of cognition and language. In Rutter, M. ed., *Infantile Autism: Concepts, Characteristics and Treatment*. Great Britain: Whitefriars Press.

————, Greenfeld, D., and Lockyer, L. (1967). A 5 to 15 year follow-up study of infantile psychosis: II. Social and behavioral outcome. *British Journal of Psychology* 113:1183-99.

————, Shaffer, D., and Shepherd, M. (1973). An evaluation of the proposal for a multi-axial classification of child psychiatric disorders. *Psychological Medicine* 3:244-50.

Savage, V. (1968). Childhood autism: A review of the literature with particular reference to the speech and language structure of the autistic child. *British Journal of Disorders of Communication* 3:75-87.

Shapiro, T., Roberts, A., and Fish, B. (1970). Imitation and echoing in young schizophrenic children. *Journal of American Academy of Child Psychiatry* 9:548-67.

————, Fish, B., and Ginsberg, G. (1972). The speech of a schizophrenic child from 2 to 6. *American Journal of Psychiatry* 128:1408-13.

Simmons, J. and Tymchuk, A. (1973). The learning deficits in childhood psychosis. *The Pediatrics Clinics of North America* 20:665-79.

Snow, C. (1972). Mothers' speech to children learning language. *Child Development* 43:549-65.

Tubbs, V. (1966). Types of linguistic disability in psychotic children. *Journal of Mental Deficiency Research* 10:230-40.

Ward, T. and Hoddinott, B. (1968). The development of speech in an autistic child. *Acta Paedopsychiatrica* 35:199-215.

Weiland, M. and Legg, D. (1964). Formal speech characteristics as a diagnostic aid in childhood psychosis. *American Journal of Orthopsychiatry* 34:91-94.

Wing, J. (1966). Diagnosis, epidemiology, aetiology. In Wing, J. ed., *Early Childhood Autism: Clinical, Educational and Social Aspects* London: Pergamon Press.

Wolff, S. and Chess, S. (1965). An analysis of the language of fourteen schizophrenic children. *Journal of Child Psychology and Psychiatry* 6:29-41.

CHAPTER TEN

Operant Analysis and Intervention With Autistic Children: Implications of Current Research

FRED FRANKEL
ALEXANDER J. TYMCHUK
JAMES Q. SIMMONS, III

Operant analysis and intervention are primarily derived from the work of B.F. Skinner, who originally demonstrated the relationships between environmental antecedents, the responses of organisms, and the environmental consequences in ways which permitted functional analyses of these events. Early clinical applications were directed toward suppressing or establishing single behaviors in individuals who were either psychotic or had severe behavior problems. The emphasis upon the single-behavior, single-case design was necessitated by a need to examine the lawfulness of deviant aspects of human behavior and to convince professionals of the applicability of general principles of learning to clinical problems.

C.B. Ferster, a student of Skinner's, and Miriam DeMyer, a child psychiatrist, were among the first to demonstrate that the limited behavioral repertoire of a previously unreachable autistic child could be extended through the use of food as a reinforcer (Ferster and DeMyer, 1961). From these studies the lawful effects of reinforcement schedules previously demonstrated in pigeons and rats were shown to obtain in autistic children. In a replication and extension of their original study, Ferster and DeMyer (1962) taught three autistic children to accumulate token reinforcements and to match-to-sample, a simple discrimination task. Hingtgen et al. (1965) shaped cooperative responses between three pairs of childhood schizophrenics. Thus, the behavior of seriously disturbed children could be made more "normal" through the establishment of adaptive behaviors. On the other hand, Wolf et al. (1964) showed that the elimination of maladaptive behaviors permitted previously developed adaptive behaviors to appear or allowed the acquisition of new adaptive behaviors. They further showed that the removal of these maladaptive behaviors could be accomplished quite easily by employing operant interventions. When this was accomplished, opportunities then arose for the development of adaptive alternatives.

These initial studies provided the impetus for a geometrically expanding number of experiments with this population. The results of these studies showed that an ever-widening spectrum of behaviors could be brought under environmental control. In addition, these analyses established the foundation for determining the types of events which produced and maintained both maladaptive and adaptive behaviors. It soon became apparent that the simple application of learning principles to individual behaviors had not yet taken full advantage of the operant paradigm. Rather, the application of operant analysis to areas of language, perception and social learning could be made and could lead to more effective interventions based on underlying substrates of these behaviors. Prior to discussing these applications in relationship to autism, it will be profitable to review some general principles of operant intervention.

PRINCIPLES OF OPERANT INTERVENTION

Briefly, the operant paradigm for intervention offers: (a) objective definitions of behavior to be changed (either increased or decreased), (b) a large set of intervention strategies which are based on learning experiments, and (c) an objective technique for the assessment of change which results from these interventions. Utilizing these principles, it follows that prior to the application of a treatment intervention, a systematic analysis of the environment in which the behavior occurs must be made. This allows for the specification of antecedents and consequences, and indicates behavioral goals. Basically, treatment goals are to increase low-rate adaptive behaviors and decrease maladaptive behaviors. In addition to the therapeutic value inherent in such an assessment, it also allows for the description of deviant behavioral repertoires in ways which shed light on their acquisition and maintenance. For instance, stereotyped behaviors may be observed under many environmental contingencies. From these observations one can determine the extent to which environmental consequences affect these behaviors and also the effects they have on information processing. Operant intervention strategies can be divided in accordance with two major objectives: to either increase or decrease the rate of a specified behavior.

Procedures for Increasing Behavior

The simplest technique used to increase the frequency of low-rate behaviors is that of *continuous reinforcement*. The therapist simply waits for the desired behavior to occur and then immediately reinforces each occurrence with a stimulus which has been shown to be effective with the child. For many young children, candy or preferred-food reward is often used. However, for some autistic children, many foods are not effective as evidenced by extensive histories of problems associated with eating. In these cases the therapist must first develop a rapport with the child in order that he may eventually offer effective social rewards such as pleasant verbal utterances or physical contact. In cases where food is effective, such food reward should always be preceded by social rewards in order to increase the effectiveness of these natural reinforcers. MacMillan and Forness (1970) have stressed that employing primary reinforcers when social reward is effective may hamper the development of exceptional children. They have proposed a reinforcement hierarchy on which food and social reinforcement are at the lowest levels. Task mastery is near the top of this hierarchy, and should be employed whenever effective in order to avoid the shortcomings of "reinforcement overkill."

Once desired behavior is elicited reliably on programs of continuous reinforcement, the technique should be changed to that of *partial reinforcement* in which behaviors are reinforced intermittently, e.g., every tenth time that they occur. Partial reinforcement is more "natural" in that it is more characteristic of the child's everyday environment. It is also much more resistant to the effects of extinction and thus helps to insure that desirable behaviors will continue after treatment is no longer administered.

Many common behaviors in the repertoires of normal individuals consist of strings of simpler behaviors. An effective approach is that of *behavioral chaining*. An integral part of a chaining procedure is the analyses of the components of complex behavior. These components are then established individually in the training process. For example, successful eating, a complex behavior, can be broken down into its components (holding a spoon, pushing spoon into food, bringing spoon to mouth, inserting spoon). Although most children quickly grasp the essential concept of such a behavior, some autistic children must be trained in each small segment.

Interventions using continuous reinforcement, partial reinforcement and chaining are effective if the child has a particular behavior in his repertoire although it is occurring at a low rate. However, frequently a child does not display the rudiments of a desired behavior. In this case, it is necessary to use behavior shaping and fading techniques. *Shaping* refers to the reinforcement of successive approximations to the desired goal behavior. In establishing toileting behavior, merely heading towards the toilet (but not voiding in the appropriate place) would be reinforced initially. After the child masters this approach response, reinforcement would be withheld until the child comes closer and eventually sits down. In contrast, a *fading* technique involves the therapist in the initial response. Upon observing the child preparing to void, the therapist would physically help the child over to the toilet, seat him, wait until he voids, and then reinforce him. On the next opportunity, the therapist would offer less help, i.e., take him over to the toilet, but let the child sit down by himself before giving reinforcement. Eventually the therapist would "fade out" all of his help, and the child would be reinforced for performance of the entire chain of behaviors.

Procedures for Decreasing Behaviors

As noted in the introduction, maladaptive behaviors, as well as desirable behaviors, are maintained by environmental consequences. In general, such behaviors are usually performed either to obtain the attention of caretakers or to escape situations which may be aversive to the child. Such situations commonly involve a high rate of demand. *Extinction* by ignoring the maladaptive behaviors works well in most cases. However, when used alone "ignoring" may not always be adequate. Its effect in decreasing behavior may be slow and it may often be associated with an initial increase of the target behavior. *Timeout* is a procedure which involves isolation of the child after each occurrence of an undesirable behavior. It is usually effective but is grossly ineffective for behaviors which are motivated by escape from high-demand situations. Also, some children seem to enjoy short periods of isolation. *Contingent aversive stimulation* or *punishment* is by far the most immediately effective technique. Contingent aversive stimuli range from a loud "No!" to administration of electric shock. Because many ethical and procedural problems are associated with the administration of strong aversives, their use should be limited to "last resort" situations (Simmons and Lovaas, 1969).

Two additional procedures have been used quite frequently in recent years: overcorrection and differential reinforcement (DRO). *Overcorrection* requires the child to make "restitution" for the environmental impact of his maladaptive behavior. For example, a child who throws objects would be required to pick up the objects he had thrown, and also to clean up the entire area. This procedure requires the constant attention of a caretaker until the target behavior is completely suppressed. For this reason this intervention may be impractical, although maladaptive behaviors are usually suppressed rapidly using this technique. *DRO* involves the reinforcement of behaviors other than maladaptives and the selective non-reinforcement of maladaptive behaviors. Both immediate and long-term suppression by a DRO program compare favorably with other types of interventions, including punishment. But this strategy also requires the constant attention of caretakers during the first stage of implementation.

Building Stimulus Control

Treatment goals for children with severely deficient behavioral repertoires include not only the acquisition of responses, but also teaching the child to discriminate appropriateness. For instance, a child with the words "blue" and "green" in his repertoire must be trained to correctly label the blue and green stimuli. Such discrimination learning has been achieved through two methods: trial-and-error learning and errorless learning. The traditional approach of *trial-and-error* involves the presentation of either one or multiple stimuli. In the one-stimulus case, the child names the stimulus from the many alternative responses in his repertoire, e.g., calling the appropriate stimulus "blue." When this is done, he is reinforced. If he mislabels the stimulus, he is informed that he is wrong and reinforcement is withheld. In the multiple-stimulus case, the child is presented with two or more objects and required to select the "blue" one. The consequences of correct and incorrect responses are the same as in the one-stimulus case.

In contrast to the trial-and-error technique, the *errorless* technique ideally employs only positive reinforcement. In the multiple-stimulus case, the correct stimulus is enhanced so that it will be selected; the blue stimulus is placed directly in front of and close to the child, while the incorrect stimuli are placed at a distance. The correct choice is immediately re-inforced. On successive trials, the distance between the stimuli is gradually decreased. Terrace (1966) has shown that the errorless procedure eliminates several bad side effects of trial-and-error learning (e.g., frustration), and facilitates the acquisition of discriminations. This model has also been employed in so-called programmed learning approaches (Hewett, Mayhew & Rabb, 1967).

OPERANT ANALYSIS AND INTERVENTION WITH AUTISTIC CHILDREN

This presentation will recast some of the psychological literature within the diagnostic framework of autism developed by Ornitz and Ritvo (1968). While there are differences between psychiatrists in terms of the diagnostic criteria for early infantile autism, it is felt that those offered by Ornitz and Ritvo are among the most comprehensive and will prove useful for the present discussion. The emphasis will center on research conducted within the past five years. Some of this research is still ongoing, and the findings are therefore preliminary.

Among Ornitz and Ritvo's criteria are the following areas of disturbance usually evident before the age of thirty months: (1) perceptual disturbances which result in variable responses to external stimuli; (2) language disturbance characterized by mutism or echolalia; (3) disturbed social relationships between the autistic and others in his environment; and (4) motility disturbances characterized by arm-flapping, finger-flicking, or object spinning. For purposes of the present discussion, we will also include self-destructive behavior under (4). Although an individual autistic child may not overtly display disturbances in all of these areas, most authors agree that disturbances in language and social relationships must be present in order for the child to receive the diagnosis (Rutter, 1974). Some psychological research has helped to clarify the characteristics and critical features of each of the areas of disturbance. This research has already suggested effective treatment strategies for the remediation of each of the diagnostic symptoms.

Disturbances in Perception

Initially, the primary thrust of psychological research was on the perceptual disturbances in autistic children. The first attempts were aimed at localizing gross deficits in the sensory apparatus. O'Connor and Hermelin (1965) presented autistic children and retarded control groups with either a light or a sound and recorded the percentage of responses to each of these stimuli. Their results were equivocal, since they did not find overall differences between groups as a function of stimulus modality or intensity, although all groups did respond more to intense auditory stimuli. On the other hand, Schopler (1966) found such a difference. He showed that autistic children were indifferent to both visual and tactile stimuli compared to normal children of the same chronological age and to retarded children of the same mental age. The autistic children showed no preference for visual over tactile stimuli, while both control groups spent approximately 60 percent of their time attending to the visual stimulus.

Recently, Koegel (1971) isolated a specific perceptual abnormality which he considered to have profound significance for education. Educators typically use prompt stimuli in errorless discrimination training. When prompts are faded out leaving only the relevant stimulus, e.g., blue, the autistic child may fixate on the prompt (distance) and not transfer to color. Two subsequent studies from Lovaas' laboratory (Lovaas & Schreibman, 1971; Lovaas et al., 1971b) demonstrated a more general phenomenon of overselectivity in autistic children during discrimination training. This was seen in a tendency to select an irrelevant feature of environmental stimuli and use it to govern their responses. The most convincing demonstration of overselectivity was that of Koegel and Wilhelm (1973) who paired pre-ferred-candy reward with a two-component visual stimulus. The children were subsequently tested with either one or the other component present. Normal children responded equally during the presence of either component. However, autistic children responded only to one of the two visual stimuli. The visual stimulus selected was different for each child. The original studies of `Lovaas and his colleagues also demonstrated that this effect was independent of stimulus modality and was different for each autistic child.

Research into overselectivity leaves unanswered two important questions. First, all of the above studies have matched normal controls by chronological age. Normal control groups differ from autistic children not only in lacking the diagnosis of autism, but also in the absence of functional retardation. Rutter and Sussenwein (1971) have suggested that the ideal control group for autistic children is children matched for mental age. It is entirely possible that overselectivity could be a developmental effect normally occurring in younger children. Second, the above studies did not isolate the precise origin of overselectivity. The question which arises is whether autistic children fail to respond to certain stimuli because most aspects of a complex stimulus are not perceived, or whether they per-severate in responding to one stimulus from among all those perceived. An experiment currently in progress is an attempt to resolve these two questions (Frankel et al., in preparation). In this study, young autistic children were compared with mentally retarded children equated for mental age. For both groups of children, a preferred-food reward was paired with a light-noise compound stimulus. In addition, physiological measures of the orienting response (vaso-constriction and heart rate) were monitored. Preliminary results with four autistic and three retarded children showed that the autistic children displayed overselectivity, whereas the retarded children did not. In subsequent tests of each component alone, three out of four autistic children showed physiological orienting reactions to the stimulus they failed to select. The results suggested that these children were reacting as if they perceived this stimulus for the first time, since orienting reactions occur to novel stimuli and eventually habituate upon repeated presentation (see Lynn, 1966, for a detailed discussion of the role of the orienting reaction in learning). The lack of over-selectivity in the mentally retarded children indicated that the over-selectivity in the autistic children was not simply a function of their being retarded as well as autistic.

Although research into the effects of overselectivity in autistic children is only beginning, the work cited strongly suggests that the use of prompt stimuli should be modified in the education of autistic children. The error-less technique could be changed so that the distracting effects of prompt stimuli could be minimized and overselectivity could be used to advantage to effect transfer of learning. In the case of color labeling, children would first be exposed to a blue block alone and asked simply to give the teacher the blue block. After the child performs this sucessfully, the blue block would be placed together with one incorrect stimulus, a yellow block. The child would again be asked to provide the blue block and the position of the blocks would be randomized from trial to trial. The use of the blue block alone would be a modified prompt, and would not involve any additional distracting stimuli. Thus, overselectivity would aid transfer of learning, since this stimulus would most likely be overselected during subsequent trials with the incorrect stimuli.

The phenomenon of overselectivity appears well established, but it remains for future research to develop the rules which individual autistic children use in choosing the stimuli to which they overselect. For example, if individual autistic children follow a stimulus hierarchy, knowledge of this hierarchy would be quite useful to educators. If a child prefers visual stimuli to auditory stimuli, then the approach would be to train auditory stimuli without the presence of visual stimuli in an attempt to reduce this preference.

Disturbances in Motility

Recently, considerable attention has been concentrated on behaviors generally classified as disturbances in motility. These repetitive, apparently non-goal directed motor behaviors are displayed by both retarded and autistic children. Rutter (1974) has suggested that stereotyped behaviors in retarded children appeared qualitatively different from those in autistic children. He further asserted that autistic children were more concerned with the *visual feedback*, since their behavior frequently involved repetitive motions in front of the eyes. In contrast, the stereotypies of re-tarded children seem to depend upon *motor* or *vestibular feedback*.

Perhaps the main impetus for discovering the mechanisms underlying this type of behavior lies in an experiment by Lovaas et al. (1971a). They found that autistic children were less responsive to their environment when engaged in stereotyped behaviors. In a subsequent study, Koegel and Covert (1972) demonstrated that stereotyped behaviors can significantly impair performance in discrimination learning. Recent research (Frankel et al., 1974) strongly suggests that the visual stereotypies in autistic children may have a different basis than in retarded children. In this particular study, six autistic and five mentally retarded children of equal mental age were presented with six different frequencies of photic-stimulation. For all subjects, two seconds of contingent photic-stimulation were provided for each pull of a lever. The frequency was varied between two and twenty flashes per second. Mentally retarded children did not differ in their rates of lever pulling for the six different frequencies. However, the rates for autistic children were much higher for frequencies between thirteen and twenty flashes per second. Thus in partial support of Rutter (1974), the frequency of visual stimulation was found to be a critical parameter for the autistic children only.

Other research has also demonstrated the role of repetition in the stereo typed behavior of autistic children. Sorosky et al. (1968) showed that the frequency of most stereotyped flapping behaviors exhibited by autistic children was between three and four cycles per second. Colman et al. (1975b) have demonstrated the effects of repetitive events in the immediate environment. Autistic children observed under fluorescent illumination engaged in stereotyped behavior for a larger proportion of their time than when observed under incandescent illumination of equal intensity. The salient difference between the two types of illumination was the repetitive nature of fluorescent lighting (60 flashes/second). However, this latter effect seems to be limited to an environment where other competing stimuli are not present.

Additional research is currently being conducted in an attempt to establish the uniqueness of the visual modality regarding the effects of repetitive stimuli. Freeman and Frankel (in progress) are currently comparing the effects of contingent vestibular stimulation upon autistic and retarded children of equal mental age. Children in both groups were placed in a "motorized rocking chair" which rocked at either 24.5 rpm, 40 rpm, or 56 rpm for five seconds, contingent upon lever pulling. No differences in rates of either group emerged as a function of frequency. This is clearly counter to the position of Rutter (1974). Thus, the effects of frequency may well be confined to the visual modality.

Some preliminary evidence is available to suggest that the function of stereotyped behavior is related to mental age. Frankel et al., (1975) showed that stereotyped behaviors of high versus low mental age autistic children were differentially affected by the presentation of novel stimuli. In this experiment, the percent of time that children engaged in stereotyped behavior was observed. Environmental stimuli were relatively absent in one condition and novel stimuli (Christmas-tree lights and sound-effects) were presented in the other. High mental age autistic children engaged in significantly less stereotypies during novel stimuli, but those with low mental age engaged in more stereotyped behavior in this situation. Frankel et al. (1974) also showed that the magnitude of preference which autistic subjects showed for higher frequencies of flashing light correlated better than .90 with mental age.

In view of the findings that stereotyped behavior interferes with learning and is correlated negatively with mental age, it seems that the best approach would be to suppress this behavior rather than trying to shape it into something more adaptive. Many different types of interventions have been successful. These include contingent aversive stimulation (Lovaas et al., 1973), overcorrection (Azrin et al., 1973), differential reinforcement or DRO (Herendeen et al., 1974), and reinforcement of toy play (Flavell, 1973). Herendeen et al. (1974) offer evidence that DRO may be superior to overcorrection in the reduction of rocking behavior and in obtaining high levels of appropriate behavior.

Self-destructive behavior also seems to have a high prevalence among autistic children (Green, 1967). This behavior has been reduced with virtually all of the previously described procedures. These include extinction (Jones, et al., 1974), DRO (Schofield et al., 1973), punishment (Lovaas & Simmons, 1969), and timeout (Hamilton et al., 1967). However, overcorrection has not been attempted. After a review of more than fifty studies on interventions in self-destructive behavior, Frankel and Simmons (in preparation) concluded that these different interventions are of comparable effectiveness in the short-run but that long-term follow-up has been lacking. Furthermore, it seems that children displaying more than one type of self-destructive behavior are not more difficult to bring under control than those who show only a single type.

Baumeister and Forehand (1974) asserted that self-destructive behavior and stereotyped behavior were related. They cited some superficial similarities, e.g., both being repetitive in nature and both frequently being displayed in the same children. However, observations by the present authors do not bear out this assertion. Jones et al. (1974) reported on the extinction of self-destructive behavior in a child who also possessed stereotyped behavior. Correlations between self-destructive and stereotyped behaviors were not great. One would expect high negative correlations between two classes of incompatible behaviors such as these if they were related. In this regard, Jones et al. reported high negative correlations between different classes of self-destructive behaviors, as expected. Forehand and Baumeister (1970) reported that movement restraint generally increased the occurrence of stereotypies during non-restrained periods. But, Jones et al. noticed that rates of self-destructive behavior were generally unaffected by constant restraint. It is obvious from the above that this area has received considerable clarification though operant analysis, and thus poses no particular problem for operant interventions.

Disturbances of Relatedness

Unlike the psychological research concerned with perception and motility, the results of research into disturbances of relatedness have not supported general clinical impressions. Freitag (1970) examined autistic children's performance on a simple marble-dropping task after prior manipulation of social contingencies. The experimenter was either (a) not present during preliminary sessions; (b) present and offering noncontingent reprimands; or (c) present and offering noncontingent praise. Autistic children performed best after condition (c), which indicated that autistic children were influenced by previous social experience.

One of the most obvious symptoms linked with disturbances in relatedness is the lack of eye-to-eye contact. Hermelin and O'Connor (1970) offered evidence that this resulted from a more general disturbance in attention. They observed the eye movements of autistic and equal mental age retarded children presented with two simultaneous stimuli. These stimuli varied in complexity from white squares to cut-up pictures of a human face. Both groups of subjects spent more time looking at the more complex stimuli. However, the retarded children spent a larger proportion of their time looking at the stimuli, while the autistic children tended to attend more to the background. The autistic children also showed fewer eye movements in general. They spent more eye fixation time than retarded children, who tended to look back and forth between figures.

The phenomenon of stimulus overselectivity also seems to play a direct role in deficits in the socialization process. Schreibman and Lovaas (1973) demonstrated that autistic children may have difficulty learning the identity of adults largely because they overselect irrelevant aspects of adults rather than attempting to discriminate them by facial and body features. The significance of this result cannot be underestimated when one considers the normally complex environment to which a child is exposed.

Another aspect of the disturbances in relatedness is the lack of peer interaction. This characteristic of autism has received relatively little attention in the psychology literature. Certainly the major means for normal children to interact is through play behaviors of various complexity. Perhaps the disturbance in play behaviors stems from the interference of competing maladaptive behaviors. In support of this contention, Koegel et al., (1974) observed marked increases in play behaviors after an intervention which served only to eliminate stereotyped behaviors.

Both positive and negative reinforcement have been used to build social responses. Lovaas et al., (1965) used escape from shock to achieve this end. Shock was terminated after the children approached a nurse. This intervention significantly decreased the frequency of self-stimulatory and tantrum behaviors and increased approach responses to the nurse. A final phase of this study demonstrated that the nurse had become a secondary reinforcer, since bar-pressing by the children was maintained by her contingent attention. Positive reinforcers have also been manipulated to increase social behaviors (Craighead et al., 1973; Tymchuk et al., 1974). In the latter study, ten-minute daily sessions were employed in an AB AB design. The first five minutes were free of social interaction (A), and then five minutes of commands were given by an unfamiliar adult (B). The results indicated that social interaction, spontaneous eye and physical contact occurred only during B periods. Furthermore, these effects showed incomplete reversal during the second A period.

Play behaviors have been successfully established through modeling procedures. Following a suggestion of Forness (1975), Colman et al. (1975a) utilized learning-disabled children with well-developed play skills as interactive models for other exceptional children who were seriously deficient in such skills. This resulted in an increase in the cooperative and solitary play behaviors of the unsophisticated children and decreased the time they spent unoccupied in any play activity. The ratio of sophisticated to unsophisticated children was also systematically varied. It was found that using only one sophisticated child produced the largest increase in appropriate play behaviors, while varying the number of unsophisticated children (from one to three) did not affect outcome. The results of Colman et al. may only apply to higher functioning exceptional children, since cooperative play behavior does not develop spontaneously in normal populations until quite late in childhood. Other preliminary work by one of the present authors (Tymchuk) indicates that young normal children may also serve to increase appropriate play behaviors in lower mental age autistic children. Normal children have been trained to systematically reinforce autistic children for working on a puzzle, pulling a wagon with other children in it, or rolling a ball to other children. Preliminary observations have indicated that these behaviors *increased* in autistic children. These findings have given impetus to the training of autistic children's siblings as a means of carrying over training to the home.

Disturbances in Language

The language proficiency of autistic children falls on a continuum from totally mute to somewhat efficient use of language. For purposes of this discussion, it is useful to divide autistic children into three language subgroups: those who possess no language skills, those whose speech is primarily echolalic, and those who exhibit a higher degree of language development.

Considerable longitudinal research has been conducted with the aim of linking language development to long-term prognosis. Rutter et al. (1967) were the first to correlate the language deficient subgroup with very poor long-term outcome. Somewhat earlier, Eisenberg (1956) suggested that autistic children who did not develop language by the age of five were not likely to acquire it thereafter. However, neither of these studies effectively separated the overall levels of functioning of the children in the different subgroups noted. It seems likely that children with low overall IQ would be less likely to develop speech and also would have a less favorable prognosis. In support of this, Rutter et al. (1967) also reported that autistic children with IQs of less than 60 displayed an unfavorable outcome compared to children with IQs above 60. Overall level of functioning is a vague term but can be operationalized by certain types of tests. Because some autistic children are not only unable to use language but unable to comprehend it (Rutter and Sussenwein, 1971), a fair test of such a child's overall IQ would be one which requires minimal verbal skills (e.g., the Merrill-Palmer).

The second major form of language disturbance is that of echolalia. The label of echolalia is not peculiar to autism. Phenomena referred to as echolalia are evident in normal children during the early stages of language development, in catatonic schizophrenics, and in some mentally retarded children. However, as is the case with stereotyped behaviors (even though behaviors of different clinical populations may bear some similarities and be referred to by the same name) it does not imply that they are identical phenomena.

At least three types of echolalia have been differentiated by previous authors. Kanner (1943) was the first to report the occurrence of *immediate* and *delayed* echolalia in autistic children. Fay (1967, 1969) later added *mitigated* echolalia, which was defined as the partial alteration of an echolalic phrase.

Of the three forms of echolalia, the immediate form is perhaps the easiest to subject to rigorous experimental test. This is because it is easier to formulate an objective definition of echolalia if it is the simple repetition of a recent verbal input. By contrast, both delayed and mitigated echolalia are difficult to define in terms of their antecedents. Two recent studies performed at UCLA are highly instructive in delineating the stimulus conditions which are sufficient to produce immediate echolalia. Nathanson (unpublished) studied the effects of the nature of verbal input upon the immediate echolalia of four autistic children. She presented each child with three different stimulus lists: (a) nonsense syllables; (b) the word "chair" presented to control for simple repetition effects; (c) simple questions which the child had previously been trained to answer correctly. In all four subjects, condition (c) produced the least echolalia (close to zero) and condition

(a) produced the most. Thus, *lack of previous learning* may be a major factor in the production of immediate echolalic responses.

Nathanson reported some evidence that when echolalic children are trained to say "I don't know" to questions they cannot answer, echolalia is reduced considerably. A more formal study has employed punishment and extinction of echolalic responses and prompt fading for correct responses (Risley & Wolf, 1967). However, the results of Freeman et al. (in press) indicate that response prevention coupled with concurrent partial reinforcement of appropriate verbal responses may be sufficient to suppress echolalia.

Three studies have commented upon developmental commonalities between autistics exhibiting a higher degree of language proficiency. Shervanian (1959) reported that these children lagged in the development of phonology for vowels and nasals but that they were more impaired in their use of stops, semivowels and fricatives. Baltaxe and Simmons (in press) cite evidence that autistic children are deficient in certain precursors of speech production. They displayed diminished babbling and used fewer language-related gestures. Rothman and Goldstein (1945) reported that autistic children showed an inability to comprehend basic word definitions, and such simple concepts as similarity and difference.

Other studies sought to demonstrate the more pervasive nature of the language deficiencies. Goldfarb et al., (1956) found more basic deficits involving difficulties with volume, pitch, rhythm, stress, and intonation. Simmons and Baltaxe (in press) reported that autistic children who performed poorly on a test of tonal memory also showed related disturbances in speech production. This suggests that many disturbances in speech production may be a function of speech perception. Baltaxe and Simmons (in press) suggested that although labeling is relatively intact in some autistic children, functional recognition of linguistic relationships is greatly deficient. It remains for future research to expand upon these preliminary findings of the abnormalities in the speech and language of autistic children. Operant paradigms may facilitate the investigation of the relationship between discrimination processes and language impairment. Reward can be made differentially contingent upon key stimuli in semantic differentiation, such as stress and intonation. The extent to which these auditory deficits are present in each of the three subgroups could be examined to determine the role of intellectual functioning on prognosis.

CONCLUSIONS

Many authors have considered that the five criteria used by Ornitz and Ritvo (1968) are not primary causes of the autistic syndrome but that one subset of these symptoms may produce the remainder of the cluster as secondary features. Rutter and his colleagues have alluded to a possibility that the social impairment is responsible for the other impairments (Rutter & Sussenwein, 1971), but have also pointed out that the language impairment may be primary (Rutter, 1968; Rutter et al., 1971). It also seems likely from this discussion that the phenomena of overselectivity and stereotyped behavior could be responsible for the other features of autism. Both impairments serve to restrict the effects of the environment upon autistic children. Overselectivity has pronounced involvement in perceptual impairment, and it seems likely that it may account for a large part of the perceptual inconstancy described by Ornitz and Ritvo (1968). In addition, some evidence suggests that it may have an important role to play in the lack of socialization: overselecting to irrelevant aspects of adults could be critical to the lack of relationships between parent and child (Schreibman & Lovaas, 1973). Furthermore, by implication, it is easy to see how overselectivity may play a role in language development: in order to attach meaning, the young child must be able to select individual words from the barrage of auditory and other stimuli which confront him. Thus, the building of a receptive vocabulary as well as other linguistic skills depends upon the child's ability to make simple discriminations and to select relevant stimuli to focus upon. If a child shows an impairment in this simple skill, then it is not surprising that he would have difficulty in the acquisition of language.

It is obvious that operant methodology offers a strategy to begin answering some of these questions. The focus is more on the techniques for manipulating variables (operant analysis) than upon operant intervention. It is equally apparent that the information gained from operant analysis can probably be most effectively utilized through delivery by operant intervention techniques.

REFERENCES

Azrin, N.H., Kaplan, S.J., and Foxx, R.M. (1973). Autism reversal: eliminating stereotyped self-stimulation of retarded individuals. *American Journal of Mental Deficiency* 78:241-48.

Baltaxe, C.A.M., and Simmons, J.Q. (in press). Language in childhood psychosis—a review. *Journal of Speech and Hearing Disorders*

Baumeister, A.A. and Forehand, R. (1974). Stereotyped acts. In, N.R. Ellis ed. *International Review of Research in Mental Retardation* Vol. 6 New York: Academic Press.

Colman, R., Ames, S., and Frankel, F. (1975a). The exceptional child as a teacher of cooperative play skills. Paper presented at the 99th annual meeting of the American Association on Mental Deficiency, Portland.

———, Frankel, F., and Ritvo, E. (1975b). The effects of background illumination upon stereotyped behaviors in autistic children. Paper presented at the 99th annual meeting of the American Association on Mental Deficiency, Portland.

Craighead, W., O'Leary, K., and Allen, J. (1973). Teaching and generalization of instruction-following in an "autistic" child. *Journal of Behavior Therapy and Experimental Psychiatry* 4:171-76.

Eisenberg, L. (1956). The autistic child in adolescence. *American Journal of Psychiatry* 112:607-12.

Fay, W. (1967). Mitigated echolalia of children. *Journal of Speech and Hearing Research* 10:305-10.

——— (1969). On the basis of autistic echolalia. *Journal of Communication Disorders* 2:38-47.

Ferster, C. and DeMyer, M. (1961). The development of performances in autistic children in an automatically controlled environment. *Journal of Chronic Disorders* 13: 312-45.

——— and DeMyer, M. (1962). A method for the experimental analysis of the behavior of autistic children. *American Journal of Orthopsychiatry* 32:89-98.

Flavell, J.E. (1973). Reduction of stereotypies by reinforcement of toy play. *Mental Retardation* 11:21-23.

Forehand, R. and Baumeister, A.A. (1970). Body rocking and activity level as a function of prior movement restraint. *American Journal of Mental Deficiency* 74:608-610.

Forness, S.R. (1975). Educational approaches to autism. *Training School Bulletin* 71 (3):167-172.

Frankel, F. and Simmons, J.Q. Self-destructive behavior in retarded and schizophrenic children: a review. *American Journal of Mental Deficiency* in press.

———, Chikami, B., Freeman, B.J., Ritvo, E., and Carr, E. (1974). The reinforcing effects of photic stimulation upon the behavior of autistic and retarded children. Paper presented at the 54th annual meeting of the Western Psychological Association, San Francisco.

———, Ritvo, E. and Pardo, R. (1975). The effect of environmental stimulation upon the stereotypic behavior of autistic children at two levels of mental age. Paper presented at the 99th annual meeting of the American Association on Mental Deficiency, Portland.

———, Simmons, J.Q., and Fichter, M. (in preparation). Physiological correlates of stimulus overselectivity in autistic and retarded children.

Freeman, B.J. and Frankel, F. (in progress). The effects of response-contingent vestibular stimulation upon the behavior of autistic and retarded children.

———, Ritvo, E., and Miller, R. (in press). An operant procedure to teach an echolalic, autistic child to answer questions appropriately. *Journal of Autism & Childhood Schizophrenia*

Freitag, G. (1970). An experimental study of the social responsiveness of children with autistic behaviors. *Journal of Experimental Child Psychology* 9:436-53.

Goldfarb, W., Braunstein, P. and Lorge, I. (1956). A study of speech patterns in a group of schizophrenic children. *American Journal of Orthopsychiatry* 26:544-55.

Green, A.H. (1967). Self-mutilation in schizophrenic children. *Archives of General Psychiatry* 17:234-44.

Hamilton, J., Stephens, L., and Allen, P. (1967). Controlling aggressive behavior in severely retarded institutionalized residents. *American Journal of Mental Deficiency* 71:852-56.

Herendeen, D.L., Jeffrey, B.D., and Graham, M.L. (1974). Reduction of self-stimulation in institutionalized children: overcorrection and reinforcement of nonresponding. Paper presented at the 8th annual meeting of the Association for Advancement of Behavior Therapy, Chicago.

Hermelin, B. and O'Connor, N. (1970). *Psychological Experiments with Autistic Children.* Oxford: Pergamon.

Hewett, F., Mayhew, D., and Rabb, E. (1967). An experimental reading program for neurologically impaired, mentally retarded and severely emotionally disturbed children. *American Journal of Orthopsychiatry* 37:35-48.

Hingtgen, J.N., Sanders, B.J., and DeMyer, M.K. (1965). Shaping cooperative responses in early childhood schizophrenics. In L.P. Ullman & L. Krasner eds., *Case Studies in Behavior Modification.* New York: Holt, Rinehart & Winston.

Jones, F.H., Simmons, J.Q., and Frankel, F. (1974). An extinction procedure for eliminating self-destructive behavior in a 9-year-old autistic girl. *Journal of Autism & Childhood Schizophrenia* 4:241-50.

Kanner, L. (1943). Autistic disturbances of affective contact. *The Nervous Child* 2:217-50.

Koegel, R.L. (1971). Selective attention to prompt stimuli by autistic and normal children. Unpublished doctoral dissertation. UCLA.

――― and Covert, A. (1972). The relationship of self-stimulation to learning in autistic children. *Journal of Applied Behavior Analysis* 5:381-88.

――― and Wilhelm, H. (1973). Selective responding to the components of multiple visual cues. *Journal of Experimental Child Psychology* 15:442-53.

―――, Firestone, P.B., Kramme, K.W., and Dunlap, G. (1974). Increasing spontaneous play by suppressing self-stimulation in autistic children. *Journal of Applied Behavior Analysis* 7:521-28.

Lovaas, O.I. and Schreibman, L. (1971). Stimulus overselectivity of autistic children in a two-stimulus situation. *Behavior Research & Therapy* 2:305-10.

――― and Simmons, J.Q. (1969). Manipulation of self-destruction in three retarded children. *Journal of Applied Behavior Analysis* 2:143-57.

―――, Koegel, R., Simmons, J.Q., and Long, J.S. (1973). Some generalization and follow-up measures on autistic children in behavior therapy. *Journal of Applied Behavior Analysis* 6:131-66.

―――, Litrownik, A., and Mann, R. (1971a). Response latencies to auditory stimuli in children engaged in self-stimulatory behavior. *Behavior Research & Therapy* 9:39-49.

―――, Schaeffer, B., and Simmons, J.Q. (1965). Building social behavior in autistic children by use of electric shock. *Journal of Experimental Research in Personality* 1:99-109.

―――, Schreibman, L., Koegel, R. and, Rehm, R. (1971b). Selective responding of autistic children to multiple sensory input. *Journal of Abnormal Psychology* 77: 211-22.

Lynn, R. (1966). *Attention, Arousal and the Orientation Reaction.* London: Pergamon Press.

MacMillan, D. and Forness, S. (1970). Behavior modification: limitations and liabilities. *Exceptional Children* 37:291-97.

Nathanson, L.S. (unpublished). Stimulus control and extinction of immediate echolalia in autistic children. Unpublished manuscript, UCLA Department of Psychiatry.

O'Connor, N. and Hermelin, B. (1965). Sensory dominance in autistic imbecile children and controls. *Archives of General Psychiatry* 12:99-103.

Ornitz, E.M. and Ritvo, E.R. (1968). Perceptual inconstancy in the syndrome of early infantile autism and its variants. *Archives of General Psychiatry* 18:76-98.

Risley, T. and Wolf, M.M. (1967). Establishing functional speech in echolalic children. *Behavior Research & Therapy* 5:73-88.

Rutter, M. (1968). Concepts of autism: a review of research. *Journal of Child Psychology and Psychiatry* 9:1-25.

——— (1974). The development of infantile autism. *Psychological Medicine* 4:147-63.

——— and Sussenwein, F. (1971). A developmental and behavioral approach to the treatment of preschool autistic children. *Journal of Autism & Childhood Schizophrenia* 1:376-97.

———, Bartak, L., and Newman, S. (1971). Autism: a disorder of cognition and language. In M. Rutter ed. *Infantile Autism: Concepts, Characteristics, and Treatment.* Edinburgh: Churchill Livingstone.

———, Greenfeld, D., and Lockyer, L. (1967). A five to fifteen year follow-up study of infantile psychosis: II. Social and behavioral outcome. *British Journal of Psychiatry* 113:1183-99.

Scheerer, M., Rothman, E. and Goldstein, K. (1945). A case of idiot savant: an experimental study of personality organization. *Psychological Monographs* Whole No. 58.

Schofield, S., Moss, D. and Frankel, F. (1973). Operant procedures for eliminating the deviant behaviors of a mentally retarded child in a preschool setting. Paper presented at the 52nd annual meeting of the California Educational Research Association, Los Angeles.

Schopler, E. (1966). Visual versus tactile receptor preference in normal and schizophrenic children. *Journal of Abnormal Psychology* 71:108-14.

Schreibman, L. and Lovaas, O.I. (1973). Overselective response to social stimuli by autistic children. *Journal of Abnormal Child Psychology* 1:152-68.

Shervanian, C. (1959). The speech development level of pre-communicative psychotic children. Unpublished doctoral dissertation, University of Pittsburgh.

Sorosky, A.D., Ornitz, E.M., Brown, M.B. and Ritvo, E.R. (1968). Systematic observation of autistic behavior. *Archives of General Psychiatry* 18:439-49.

Simmons, J.Q. and Baltaxe, C. (in press). Language patterns of autistic children who have reached adolescence. *Journal of Autism & Childhood Schizophrenia.*

——— and Lovaas, O.I. (1969). Use of pain and punishment as treatment techniques with childhood schizophrenics. *American Journal of Psychotherapy* 23:23-35.

Terrace, H.S. (1966). Stimulus control. In W.K. Honig ed., *Operant Behavior: Areas of Research and Application* New York: Appleton-Century-Crofts.

Tymchuk, A.J., Insul, A., and Berger, D. (1974). Development of social interaction between an autistic boy and an unfamiliar adult. Paper presented at the 98th annual meeting of the American Association on Mental Deficiency, Toronto.

Wolf, M.M., Risley, T., and Mees, H.L. (1964). Application of operant conditioning procedures to the behavior problems of an autistic child. *Behavior Research & Therapy* 1:305-12.

CHAPTER ELEVEN

Genetic Studies

M. ANNE SPENCE

In a review article of autism, Rutter (1968) stated: "The importance of genetic factors remains unknown." In 1975, that continues to be a true statement. A number of recent articles (Rutter and Bartak, 1971; Spence et al., 1974) do allude to the *possibility* of a genetic etiology; a reasonable amount of information is available relevant to the issue of a genetic involvement in this syndrome. Therefore, in this discussion we will utilize the existing information to explore three basic questions:

(1) What are the possible genetic factors?
(2) How do you test for presence of these factors?
(3) How much has been accomplished to date?

CHROMOSOMAL ABNORMALITIES

The first and most obvious genetic factor to consider is the chromosomes. Each individual has forty-six chromosomes, twenty-two pairs of autosomes and one pair of sex chromosomes. With the recently developed technique of trypsin-Giemsa staining (Seabright, 1972), the bands for each chromosome pair are unique and sufficient to identify the specific chromosome. Variations in chromosome number or shape may alter the phenotype of the individual. An example of this is Down's syndrome, where these individuals have an extra number 21 chromosome and exhibit a constellation of physical features and mental retardation (Hamerton, 1971).

A number of studies have reported chromosome analysis of autistic children and failure to detect any chromosome abnormality (Biesele et al.,

169

1962; Böök et al., 1963; Judd and Mandell, 1968). A total of thirty-one children were evaluated in these studies, a sufficiently large sample to rule out the possibility of a chromosomal variant contributing to any significant portion of the cases of autism. The report of a long Y chromosome by Judd and Mandell (1968) is less relevant now because more recent work has shown the length of the Y chromosome to be highly variable in normal individuals (Lubs & Ruddle, 1970).

Application of the new banding trypsin-Giemsa technique has not yet been reported for autistic children. However, our own studies of four autistic children, using banding, have also failed to reveal any abnormalities (Crandall and Sparkes, 0000).

GENE VARIATIONS

Genes may be simply defined as units of the DNA molecule which are responsible for the production of molecules such as enzymes and proteins required for our biochemical functions. Almost 2000 variations (mutations) in gene function have been described for man (McKusick, 1971). However, these mutations are not visible as changes in the chromosomes which carry the genes. More complete discussions are available (Thompson and Thompson, 1973). The effects of the mutant or altered genes are classified by their pattern of inheritance in families. Examples of each type of inheritance are discussed below and contrasted to our available information on autism.

X-linked inheritance

A proportion of the genes are carried on the X chromosome, or sex chromosome. Females have two X chromosomes, while males have only one X and a Y chromosome. Therefore, a primary feature of an X-linked mutation is that they occur more frequently in males. Examples of known X-linked diseases are hemophilia and Duchenne's muscular dystrophy (McKusick, 1971).

All studies of autistic children report an excess of affected males. Kanner (1954) reported a male-to-female ratio of 4:1, while Lotter's study (1966) reported a ratio of 2.5:1. Our own study of fifty-two autistic children reported a ratio of 4.8:1 (Spence et al., 1973).

The predicted ratio of males to females for an X-linked inheritance model for autism can be computed directly from the frequency of the disease in the population (Thompson and Thompson, 1973, p. 279). The frequency reported by Lotter (1966) is approximately 4/10,000. The frequency in males is approximately 3/5,000, which we will call q. The ratio of males to females, as predicted by genetic theory, is 1:q, and this ratio is approximately 1700:1. Therefore, for a trait as rare as autism, the ratio of affected males to affected females would have to be considerably larger than the reported ratio. For this reason, an X-linked type of inheritance can be excluded as a contributing factor for autism.

Autosomal dominant inheritance

The majority of our genes are carried on the autosomes, or non-sex chromosomes. When the presence of one copy of the mutant gene is sufficient to produce the trait, then that mutant gene is said to be dominant. Examples of conditions known to be inherited in an autosomal dominant fashion are Huntington's chorea, Marfan's syndrome, and certain forms of dwarfism (McKusick, 1971). With a dominant gene, the usual pattern of inheritance is: affected individuals in generation after generation (equal numbers of affected in the two sexes), and about one-half of the children of an affected parent also affected. If we treat the syndrome diagnosed as autism as our trait in question, then obviously we do not see this pattern of inheritance. That is sufficient evidence to exclude a dominant form of inheritance for autism.

Autosomal recessive inheritance

A gene carried on an autosomal chromosome is said to be recessive when two copies of the same mutant gene are required before the individual expresses the trait. Examples of conditions inherited in this way are cystic fibrosis, phenylketonuria (PKU), and the O type for the ABO blood group (McKusick, 1971).

In a family where a recessive trait is present, we see three important features. First, the parents are completely normal in appearance. It is possible with a few diseases, like Tay-Sachs, to detect parents who carry the mutant gene through an enzyme assay (O'Brien et al., 1970). Second, the disease may reoccur in the family, usually within the same sibship, where approximately 25 percent of the children are affected. And finally, it is the case that parents of children with recessive diseases are more often related to each other, e.g., a consanguinous marriage between first cousins, than is seen in the general population.

In families with autistic children, the parents are most often normal with minimal variation, such as a higher education level (Lowe, 1966), but not autistic (Rutter, 1968). However, the recurrence risk reported for sibs of autistic children is about 2 percent (Rutter, 1968). This figure is far below the predicted 25 percent. In addition, there is no evidence to date that consanguinity occurs more often among parents of autistic children. These reasons present a strong case for excluding recessive inheritance as the genetic factor in autism.

COMPLEX GENETIC MODELS

The evidence cited is sufficient to safely reject the proposed single gene hypotheses and the possibility of chromosome involvement for autism. However, this information has not yet been applied to more complicated alternatives. The simplest extension is to consider the situation where the presence of several genes is required to produce the trait. Examples of this type of inheritance are well known in experimental animals, but few examples are known in man, one being the interaction between the ABO and secretor genes (Thompson and Thompson, 1973). An example of this would be an hypothesis which requires three genes to be present, all in the double dose recessive form, to produce the trait. Such a situation would predict 1.6 percent affected sibs, which is strikingly close to the reported 2 percent (Rutter, 1968). However, this expanded autosomal hypothesis would not explain the different rate of affected in the two sexes.

An additional hypothesis which remains to be explored is that of polygenic or multifactorial inheritance. The concept is that many genes affect the expression of the trait. The first attempt to apply this in human conditions was by Falconer (1965). Carter (1971) then extended this suggestion to many of the congenital malformations such as cleft lip and palate, club foot, and pyloric stenosis. This hypothesis has been further developed by Smith (1972) and Reich et al. (1972).

The expected situation under this hypothesis is the same as if a large number of individuals are measured for a trait. Then, we see an approximately normal or bell-shaped distribution of individuals. The trait measured could be height, weight, or a theoretical liability for a disease or condition like autism. If the situation is height or weight, all individuals can be measured and categorized. For the situation like autism, we actually see only two categories, affected and normal. The break point between these two is called the threshold on the liability scale. If the individual has enough contributions from genes *and* environment, his own liability value will fall above the threshold point, and that individual will be classified as affected. With this model, it is possible to account for the small recurrence risk in families and the slightly different rate in the two sexes. Carter (1973), in an excellent chapter describing this model, provides examples from data on the congenital malformations.

The complication resulting in delay in testing this hypothesis for autism is a statistical one described by Reich and his colleagues (1972). In order to test the goodness of fit to the data, it is necessary to impose at least two threshold points, i.e., to define at least three categories. Since a milder form of autism has not been described in the relatives of affected children, it will be necessary to collect family data on specific, measured variables where this type of analysis can be applied.

SUMMARY

Evidence from a supplementary type of study, comparisons of identical (monozygotic) and fraternal (dizygotic) twins, suggests a possible genetic mechanism for autism. The measured concordance rate, i.e., proportion of co-twins affected given the first affected twin, is probably higher in monozygotic twins, as expected if genes play a role in the etiology of the condition. The difficulty with interpreting these studies is discussed in some detail by Ornitz (1973) and Rutter (1967). Obtaining a definitive answer is dependent upon both an unquestionable diagnosis of both twins and an unquestionable resolution to their zygosity. If, however, the correct concordance rate is 80 percent among monozygotic twins and 20 percent among dizygotic twins, then the evidence favors genetic involvement.

Several complications arise in testing the genetic hypotheses. One complication is the lack of sufficient data. Where much of the current research relates directly to the affected individuals, genetic analyses require detailed information on all family members. This is particularly true in the case with multifactorial inheritance where data is required from many different types of relatives, e.g., parents, sibs, cousins, grandparents, etc.

The second complication is by far the most difficult. Throughout this discussion, the genetic hypotheses were tested against data on the presence versus absence of autism. Yet, it is well known that the specific set of symptoms which are included within the diagnosis "autistic" represent a complicated structure of many variables (Ornitz, 1973). Each affected child may present a different aggregation of these symptoms.

Therefore, it may be that a single genetic mechanism is not responsible for autism. It may be that several mechanisms are responsible for some or all of the cases. Or, it may be that only certain aspects, symptoms, of the condition are inherited. Since these possibilities exist, each symptom of the condition and cluster of the symptoms will have to undergo separate genetic analyses, testing the data against the existing genetic hypotheses.

The three situations in the families of autistic children of normal parents, low recurrence risk, and an altered sex ratio among affected are not evidence against genetic involvement in the etiology of the condition. The evidence from twin studies is weak but supportive of a role for genes. However, at this time no evidence exists which points to a specific genetic mechanism for autism.

REFERENCES

Biesele, J.J. and Schmid, W. (1962). Mentally retarded schizoid twin girls with 47 chromosomes. *Lancet* 3:403-05.

Böök, J.A., Nichtern, S, and Gruenberg, E. (1963). Cytogenetical investigation in childhood schizophrenia. *Acta Psychiatrica Scandinavia* 39:309-23.

Carter, C.O. (1971). Genetics of common malformations. In D. Gairdner and D. Hull, eds., *Recent Advances in Paediatrics* London: Churchill.

—— (1973). Multifactorial genetic disease. In V. McKusick and R. Claiborne, eds., *Medical Genetics* New York: H.P. Publishing Co., Inc.

Crandall, B.F. and Sparkes, R.S. (0000). Personal communication.

Falconer, D.S. (1965). The inheritance of liability to certain diseases, estimated from the incidence among relatives. *Annals of Human Genetics* 29:51-76.

Hamerton, J.L. (1971). *Human Cytogenetics* Volume II, New York: Academic Press.

Judd, L.J. and Mandell, A.J. (1968). Chromosome studies in early infantile autism. *Archives of General Psychiatry* 18:450-57.

Kanner, L. (1954). To what extent is early infantile autism determined by constitutional inadequacies. *Proceedings of the Association for Research on Nervous and Mental Diseases* 33:378-85.

Lotter, V. (1966). Epidemiology of autistic conditions in young children. *Social Psychiatry* I:124-37.

Lowe, L.H. (1966). Families of children with early childhood schizophrenia. *Archives of General Psychiatry* 14:26-30.

Lubs, H.A. and Ruddle, F.H. (1970). Applications of quantitative karyotypy to chromosome variation in 4400 consecutive newborns. In P.A. Jacobs, W.H. Price and P. Law, eds., *Human Population Cytogenetics* Baltimore: The Williams and Wilkins Company.

McKusick, V. (1971). *Mendelian Inheritance in Man* Baltimore: Johns Hopkins Press.

O'Brien, J.S., Okada, S., Chen, A., and Fillerup, D. (1970). Tay-Sachs disease: detection of heterzygotes and homozygotes by serum hexosaminidase assay. *The New England Journal of Medicine* 283:15-20.

Ornitz, E.M. (1973). Childhood autism: a review of the clinical and experimental literature. *California Medicine* 118:21-47.

Reich, T., James, J.W., and Morris, C.A. (1972). The use of multiple thresholds in determining the mode of transmission of semi-continuous traits. *Annals of Human Genetics* 35:163-84.

Rutter, M. (1967). Psychotic disorders in early childhood. In A.J. Copper and A. Walk, eds., *Recent Developments in Schizophrenia—A Symposium* London: RMPA.

—— (1968). Concepts of autism: a review of research. *Journal of Child Psychology and Psychiatry* 9:1-25.

—— and Bartak, L. (1971). Causes of infantile autism: some considerations from recent research. *Journal of Autism and Childhood Schizophrenia* I, 1:20-23.

Seabright, M. (1972). Human chromosome banding. *Lancet* 1:967.

Smith, C. (1972). Correlation in liability among relatives and concordance in twins. *Human Heredity* 22:85-91.

Spence, M.A., Simmons, J.Q., Brown, N.A., and Wikler, L. (1973). Sex ratios in families of autistic children. *American Journal of Mental Deficiency* 77:405-407.

Spence, M.A., Simmons, J.Q., Wikler, L., and Brown, N.A. (1974). Dermatoglyphics of childhood psychosis: a family study. *Human Heredity* 24:82-87.

Thompson, J.S. and Thompson, M.W. (1973). *Genetics in Medicine* Philadelphia: W.B. Saunder, Co.

CHAPTER TWELVE

Biological Disorders in Infants at Risk for Schizophrenia

BARBARA FISH

Evidence from many sources (Ornitz and Ritvo, 1968; Fish, 1975) suggests that children only develop schizophrenia and early infantile autism if they have an underlying biological disorder which predisposes them to these illnesses. It would advance our research in this area if we could study these disorders in infants before they show the gross manifestations of psychosis. In this way, we would begin to understand the mechanisms by which the biological disorders evolve into specific symptoms. This could enable us to begin treatment at a much earlier stage of the illness and possibly prevent some of the later handicaps.

In this chapter, I shall discuss evidence from my research on neurological abnormalities in infants who are at risk for schizophrenia. I use the term "childhood schizophrenia" to refer to children with infantile autism and those with milder forms of the disease whom others call schizophrenic. The childhood schizophrenics who have an onset of withdrawal before two years of age show a clinical picture similar to infantile autism. They constitute the most severe subgroup of childhood schizophrenics (Fish, 1975). Genetic studies of these children show that their families have the same incidence of the adult form of the disease as is found in families of adult schizophrenics. The childhood form is the most severe and closest to the chronic adult form (Goldfarb, 1968; Kallman, 1956). Follow-up studies show that, as adults, almost all of these childhood schizophrenics clinically resemble chronic adult schizophrenics (Annell, 1963; Bender and Faretra, 1972). I do not believe that all children with infantile autism are childhood schizophrenics. Some of them diagnosed as autistic have an illness secondary to a more specific organic brain syndrome. It is unlikely that we will be able to separate out reliably these different forms of autism until we can identify the underlying specific organic brain syndromes in the same manner as we now can with PKU. The outcome of these children depends on the nature of their underlying organic brain disease. Their defects may be stable or may show deterioration. My research does not apply to these children, but only to those autistic children who are part of the larger schizophrenic group.

I was able, in two studies conducted since 1952, to identify pre-schizophrenic infants as early as one month of age. The children and controls were independently evaluated by psychiatrists and psychologists who were unaware of the infancy data. They saw the children at ten years of age and again at eighteen years. I will summarize the evidence which identified the presence of a biological disorder in these children and then discuss possible leads for treatment.

TWO PROSPECTIVE STUDIES

Two infant studies were begun, one in 1952 and a second in 1959. The subjects, methods, predictions, and detailed findings have been reported for the first group (Fish et al., 1957, 1959, 1965, 1966) and for the second group (Fish et al., 1962, 1963, 1973). In summary, the infants born in 1952 to 1953 and in 1959 to 1960 comprise a group of twenty-four of whom over half are now twenty-two years old. The 1952 to 1953 group was randomly selected from a well-baby clinic which served a lower class neighborhood, high in social and psychiatric pathology. There was also a high incidence of pregnancy and birth complications in this group. Mothers of the 1959 to 1960 infants were chronically hospitalized schizophrenic patients. Most of these children were reared in carefully selected permanent adoptive or foster homes.

The assessment of infant development was based on standard infant tests and measurements repeated at key ages ten times between birth and two years of age. Height, weight, head circumference, and overall body growth were plotted on the Wetzel grid (1946). This enables one to quantify changes in an infant's growth curve compared to his earlier pattern. Separate developmental quotients (DQs) were also obtained for gross motor, visual motor and language development using the Gesell examination (1947). The analysis of serial DQs in different areas is comparable to following serial changes in IQs in older individuals.

In the 1959 to 1960 study, methods were developed for measuring the infant's behavioral state of arousal, that is, quantifying how irritable or how apathetic each infant was (Fish et al., 1962, 1963). In addition, each infant's response to vestibular tests was measured. The vestibular apparatus normally registers body movements in space and adjusts the compensating movements which maintain erect posture and equilibrium. Vestibular responses have been shown to be decreased in autistic and schizophrenic children, and it has been suggested that this may be responsible for some of the abnormalities in movement which these children show (Pollack and Krieger, 1958; Colbert et al., 1959; Ritvo et al., 1969).

Independent psychological and psychiatric assessments were made when the children were ten and eighteen years of age. They were given intelligence tests, educational assessments, projective tests, a standard psychiatric diagnosis, and global severity ratings, and ranked in order of severity. Two were diagnosed as schizophrenic at follow-up. Brief clinical summaries of these two schizophrenic children have been published previously (Fish, 1957, 1966, 1973). Peter, born in 1952, has made a marginal social adjustment. He has never been hospitalized. Linda, born in 1959, was hospitalized from ages seven to ten and then transferred to a residential treatment center where she remains today at age fifteen. The disorder of these children was never severe enough to warrant the diagnosis of infantile autism. The four children diagnosed as having "severe personality disorders" have disorders of thinking, identification, and personality organization which resemble schizophrenia. However, they did not show gross psychotic disruptions.

PANDEVELOPMENTAL RETARDATION: EVIDENCE FOR A NEUROBIOLOGICAL DISORDER

In the two childhood schizophrenics, analysis of their developmental curves indicates an early biological disorder. In both infants there was a major disorganization of neurologic maturation. It involved gross motor, visual-motor, and physical development as early as the first month of life. There was no fixed neurologic defect. Rather, disorders of timing, integration, and organization of neurologic maturation were observed.

The pattern of this disorganization is not seen in the usual forms of retardation. First, there was an unusual fluctuation in the rate of development, with marked acceleration and marked retardation succeeding one another. Peter's gross motor development dropped to 45 percent of normal at nine months of age. Then, without any change in his external circumstances, it suddenly accelerated and he achieved five months' development in the next two months, so that he reached normal levels at thirteen months.

Other features also distinguished this from usual patterns seen in chronic brain syndromes. First, they sometimes showed a temporary loss of a previously acquired ability. Second, unlike normal babies who show development of head control before control of bodies or legs, these two children sometimes showed a complete reversal of this pattern. Third, in visual-motor development, they often passed more difficult items on the same examination on which they failed easier items. This is the reverse of the pattern one sees in chronic brain disorders. However, this erratic functioning is exactly what one sees in older schizophrenic patients who fail easy items on an intelligence test and then succeed on more advanced items during the same testing session.

The most severe form of the retardation involved physical growth as well as gross-motor and visual-motor development. The severity of "pandevelopmental retardation" was related to the severity of psychiatric disorders seen at ten years of age. It was most severe in the two preschizophrenic infants and most extreme in Peter. His onset of symptoms was earlier and his later intellectual and perceptual disturbances were more severe than Linda's. Children in whom pandevelopmental retardation was milder and shorter were ranked just below the two schizophrenic children in the severity of psychiatric disturbance at ten years of age. Children who had no retardation of physical growth had still milder disorders at ten years.

None of the children with pandevelopmental retardation had histories of pregnancy or birth complications. Those control infants who had pregnancy or birth complications showed brief lags in early development. These completely subsided and were totally different in pattern from the erratic development in the disturbed children. The incidence of pandevelopmental retardation was significantly related to a genetic history for schizophrenia (Fish, 1975).

It is this peculiar pattern of disorganization of early neurologic development which appears to reflect a biological vulnerability to schizophrenia. Whether a vulnerable child became psychotic or developed a less severe personality disorder depended upon the severity of his early neurologic deviations interacting with his particular environment. A genetically determined biological vulnerability is just that. It can be exaggerated by a destructive and/or impoverished environment and can be compensated for by a constructive environment. Only when the initial neurobiological disorder is of devastating proportions is it the overriding determinant of outcome.

Several large-scale controlled studies have demonstrated early motor symptoms or neurologic disorders in the histories of children with severe personality disturbances who later developed adult schizophrenia (O'Neal and Robins, 1958; Robins, 1966; Watt, 1974; Ricks and Berry, 1970). Furthermore, in two large-scale studies of children at risk for schizophrenia, Mednick (1971) found motor retardation at one year of age and Marcus

(1974) found soft neurologic signs at seven to ten years of age occurring significantly more often than in the controls.

In order to understand the nature of the early neurologic disorder, one must do prospective studies and follow development in much more detail. Our observations indicate that there is a *disorder of the overall regulation and patterning of the orderly progress of maturation.* There were not simply disorders of isolated traits or responses. Furthermore, the disorder affects many systems under control of the central nervous system including physical growth, gross motor, visual-motor, vestibular functioning, and possibly arousal. The biological dysfunction in vulnerable infants is a disorder of the total organism. In the infant studies, the more severe developmental deviations preceded the more severe psychiatric disorder. Similarly, studies of adult schizophrenics have shown that the most severely disabled patients had the highest frequency of early motor disorders and the earliest onset of severe cognitive impairment. The childhood schizophrenics whom we call autistic, have an onset before two years and are at the furthest extreme of severity. Overt signs of the neurologic dysfunction change with maturation. In the first two years of life pandevelopmental retardation occurs, with gross motor retardation and delays and disorders in the development of reaching and manipulation of objects. These are succeeded by disorders of visual-motor and perceptual function and soft neurological signs up to about ten years of age. The delays and distortions of early speech development in the second year are succeeded by more specifically schizophrenic thought disorders. There appears to be a continuity between the early disorganization of neurological development and the later integrative deficits. As these children grow older, erratic functioning occurs in higher cognitive skills. For instance, they show isolated problem solving, as in puzzles or in rote vocabulary and memory for associations, but none of these abilities becomes integrated into useful goal-directed activity. They remain non-adaptive, haphazard or stereotyped fragments of behavior. In the same way, many of these children begin to say words by one to one-and-a-half years and may speak in phrases or sentences by two to two-and-a-half years. However, from the start, their comprehension is poor and their speech is echolalic and fragmented and is rarely if ever used for communication.

Assessment of pandevelopmental retardation could be used as a kind of marker in designing studies of underlying biological disorders in schizophrenia. Pandevelopmental retardation would identify those infants most vulnerable to later development of schizophrenia or to severe personality disorders. The periods of most severe panretardation most likely reflect increased activity of the schizophrenic process. These measurable fluctuations in development could therefore underscore the significance of any concurrent neurophysiologic or biochemical changes. In the same way, as we develop methods for early treatment of these vulnerable children, we could use the fluctuations in development to indicate which children are in need of help.

ABNORMALLY "QUIET" STATE

In addition to pandevelopmental retardation, several other patterns give evidence of an underlying biological disorder. The first is an "abnormally quiet" state found in infants of schizophrenic mothers. In the first month, when normal waking infants cry and thrash vigorously, these infants were abnormally inactive and showed little or no crying even with vigorous muscular stimulation. They also had flaccid muscle tone, appearing soft to the touch and very floppy when moved. This abnormal state was accompanied by decreased vestibular responses. This suggested that there may have been some type of associated central nervous system depression. However, these infants showed normal or precocious visual responses and attention. This was not, therefore, a general sleepiness, but some form of apathy or lethargy limited to certain systems. Three out of the four abnormally quiet infants went on to develop severe psychopathology after ten years. However, only one of the two later schizophrenics had been abnormally quiet.

The abnormally quiet and lethargic state is reminiscent of apathetic behavior seen in very young schizophrenic and autistic children. Some of these were initially alert and active but became inactive, toneless, and apathetic at eight to thirty months, when their development regressed. They became withdrawn and showed decreased and psychotic speech (Fish, 1960, 1971). In young psychotic children, this early lack of energy (drive), attention, and affective responsiveness often confuses and distresses mothers. It disrupts early social-affective interaction. In some families, the overly quiet infants are left alone, except for the rare times when they cry. This only increases apathy and social isolation. Such apathy can affect aspects of learned behavior, in particular those behaviors which depend upon reinforcement by the infant's pleasure and that provided by the mother's responses and approval. Normal infants and children show great delight with newly acquired achievements and repeat them ad infinitum. Both the pleasure and the repetition play an important part in the learning process. However, young schizophrenic children frequently show less drive, attention, interest, and perseverence. They often ignore or appear apathetic following their success in problem-solving, and they do not practice and exploit their abilities as normal infants do. Their performance may even deteriorate rather than improve with repetition. Words may be acquired briefly and then not be heard for months or years.

Slow and delayed responsiveness in many psychotic children appears to add to their confusion. While they apparently are still dreamily responding to an earlier word or phrase, those around them chatter on at a normal conversational speed and events continue to move on at a normal pace. The original word the child is "learning" becomes misidentified with subsequent and unrelated words and events. I believe that disturbed arousal and responsiveness keeps the schizophrenic child's experience of events out of phase with the normal experience of time and reality. This adds to his confusion regarding causality. In treatment, some of these children are able to learn correct associations if one simplifies and slows down presentation of words and stimuli to match the pace of their apparent comprehension. Hopefully, in the future, neurophysiological studies will give us more direct leads regarding specific treatments for this apathetic, "dreamy state" in pre-schizophrenic and psychotic children.

VISUAL-MOTOR DISORDERS

Tests of visual-motor performance revealed severe disturbances by two years of age. There was a delay in visual attention to objects held in hand at three and four months of age, relative to attention to objects in the environment. This might be an early defect in self-awareness. Toward the end of the first year, a number of these infants showed increased gazing at their own hands at an age when normal infants have already dropped this behavior. However, this did not become a stereotyped pattern as is seen in autistic-schizophrenic children.

Several children showed severe delays in reaching and manipulation in the first year, with difficulty in imitating movements by others from the end of the first year. Gross irregularity or "scatter" in visual-motor tasks during infancy occurred only in children with severe to moderate psychiatric disorders at ten years (Fish and Hagin, 1973). Only one item, failure of bimanual integrated activity, was similarly correlated with the presence of later psychiatric disorder. The integrated functioning of one hand with the other at the midline normally begins with mutual fingering of one hand by the other at four months. This is followed by the transfer of objects from one hand to the other at six months and, finally, at nine months, by the simultaneous grasp of an object in each hand and approximating them. Failure in these specific bimanual skills occurred in all eight of the children rated as having severe to moderate psychiatric disorder at ten years, but not in the two children rated as having mild to no impairment in the high risk group (Fish and Hagin, 1973). Again, there was a significant relationship at four months and six months between decreased bimanual integration and reduced vestibular response (Fish, 1975). The pre-schizophrenic infant, Linda, had the most severe retardation in these items. Although manual dexterity developed normally, her hands did not engage in the midline like those of a normal four-month infant when she was six months. She did not transfer objects from hand to hand as a normal six-month-old, even when she was thirteen months. Instead of reaching for objects at six months, she waved her arms laterally in a movement reminiscent of the normal four-month pattern and of the peculiar flapping seen in autistic-schizophrenic children. At thirteen months, she did not grasp or manipulate objects normally, but was hesitant and preoccupied with gingerly patting and poking at their surfaces. This bizarre touching without grasping also resembles what is often seen in severely retarded autistic-schizophrenic children. Her visual-motor performance became less severely retarded at eighteen months, and by two years she performed normally with visual-motor materials.

In the schizophrenic girl, Linda, and in three others, pandevelopmental retardation appeared between six and nine months and involved failures in bimanual integration. These four children went on to show subsequent defects in visual-spatial performance, failing the Gesell form-board in the second year, and the block design subtest of the Weschler Intelligence Scale for Children at ten years (Fish, 1975). Pandevelopmental retardation in this critical period of six to nine months had serious perceptual sequelae in these four children. At six months, decreased vestibular responses occurred only in these four children and tended to show a relationship to later failures in visual-spatial performance.

The vestibular apparatus normally anchors awareness of the body's direction relative to gravity and thereby orients the three dimensions of body space: up-down, right-left, and front-back (Gibson, 1966). It also orients the perception of vertical and horizontal in external space which are bound to the awareness of one's own body position. It may not, therefore, be entirely coincidental that disruption of vestibular responsiveness was associated with the disturbances in visual-spatial performance. The nature of this possible relationship is highly speculative. However, there are studies of adult schizophrenics which suggest that unstable spatial perception may accompany the acute onset of schizophrenic activity (Chapman, 1966).

The nature of early visual-motor disorders in vulnerable children suggests that they might be amenable to early treatment and remediation. We are currently studying functions of early manipulation and reaching in more detail, in the hope that this may eventually lead to methods of early therapeutic intervention.

REFERENCES

Annell, A. (1963). The prognosis of psychotic syndromes in children. A followup of 115 cases. *Acta Psychiatrica Scandinavica* 39:235-297.

Bender L. and Faretra G. (1972). The relationship between childhood schizophrenia and adult schizophrenia. In Kaplan, A.R., ed., *Genetic Factors in Schizophrenia* Springfield: Charles C. Thomas.

Chapman, J. (1966). The early symptoms of schizophrenia. *British Journal of Psychiatry* 112:225-251.

Colbert, E.G., Koegler, R.R., and Markham, C.H. (1959). Vestibular dysfunction in childhood schizophrenia. *Archives of General Psychiatry* 1:600-617.

Fish, B. (1957). The detection of schizophrenia in infancy. *Journal of Nervous and Mental Disease* 125:1-24.

——— (1959). Longitudinal observations of biological deviations in a schizophrenic infant. *American Journal of Psychiatry* 116:25-31.

——— (1960). Involvement of the central nervous system in infants with schizophrenia. *Archives of Neurology* 2:115-21.

——— (1963). The maturation of arousal and attention in the first months of life: a study of variations in ego development. *Journal of the American Academy of Child Psychiatry* 2:253-70.

——— (1971). Contributions of developmental research to a theory of schizophrenia. In Hellmuth, J., ed., *Exceptional Infant. Volume 2, Studies in Abnormalities* New York: Brunner and Mazel pp. 473-82.

——— (1975). Biologic antecedents of psychosis in children. In Freedman, D.X. ed., *The Biology of the Major Psychoses: A Comparative Analysis*. Association for Research in Nervous and Mental Disease, Publication No. 54, New York: Raven Press pp. 49-80.

——— and Alpert, M. (1962). Abnormal states of consciousness and muscle tone in infants born to schizophrenic mothers. *American Journal of Psychiatry* 119:439-45.

——— and Alpert, M. (1963). Patterns of neurological development in infants born to schizophrenic mothers. In Wortis, J., ed., *Recent Advances in Biological Psychiatry* Volume 5, New York: Plenum Press pp. 37-42.

——— and Hagin, R. (1973). Visual-motor disorders in infants at risk for schizophrenia. *Archives of General Psychiatry* 28:900-904.

———, Shapiro, T., Halpern, F., and Wile, R. (1965). The prediction of schizophrenia in infancy: III. A ten-year follow-up report of neurological and psychological development. *American Journal of Psychiatry* 121:768-75.

———, Shapiro, T., Halpern, F., and Wile, R. (1966). The prediction of schizophrenia in infancy: II. A ten-year follow-up of predictions made at one month of age. In Hoch, P. and Zubin, J., ed., *Psychopathology of Schizophrenia* New York: Grune and Stratton. pp. 335-53.

Gesell, A. and Amatruda, C.S. (1947). *Developmental Diagnosis: Normal and Abnormal Child Development, Clinical Methods and Pediatric Applications*, 2d. ed., New York: Paul B. Hoeber.

Gibson, J.J. (1966). *The Senses Considered as Perceptual Systems*. Boston: Houghton-Mifflin.

Goldfarb, W. (1968). The subclassification of psychotic children: application to a study of longitudinal change. In Rosenthal, D. and Kety, S.S. ed., *The Transmission of Schizophrenia*. London: Pergamon Press pp. 333-42.

Kallman, F. and Roth, B. (1956). Genetic aspects of preadolescent schizophrenia. *American Journal of Psychiatry* 112:599-606.

Marcus, J. (1974). Cerebral functioning in offspring of schizophrenics. A possible genetic factor. *International Journal of Mental Health* 3:57-73.

Mednick, S.A., Mura, M., Schulzinger, F., and Mednick, B. (1971). Perinatal conditions and infant development in children with schizophrenic parents. *Social Biology* 18:S103-13.

O'Neal, P. and Robins, L.N. (1958). Childhood patterns predictive of adult schizophrenia: a 30-year follow-up study. *American Journal of Psychiatry* 115:385-91.

Ornitz, E.M., and Ritvo, E.R. (1968). Perceptual inconstancy in early infantile autism. *Archives of General Psychiatry* 18:76-98.

Pollack, M. and Krieger, H.P. (1958). Oculomotor and postural patterns in schizophrenic children. *Archives of Neurology and Psychiatry* 79:720-26.

Ricks, D.F. and Berry, J.C. (1970). Family and symptom patterns that precede schizophrenia. In Roff, M. and Ricks, D.F. eds., *Life History Research in Psychopathology* Volume I, Minneapolis: Minnesota Press, pp. 31-50.

Ritvo, E.R., Ornitz, E.M., Eviatar, A., Markham, C., Brown, M., and Mason, A. (1969). Decreased postrotatory nystagmus in early infantile autism. *Neurology* 19:653-58.

Robins, L.N. (1966). *Deviant Children Grown Up.* Baltimore: Williams and Wilkins.

Watt, N.F. (1974). Childhood and adolescent routes to schizophrenia. In Ricks, D.F., Thomas, A., and Roff, M. eds., *Life History Research in Psychopathology* Volume III, Minneapolis: University of Minnesota Press, pp. 194-211.

Wetzel, N.C. (1946). The baby grid. *Journal of Pediatrics* 29:439-54.

CHAPTER THIRTEEN

Experimental Studies of
Autistic Children in the Classroom
FRED FRANKEL

Close inspection of the behavioral repertoires of autistic children reveals that they lack many specific skills which normal children acquire before they are of age to be enrolled in elementary classes. For this reason, educational therapy may be of much value to preschool autistic children. But what sort of educational therapy? Much research has shown that individual autistic children are quite different from one another in the skills they possess and the maladaptive behaviors they display. Based upon these observations, it has been proposed that educational interventions should be of a prescriptive or prosthetic nature (Gilhool, 1974; Lindsley, 1964). The underlying philosophy is that each child has certain specific handicaps, cognitive and/or behavioral in nature, which must first be determined. The obligation of education is to provide an environment within which each child can function to his maximum potential despite his handicaps. The goal is to eliminate the need for special environments for those children who improve sufficiently.

From the very outset the education of the autistic child must therefore be concerned with assessment. Initially, the goal of assessment should be prescriptive: it should suggest practical means of arranging the educational environment to take the maximum advantage of skills and behaviors which individual autistic children possess and it should suggest specific curricula designed to train skills which the individual autistic child does not have.

This chapter will be concerned with current research into initial behavioral assessment of autistic children and subsequent evaluation of gains which they make. This research has been concerned with (1)

185

delineations of the optimal educational environment for each autistic child, (2) observation of the child's behavioral repertoire to determine the prevalence of behavior patterns compatible or incompatible with good academic performance, and (3) long-term assessment of the outcome of educational intervention.

INITIAL ASSESSMENT

Assessment of the optimal educational environment provides information relevant to the delivery of the curriculum, the best type of reinforcement for each child, and the effects of the presence of other children in the same teaching situation. The teacher of the autistic child often has two environmental options available which may have marked effects on the academic performance of autistic children: teacher-to-child ratio and type of reinforcer. Many researchers have made the generalization that a 1:1 teacher-to-child ratio will produce optimal rates of learning in autistic children (e.g., Coffey and Weiner, 1967; Hewett and Blake, 1973). On the other hand, Blatt and Garfunkel (1973) have taken the position that children are generally not influenced by this parameter.

The use of contingent food reinforcement in addition to praise is reported by many to enhance the performance of autistic children over the use of praise alone (Koegel and Rincover, 1974; Hudson and DeMyer, 1968). Conversely, it has been reported that at least some autistic children can be effectively reinforced with praise alone (Freitag, 1970). MacMillan and Forness (1973) have stressed the shortcomings of reinforcement "overkill" or the error of providing children with too primitive a reinforcer, when they can function well or perhaps better with a more natural reinforcer.

Despite the above misgivings in the literature, many special educators strive for the 1:1 teacher-to-child ratio and the addition of food reinforcement in trying to promote the optimal degree of learning for autistic children. Intuitively, it seems quite reasonable that two types of reinforcers (food and praise) should be better than praise alone and that a child will work better under the teacher's undivided attention as opposed to when the attention is shared with others. Casual observations often reveal that a child seems more "motivated" when contingent food reward is introduced into the situation. On the other hand, at least for some children, food reward seems to be more of a distractor than an aid to better performance. For instance, a child may enjoy solving puzzles simply for mastery of the task (MacMillan and Forness, 1973), and may be quite proficient and attentive if left to himself. If that same child is working for food reward, his behavior may deteriorate since he is no longer working for task mastery but in order to get the task completed as soon as possible in order to obtain the food. In fact, an observation such as this was made in Harlow's laboratory about monkeys who were given raisins to solve puzzles which they were fond of manipulating. The result was a *marked deficit* in the previously flawless performance of these monkeys.

The number of other children with which a child must share teacher's attention may be expected to influence the performance of autistic children only to the extent that (a) the other children interfere with contingencies upon the child's maladaptive and adaptive behaviors or (b) to the extent that the child actually perceives the presence of the other children. It seems reasonable that a teacher can be more effective in administering contingencies to one child versus many (certainly one child versus seven or eight), but does the addition of one or two other children significantly impair this capacity? Clinical observation indicates that autistic children may not, in fact, recognize other children as such, reacting to them as they would to other inanimate objects (Hermelin and O'Connor, 1970).

Researchers advocating the 1:1 teacher-to-child ratio and the addition of food reward have not to date offered any direct evidence that either condition is preferable for all autistic children. An investigation of the effect of each of these conditions would appear long overdue. Why should 1:1's be utilized if they offer no distinct advantages over 1:3's? Certainly the latter is more economically feasible, and is used more widely (in fact, 1:6's are not uncommon). Thus, if direct comparison for individual children reveals no distinct advantages for the 1:1, it should be preferable to place the child with a number of other children.

Frankel and Graham (in press) attempted to answer these questions with systematic observations of three different types of child behaviors in 1:1 versus 1:3 situations and with praise—with or without the addition of food reinforcers.

Twelve children, six diagnosed as autistic by the criteria of Ornitz and Ritvo (1968), and six not meeting these criteria but mentally retarded, were observed individually and in groups for over one week. The children were all inpatients at the Neuropsychiatric Institute and had been there for at least two weeks prior to these observations. During this initial period teachers had adequate opportunity to (1) establish some minimal rapport with each child; (2) place each child within a range of mental ages (referred to as "level of functioning"); and (3) ascertain from ward staff each child's preferred food reward.

Table I shows the types of behaviors which were assessed within each of several behavioral categories. *Adaptive behavior* was measured as either the proportion of teacher demands which the child attempted to answer (response) or the proportion of his or her responses which were correct.

Table I.
Definitions of Behaviors Observed (Frankel and Graham, in press)

(A) Teacher Behavior

1. Demand – Each time the teacher instructed the subject as to the goal of the task.

2. Prompt – Simplification of a demand, eliminating at least one requirement to be met by the subject.

(B) Adaptive Performance*

1. Response – Number of times the subject initiated touching responses with materials involved in the task.

2. Correct – Number of correct responses made without the assistance of prompts. A demand could be repeated more than once if no response occurred and a correct could be scored as long as prompt was not employed.

(C) Attention

1. Re-directs – Number of times subject either looked away from task material or was out of seat and therefore directed to the task by the teacher.

2. Attending to Teacher – Duration of time spent looking at teacher's face or upper part of teacher's body.

3. Attending to Task – Duration of time spent looking at materials involved in task.

(D) Maladaptive Behaviors

1. Tantrum – The total duration and number of recurrences of crying, whining, screaming or agitation.

2. Aggression – The total number of acts of hitting, pinching or biting directed towards the teacher or peers.

3. Stereotyped behaviors – The total duration and number of repetitive behaviors involving either objects or parts of the body, which were not appropriate and without apparent goal.

*Number of responses and number of correct were converted into percentages by dividing the number of *demands* and number of *responses* respectively. This was done to account for the different rates of responding for different children, as number of demands per three-minute segment was not controlled. Maladaptive behaviors were ignored by the teacher, i.e., the teacher acted as if they did not occur.

Attention was measured as the number of times a teacher verbally or physically redirected the child to the task (redirect), as the proportion of time the child made eye contact with the teacher (attention to teacher), and as the number of times the child made eye contact with the materials constituting the task (attention to task). *Maladaptive behaviors* included the frequency and duration of tantrums, aggressive acts, and stereotyped behaviors.

During six days of formal assessment each child was seen for six twenty-minute daily sessions. These sessions were kept short so as to limit the effects of fatigue on child and teacher performance. During half of these sessions the child was observed in a 1:1 situation and during the other half in a 1:3 situation. The two other children in the 1:3 situation had been judged to be functioning approximately at the subjects' level and they had been enrolled in the school program for at least one month prior to the experimental sessions. Level 1 children were functioning at approximately eleven months of age, level 2 at twenty months and level 3 at forty-seven months. Only the level 3 subjects of both diagnostic categories possessed any speech.

During each daily session the children were presented with at least four different three-minute tasks which were part of the regular school curriculum. These tasks were similar to those included within the six areas of functioning assessed by the EPEC (see Chapter Fifteen). Each task was presented on four occasions. On two occasions only praise was used as a reinforcement for correct responses while on the other two occasions, both food and praise followed each correct response.

Percent correct and *percent response* data were analyzed separately for each child using an analysis of variance (Winer, 1962). Table II shows the results of this analysis. Entries in the Table indicate the percentage difference between the entries in the extreme left-hand column. Each entry represents data gathered from forty-two individual observations of each child. Thus, the entry in row 1, column 1 of 25.8 indicates that the 1:1 produced 25.8 percent higher *correct response* than the 1:3 situation for autistic subject #1. Furthermore, this difference was statistically significant ($p < .05$). Because it was preferable to conclude that there was a genuine difference when really there was none (an "*a*" error) rather than to conclude that there was no difference when there really was one (a "B" error), marginally significant findings ($p < .10$) are also reported.

It is evident from Table II that the situation variable affected the *percent response* observations of only two autistics and none of the retarded children. Furthermore, the 1:1 situation increased *percent response* only in one autistic (subject #1) but decreased *percent response* in autistic subject #5. The same divergent effects of situation were also evident in *percent correct*. Autistic and retarded subjects #1 showed 27 percent and 36.8 percent increase in *percent correct* but retarded subject #3 showed a decrease of 16.8 percent in the 1:1 situation. Thus, as expected, the effects of situation are specific to the child being observed.

Also evident in Table II is the general lack of differences produced by the addition of food reinforcement. The presence of food decreased the *percent response* of autistic subject #4 by 8.3 percent and increased the *percent correct* for retarded subject #2 by 23.5 percent. Finally, reinforcement interacted with task only in one subject but task and situation

Table II.
Individual comparisons of each autistic and retarded child. Marginally significant findings
($p < .10$) are also reported (Frankel and Graham, in press)

Percent Response

Comparison	Autistic						Retarded						df
	1	2	3	4	5	6	1	2	3	4	5	6	
1:1 – 1:3	25.8**	–.2	11.8	7.1	–5.8**	1.3	6.7	22.6	–16.4	–17.8	6.6	–3.7	1,1
Food – No Food	–4.2	–15.0	–11.5	–8.3*	2.5	4.0	–1.8	34.3	–9.8	3.7	–.1	3.7	1,1
Task	ns	$p < .10$	ns	$p < .10$	ns	ns	ns	$p < .05$	$p < .01$	ns	ns	ns	4,4
Situation x Reinforcer	ns	ns	$p < .10$	ns	ns	ns	ns	$p < .10$	ns	$p < .10$	ns	ns	1,1
Task x Reinforcer	ns	ns	ns	ns	ns	ns	ns	ns	ns	ns	ns	ns	4,4
Mean	39.9	41.7	68.0	46.4	83.5	94.7	90.1	66.8	57.1	73.8	94.5	98.1	

Percent Correct

Comparison	Autistic						Retarded						df
	1	2	3	4	5	6	1	2	3	4	5	6	
1:1 – 1:3	27.0**	–5.0	–22.8	–10.4	–5.8	.6	36.8*	26.8	–16.8*	–33.5	–6.5	–27.9	1,1
Food – No Food	–10.2	–5.5	–6.8	–2.5	–1.2	12.8	6.5	23.5**	4.2	–.4	11.5	–.3	1,1
Task	ns	$p < .05$	ns	$p < .10$	$p < .05$	$p < .10$	$p < .05$	$p < .10$	$p < .05$	$p < .05$	ns	ns	4,4
Situation x Reinforcer	ns	ns	ns	$p < .10$	ns	ns	ns	ns	ns	ns	ns	ns	1,1
Task x Reinforcer	ns	ns	ns	ns	ns	ns	ns	ns	ns	ns	ns	ns	4,4
Mean	27.5	28.3	27.3	28.1	55.4	63.5	64.5	56.5	38.7	33.3	56.6	77.9	

*$p < .10$
**$p < .05$

interacted in three subjects. Overall results indicated that the presence of food reinforcement *significantly* aided the performance of retarded subjects but had much less effect upon the autistics, except for an overall decrease in tantrums in the autistic group ($p < .05$) and a decrease in the use of redirects ($p < .05$).

In order to determine if any specific behaviors might be predictive of academic competence in autistic and retarded children, six of the ten behaviors observed were compared using partial correlation coefficients. Partial correlation coefficients differ from the commonly used Pearson and Spearman coefficients in that the effects upon correlations of extraneous variables are mathematically partialed out. Thus, the partial correlation between *teacher attention* and *percent response* in this analysis partials out the correlations between *percent response* and each of the other five variables. As a result of this, a lower correlation coefficient is required for statistical significance. Table III shows the results of this analysis. Correlations between each variable and *percent response* are shown in the left three columns. The first column shows overall partial correlations over both groups and the second and third columns show correlations for autistic and retarded children separately. The most important outcome of this analysis is that *attention to task*, rather than *attention to teacher* showed the highest overall correlation with both *percent correct* and *percent response*. These latter correlations were all in a positive direction. Thus, the more the child looked at the materials involved with the task, the more the child attempted to respond to the task and the more correct responses he made. In striking contrast to this, *attention to teacher* did not correlate significantly with *percent correct*, but correlated negatively and significantly with *percent response* in the retarded children. Thus, looking at the teacher's face did not have a significant impact upon autistic children. Retarded children tended to look at the teacher (perhaps for assistance) when they were unable to respond.

These results suggest that training *attention to task* may be a much better tactic than training *attention to teacher*, especially for retarded children. The high partial correlations between *percent correct* and *percent response* strongly suggest that both of these measures reflect the same phenomenon. If a child does not respond it is most likely because he doesn't know the correct answer rather than that he is simply being oppositional.

ASSESSMENT OF OUTCOME

Systematic observation techniques were next applied to assess changes produced by participation in the structured educational program at the Neuropsychiatric Institute. For this purpose, four autistic children and four

Table III.

Partial correlation coefficients between percent response, percent correct and each of five other dependent variables
(Frankel and Graham, in press)

Variable	Percent Response			Percent Correct		
	Overall	Autistic	Retarded	Overall	Autistic	Retarded
Teacher Attention	−.07	.07	−.26**	−.01	−.11	.06
Task Attention	.41**	.41**	.22**	.10*	.12	.09
Tantrum	.11*	.08	.08	.00	−.08	.06
Percent Response	—	—	—	.58**	.60**	.55**
Percent Correct	.58**	.60**	.55**	—	—	—
Redirect	−.06	.07	−.37**	.04	.05	.09
N	288	144	144	288	144	144

*p <.05
**p <.01

mentally retarded children, matched for levels of functioning and length of participation in the NPI Preschool program, were compared. The average length of stay for both groups of children was 6.56 months. Each group contained three children functioning at level 2 and one child functioning at level 5. The present comparison was limited to children who did not improve sufficiently to be tested on a higher level of functioning at the end of a six-month period. Thus, conclusions from this data are restricted to those children showing minimal gains.

Analysis of variance performed on each of the observed behaviors revealed that adaptive and attention behaviors increased while maladaptive behaviors decreased significantly from pre- to post-testing. *Percent response* increased from 70.6 percent to 84.3 percent and *percent correct* increased from 42.9 percent to 66.9 percent. *Attention to task* showed a marked increase from 58.0 to 70.0 seconds, *attention to teacher* showed a smaller increase from 3.4 to 6.9 seconds (all *ps* <.05), while *redirects* did not change significantly. Finally, *tantrums* decreased from 3.3 to 1.1 seconds (*p* .05), *aggression* decreased from .67 acts to .12 acts (*p* <.01), but *stereotyped behavior* did not change from its initially low rate of occurrence (1.6 acts and 4.1 seconds average duration per three-minute interval). One surprising result was that *attention to task* improved much more in the 1:1 situation than in the group situation so that differences were significant upon post-test which were not in pre-testing. Examination of individual protocols revealed that three autistic children and one retarded child increased *percent response* or *correct* upon post-testing beyond the $p < .05$ level of significance and two other retarded children increased their percentages beyond the $p < .10$ level.

SUMMARY

Direct and systematic observation of autistic and mentally retarded children generally supported our initial hypothesis that the effects of teacher-to-child ratio and the presence of food reinforcement were *highly individual*. In fact these two parameters did not have any overall effects on the adaptive performance of the autistic group, although food reinforcement decreased the number of tantrums and increased one measure of attention. These results are not intended to suggest the abandonment of food reinforcement and the 1:1 situation, but rather the assessment of their effects upon the adaptive and attentive behaviors of each child in a manner similar to that utilized here. High correlations between percent response and percent correct suggest that these two measures are strongly related; children are not inclined to respond to demands unless they already know the correct response. Thus, changes in either of these adaptive behaviors should be considered during evaluation.

The effects of food reinforcement upon such maladaptive behaviors as tantrums should not be of practical concern. It is far more effective to use specific programs to decrease tantrum behaviors (Williams, 1959), stereotyped behaviors (Azrin et al., 1973), and aggression (White et al., 1972), than to use food contingent upon correct responses.

Post-testing for eight children revealed that six months of participation in the NPI Preschool program was sufficient to increase attentive and adaptive behaviors and to decrease maladaptive behaviors. Furthermore, improvement in adaptive performance was evident in the individual analyses of six of the eight children. This suggests not only that the school program as a whole was effective for most children, but also offers an objective criterion of effectiveness for individual children. Such objectivity is essential in the eventual isolation of critical features of the program which lead to such success. It is also initially useful as a method of selecting the type of child with whom the program would be most effective. Additionally, assessment at regular six-month intervals after admission could be most informative with respect to the progress of individual children. Such assessment would reveal when children are ready to move on from food reinforcement to higher level reinforcers such as praise and task mastery, and from a 1:1 situation to that of a group.

REFERENCES

Azrin, N.H., Kaplan, S.J., and Foxx, R.M. (1973). Autism reversal: eliminating stereotyped self-stimulation of retarded individuals. *American Journal of Mental Deficiency*, 78: 241-48.

Blatt, B. and Garfunkel, F. (1973). Teaching the mentally retarded. In R.M. Travers ed., *Second Handbook of Research on Teaching*. Chicago: Rand McNally.

Coffey, H.S. and Weiner, L.L. (1967). *Group Treatment of Autistic Children*. Englewood Cliffs, New Jersey: Prentice-Hall.

Frankel, F. and Graham, V. (in press). Systematic observation of classroom behaviors of retarded and autistic preschool children. *American Journal of Mental Deficiency*.

Freitag, G. (1970). An experimental study of the social responsiveness of children with autistic behaviors. *Journal of Experimental Child Psychology* 9:436-53.

Gilhool, T.K. (1974). "Innovation." keynote address at the 98th annual meeting of the AAMD, Toronto.

Hermelin, B. and O'Connor, N. (1970). *Psychological Experiments with Autistic Children*. Oxford: Pergamon.

Hewett, F.M. and Blake, P.R. (1973). Teaching the emotionally disturbed. In R.M. Travers ed., *Second Handbook of Research on Teaching*. Chicago: Rand McNally.

Hudson, E. and DeMyer, M.K. (1968). Food as a reinforcer in educational therapy of autistic children. *Behavior Research and Therapy* 6:37-43.

Koegel, R.L. and Rincover, A. (1974). Treatment of psychotic children in a classroom environment: I. Learning in a large group. *Journal of Applied Behavior Analysis* 7:45-60.

Lindsley, O.R. (1964). Direct measurement and prosthesis of retarded behavior. *Journal of Education* 147:62-81.

MacMillan, D.L. and Forness, S.R. (1973). Behavior modification: Savior or savant? *American Journal of Mental Deficiency* Monograph Series No. 1, 197-210.

Ornitz, E.M. and Ritvo, E.R. (1968). Perceptual inconstancy in the syndrome of early infantile autism and its variants. *Archives of General Psychiatry* 18:76-98.

Williams, C.D. (1959). The elimination of tantrum behavior by extinction procedures. *Journal of Abnormal and Social Psychology* 59:269.

Winer, B.J. (1962). *Statistical Principles in Experimental Design*. New York: McGraw-Hill.

White, G.D., Nielsen, G., and Johnson, S.M. (1972). Time out duration and the suppression of deviant behavior in children. *Journal of Applied Behavior Analysis* 5:111-20.

PART IV

*Management of Autistic
Persons in Schools*

CHAPTER FOURTEEN

Educational Approaches at the NPI School:

The General Program
VICKI L. GRAHAM

THE GENERAL PROGRAM

Since 1961, the Neuropsychiatric Institute (NPI) Preschool, has operated as an integral part of the Children's Division of the UCLA Department of Psychiatry. The school staff are members of the interdisciplinary treatment team. In this role they are responsible for each child's educational program and its coordination with a variety of other specialists. Since traditional medical diagnosis rarely offers a clear-cut plan for educational and behavioral treatment (Hewett, 1974; Rutter et al. 1967), the Preschool staff relies upon assessment of social/emotional learning and cognitive needs of each patient. To do this, a type of "non-categorical grouping"—along the lines of the new master plan for special education in California—is employed. This concept, which disregards traditional labels and placement by age, has proven beneficial in two major ways. First, it requires that children be grouped by developmental needs rather than by artificial medical-based categories or educational labels. For example, at the NPI Preschool program, remediation of fine motor disabilities occurs in a heterogeneous group with respect to medical diagnosis. Thus, all the children in this group share only one factor—the need for fine motor training.

Second, placing children with different needs and learning styles in the same classroom requires a teacher to be highly flexible. One must be able to adapt materials to children with different learning disabilities. One must be sensitive to each child's level of competence and to the next steps in his development along a number of dimensions.

STUDENT POPULATION

The student population of the NPI Preschool is composed of residential and day-care patients with many different diagnoses. If a child's social and intellectual level of functioning is between six months and six years, he is placed in the Preschool. Although chronological age is not a limitation, the students generally range between two and eight years. Since many have been excluded from schools because of unacceptable behaviors, one of the first goals is to aid the pupil's adjustment to the classroom setting. Once this is accomplished, the staff can then provide an accurate assessment of his actual abilities and disabilities—factors which previously may have been marked by maladaptive behaviors.

The duration of a child's stay in the hospital is decided in a multi-disciplinary team meeting. In making this decision the following key questions are asked: (1) Is the child making demonstrable progress in the program? (2) Is the program providing services which cannot be duplicated within the community? If the answers are in the affirmative, the recommendation is that the child will remain, pending his next periodic re-evaluation.

STRUCTURE OF THE PROGRAM

Each child is assigned a "primary teacher" who is responsible for his initial evaluation, monthly progress assessments and a discharge evauation. The teacher is also responsible for designing, coordinating, and implementing programs. A permanent record of each child's status in school is kept. These reports are relayed to the interdisciplinary team and the school's community liaison person who initiates and arranges appropriate school placement prior to discharge. This process may involve a visit by the primary teacher to a prospective community school. When indicated, the primary teacher arranges to attend school with the child in order to facilitate the transition. She also assists the community teacher in planning for the child.

A typical school day consists of three one-hour sessions. Each session contains a one half-hour work period and a one half-hour play or music period. In less structured periods, teachers help the children learn to play appropriately. For example, if a child's skill is at the twelve-month level, the teacher provides materials, supervision, and social interaction appropriate for that age. For those at the two- to five-year level, programs to increase appropriate peer interaction and to teach more sophisticated use of toys is employed. These periods are monitored by adults using both directive and modeling techniques. These play and music periods are used to encourage transfer and generalization of skills learned in the structured work periods.

The NPI Preschool has been awarded a Federal Compensatory Education Title I grant. This provides funds to supplement the staff-to-student ratio. Teachers take children on outings to zoos, parks, and other extramural educational facilities to provide an opportunity for the generalization of behaviors and skills learned in the classroom.

CONTENT OF THE PROGRAM

The Preschool program content is based upon research of Hewett, (1964, 1965; Hewett et al., 1967), Lovaas and Simmons, (1966; Lovaas, 1966a, 1966b), Rabb and Hewett (1966), and Rabb and Busch (1968). Specifically, previous techniques primarily used an operant approach. Results indicated that while children increased specific skills, they did not "learn to learn." This is important if further expansion of skills and the development of incidental learning is to occur. A review of child development research (Gesell et al., 1940; Gesell and Amatruda, 1947; Bayley, 1969; Caldwell and Richmond, 1962; Caldwell, 1968; Doll, 1946) formed the basis for our redesigned program. Our new curriculum and evaluation schema are based principally on developmental hierarchies. Learning tasks follow normal development sequences in which children develop skills and abilities based upon previous learning. Thus, staff are able to concentrate on specific areas of disability without neglecting areas of strength or previous learning. At this time, the Preschool staff discontinued taking data on the correct responses made by a child during teaching sessions. This step was taken for three reasons. (1) Taking the data interfered with the teacher/child relationship because the teacher had to spend time during the sessions recording responses rather than interacting with the child. (2) Teaching became much too cumbersome when the teacher had to present materials as well as manipulate pen and paper. (3) The use of a pretest, periodic evaluations, and a post-test resulted in the same information as did constant data taking.

Concurrent with these changes, reliance upon operant conditioning has shifted and it is now only one aspect of management. At present, contingencies are established for each child, based on his capabilities, which he can understand and which he can control. Thus, a child learns that he can manipulate his environment in an adaptive fashion, that he is responsible for his behavior, and that he can control the consequences thereof.

We feel that the most desirable way of rewarding adaptive classroom behavior is by praising. However, some of our children need specific concrete reinforcers, (e.g., candy) in order to begin to learn acceptable behavior. Tangible reinforcers are viewed as temporary measures and as children advance they are eliminated in favor of social reinforcers such as praises and smiles.

The specific curricular tasks we emphasize are those which children must have if they are to be accepted and remain in community school programs. For example, we stress attending to tasks, peers and teachers, sitting quietly in a chair, raising hands for attention during lessons, taking turns, sharing, lining up for transitions from room to room, working independently and following directions. These behaviors are systematically positively reinforced in accordance with a program designed for each child. Behaviors which inhibit children from learning, which could result in their exclusion from school, are systematically decreased or eliminated. These include noncompliance, tantrums, aggression, self-destructive behavior and motility disturbances. Either extinction or suppression techniques are specifically designed for the child and his target behavior objectively defined. Suppression techniques include short periods of restriction to a chair in a corner of the room. In the event that a request for chair restriction is ineffective, the child may be held in the chair by the teacher. If that is not appropriate, then he may be restricted briefly in a time out room. Direct physical punishment is *never* used.

Motility disturbances or stereotypic behaviors warrant special mention. While a child is in school, either during a structured work period or play or music period, we attempt to suppress motility disturbances. This approach is utilized because we have determined that they have a deletereous effect on learning. Research has shown (Lovaas et al., 1971; Koegel and Covert, 1972) that children involved in such behaviors do not attend as well to learning tasks, that the latency between demands and responses are lengthened, and learning rates are depressed. To aid this goal, adaptive behaviors which directly interfere with the child's motility disturbances are taught and systematically reinforced. Such competing behaviors also can serve to increase a child's normal behavioral repertoire. In short, we try to increase those behaviors which will influence significant adults and peers to interact with these children and decrease those behaviors which have the opposite effect.

Preschool Assessment

REBECCA FLAHARTY

PRESCHOOL ASSESSMENT

Each patient on the Neuropsychiatric Institute Inpatient's Service attends the school program. Each receives three types of assessments; academic, behavioral, and language. In this section we shall present an overview of these areas of evaluation and discuss their usefullness for the program.

BEHAVIORAL EVALUATION

The behavioral evaluation begins shortly after admission to the school and takes four days to complete (Frankel, 1975). Two trained observers simultaneously record ten behaviors for twenty-minute periods each day. They observe the child via a one-way mirror and data is recorded on an Esterline-Angus Multiple-Pen Recorder. The behaviors that are chosen are those which are thought to be most relevant for establishing an appropriate learning situation and behavioral program for the child. (Frankel and Graham, 1975). During these observarions, learning situations and re-inforcement variables are systematically manipulated to determine what learning situation is best for the child. Thus, an attempt is made to determine whether a given child will benefit more from a one-to-one teaching situation or if he will do better when involved with other children in a group situation. Also, an attempt is made to determine whether a given child will more readily respond to social reinforcement alone or is the addition of a tangible reinforcement necessary to insure initial progress.

Groups of tasks, specifically chosen for each child, are also systematically varied during these intital observation periods. A child's rate of performance on each is determined to assess task-related effect. For example, does the child exhibit maladaptive behaviors more frequently during tasks which are basically manipulative in nature—such as puzzles or blocks—or during tasks which require a more cognitive or verbal response—such as body image, number, or color-tasks? Do tantrums, motility disturbances, self-destructive or other manipulative behaviors occur more frequently in certain situations or following some specific events? The answers to these questions, plus observations of idiosyncratic behaviors provide the basis for prescribing a learning environment and behavioral intervention program for each child. At periodic intervals during a child's hospitalization, behavioral reassessments are made by repeating the initial objective observation procedures. Indicated changes are then implemented.

An attempt is always made to move children quickly from a one-to-one situation to small group learning situations. These more closely approximate community classroom environments and thus are more desirable.

We are frequently asked about our use of food reinforcers. Our philosophy is to consider them as "last resort" measures to be used only on a short-term basis with children who do not respond to social reinforcers such as playtime, praise, hugs, and tickles.

ACADEMIC EVALUATION

An academic evaluation takes place during the first few days of each child's school assessment period. The Evaluation and Prescription for Exceptional Children (EPEC) (Flaharty, 1975) is administered to determine developmental level in fifteen skill areas. These include puzzles, blocks, numbers and colors, fine and gross motor skills, language, visual and auditory memory, play, socialization and cognitive skills. Tasks in each of these areas were taken from previously standardized developmental and intelligence tests—in particular the Stanford-Binet, Bayley, Merrill-Palmer, Gesell, and Cattell tests. Items are divided not only into the fifteen skill areas but also arranged along the developmental hierarchy from birth to seven years. Developmental levels and profile of abilities is obtained which shows areas of strengths and weaknesses. This pattern is used to determine the academic program for each child (Flaharty and Schofield, 1975).

In summary, the academic assessment allows the teacher to procure an individualized prescriptive program for each child. Deficient areas are defined and skills taught along a developmental continuum. Programs are also instituted to insure progress in other areas as well, thus avoiding disproportionately high levels of competence or "splinter skills."

LANGUAGE EVALUATION

A language evaluation takes place after the child has had the opportunity to adjust to the social demands and structure of the total preschool program, and has developed rapport with his primary teacher. This takes into account the fact that language production is highly dependent upon social variables. The language evaluation determines the type of remedial and linguistic program for the child.

SUMMARY

Each child in the NPI Preschool has an individualized curriculum designed specifically for him. It is based on results obtained from multiple assessments in three areas: behavioral, academic, and language. The behavioral evaluation defines the best learning situation for each child (one-to-one or small groups, tangible or social reinforcers, and specific task areas which are associated with maladaptive behaviors). Academic (or skill area) evaluation defines areas and patterns of strength, weaknesses, and the content for remedial programs. Finally, language evaluations define programs for correcting receptive and expressive deficits in specific patients.

The Language Program

ELLEN RICHEY

THE LANGUAGE PROGRAM

Language, as generally defined by psycholinguists, is a cognitive process involving conceptualization, symbolization, comprehension and production. This process leads to the creation of novel utterances which express concrete and abstract material within the framework of rules of vocabulary, grammar and syntax (Sapir, 1921; Osgood and Sebeok, 1967; DeVito, 1970).

Language can be expressed through various modes such as speech, writing, and sign language. This conceptualization of language (which places it beyond a simply-defined behavioral phenomenon) underlies our thinking and formed the basis for the development of our language therapy program. Previous investigators have attempted to design therapy programs to establish verbal skills in autistic children, as described by Garcia and DeHaven (1974). Initially, we utilized programs using reading (Rabb and Busch, 1968), the Premack symbol language (Premack and Premack, 1972), traditional operant therapy techniques (Lovaas, 1966; Sailor et al., 1973; Stark et al., 1973), and American Sign Language (Stokoe et al., 1965). Each of these approaches had only limited success. The Premack symbol language utilized combinations of arbitrarily defined symbols arranged on a magnetic board. The American sign language, developed primarily for the deaf, utilized gestures of the arms and hands. However, neither of these systems employed vocalization. Furthermore, they were not understandable by untrained individuals and thus were not useful for everyday communication. Also, their use called attention to the child.

Operant-based therapy programs were primarily unsatisfactory since they did not teach the children how to produce novel responses, either in form or content. We found that a child could be easily trained to respond in a complete grammatical sentence to a specific verbal prompt. However, this response would not generalize to other situations nor to untrained specific stimuli. When trained to answer a specific stimulus question such as, "What is this?" and being shown a cookie, they would be rewarded for saying, "This is a cookie." However, when given a different stimulus question as, "What is in the box?" they would not be able to use the appropriate verbal response and a new response would have to be taught independently. Furthermore, operant programs did not develop language to the point where the children could learn semantic differences. This difficulty has also been reported by Breger and McGaugh (1965).

We also assessed developmentally based programs such as the *Manual for Assessment of Children's Language Comprehension* (Foster et al., 1972) and *Emerging Language* (Hatten et al., 1973). We found they had two major drawbacks. First, they did not extend below the two- to three-year level of language development. Normal children of this age have a wide vocabulary and have begun to combine words into two- and three-word phrases. In contrast, our primary concern was with children who did not use words and thus, mistakenly might have been thought to have no linguistic skills. Also, the increments between levels of development in these programs were large, often encompassing periods of a year of more and did not include tasks necessary to establish all skills known to exist at each level of language acquisition. For example, a program might include the combination of words into a two-word phrase known to occur at the twenty-one-month level

(Bayley, 1969), but might not include the ability to use "yes" appropriately, a skill which also occurs at this age (Lewis, 1963).

Previous authors of operantly-based programs (Rutter and Sussenwein, 1971; Gray and Ryan, 1973) have attempted to utilize developmental sequencing. These also have two major limitations. First, sequences of trained material were not sufficiently detailed. Second, when non-verbal children were encouraged to produce sounds to receive food reinforcers, natural language did not evolve. Instead, ungeneralized, stilted speech patterns were produced. We believe this unfortunate result occurred because a major basic ingredient of normal language development was not present. This ingredient is a social relationship with an adult, usually the mother, who does not provide *only* contingent tangible rewards (Menyuk, 1971).

NPI SCHOOL LANGUAGE PROGRAM

In view of the lack of success with previously designed programs we were motivated to develop our own. We began by assembling a detailed evaluation scale from the developmental point of view. The research of Bayley (1969), Menyuk (1971), and Lenneberg (1967) (see Appendix) were extensively utilized. This scale contains elements of normal language from birth to thirty months and is divided into expressive and receptive components. Each component is subdivided into a hierarchy of seven levels spanning no more than six months each. This scale is administered to each of our children over several sessions lasting approximately one half-hour. Both observational data and responses to specific tasks are recorded by an independent observer. We frequently find marked divergence between levels of receptive and expressive language in an autistic child, with the receptive area usually being the more advanced. This phenomenon also occurs in normal individuals (as when learning a new language), but is much more pronounced in autistic children.

Based on this evaluation, language levels are established and a language therapy program is designed by choosing specific tasks according to the level of functioning of the child. Each child's school program then includes a half-hour daily language session. An integral part of this program is the formation of rapport between child and teacher, which resembles as closely as possible the normal mother-child relationship. This relationship is also viewed and structured developmentally. For example, a three-year-old child with expressive language skills at the six-month level would be treated by his primary teacher as a mother would treat her six-month-old child. In addition to these structured sessions, the primary teacher spends as much additional time as possible with the child in order to solidify and further develop their positive relationship. An initial goal in the early stages of the language program is to teach the child that he can use his voice in a social interaction. The next step is to aid him in organizing his verbalizations in a systematic way. As the child accomplishes this, he advances up the expressive and receptive hierarchy of language development (see Appendix) at his own learning rate. A child is never required to make specific verbalizations and food reinforcers are not used. However, behavioral programs are instituted concurrently. They are designed to eliminate maladaptive behaviors such as temper tantrums, aggression, or self-destructive behavior, and to build in other social and behavioral skills. After the child has passed the eighteen-month expressive level, we may place contingencies on his verbal performance. For example, if a child has developed reliable labeling skills, he may be required to ask for a desired object by name.

Articulation training is not a routine part of our program. It is only introduced after a child has established expressive skills past the twenty-four-month level and demonstrates grossly aberrant articulation.

One significant practical advantage of our program is that it can be implemented, under supervision, by individuals with a minimum of professional training. This is in contrast to other programs which can only be conducted by highly trained personnel such as speech therapists and psycholinguists.

PHILOSOPHIES OF LANGUAGE DEVELOPMENT

Our language therapy program is based on the theoretical view that language—creative communicative language—cannot be trained or taught. Rather, it may be elicited from an autistic child by using a developmental therapeutic approach. Some researchers believe that normal children have an innate capacity for and a need to develop language skills (Lenneberg, 1964; deSaussure, 1959). Others believe that infants do not have this innate quality and develop language only by imitating adult models (Skinner, 1957; Mowrer, 1960). The autistic children we have seen have been provided with normal linguistic models, thus, we believe that a central nervous system dysfunction resulting in perceptual inconstancy (Ornitz and Ritvo, 1968) has rendered them unable to benefit from this modeling. Our approach stresses overemphasis of normal modeling in a systematic manner in an attempt to overcome the child's dysfunction.

Psycholinguists have divergent views as to whether expressive skills or basic concepts are acquired first. Whorf (1956) has postulated that basic expressive skills direct the development of cognition. Conversely, Piaget (1955) and others have postulated that in order for an infant to be able to develop expressive abilities, he must first have cognitive skills. Our data support this latter hypothesis.

PRELIMINARY RESULTS

To date, we have treated six autistic children for an average length of nine months each. They have all exhibited significant growth in the development of expressive and receptive language. Initially, all had receptive and expressive language functions below the one-year level as measured on our evaluation scale. Despite histories of previous language arrests each progressed at least six months' developmentally during the first six months of our treatment. We have observed a positive relationship between linguistic progress in our program and initial non-verbal IQ test scores. One child has developed language skills consonant with his chronological level. A more detailed follow-up report has been presented to the American Association on Mental Deficiency (Richey and Flaharty, 1975).

REFERENCES

Bayley, N. (1969). *Manual for Bayley Scales of Infant Development.* New York: The Psychological Corp.

Breger, L. and McGaugh, J.L. (1965). Critique on reformulation of "learning theory" approaches to psychotherapy and neurosis. *Psychological Bulletin* 63:338-58.

Caldwell, B. (1968). The fourth dimension in early childhood education. In R.D. Hess and R.M. Bear, eds. *Early Education.* Chicago: Aldine Publishing Company. pp. 71-82.

——— and Richmond, J. (1962). The impact of theories of child development. *Children* 9:73-78.

deSaussure, F. *Course in General Linguistics.* (1959). In Charles Bally and Albert Sechebaye eds. in collaboration with Albert Reidlinger, translated by Wade Baskin. New York: Philosophical Library.

DeVito, J. (1970). *The Psychology of Speech and Language: An Introduction to Psycholinguistics.* New York: Random House.

Doll, E. (1946). *The Vineland Social Maturity Scale* Minneapolis: Educational Testing Bureau.

Flaharty, R. An educational assessment tool. cf. Part II, Chapter 4.

——— and Schofield, S. (1975). A comprehensive assessment procedure for atypical preschool children. Paper presented at American Association on Mental Deficiency Annual Conference, Portland, Oregon.

Foster, R., Giddan, J., & Stark, J. (1972). *Manual for the Assessment of Children's Language Comprehension* Palo Alto, Calif.: Consulting Psychologists Press, Inc.

Frankel, F. cf. Section II, Chapter 3.

——— and Graham, V. (in press). Systematic observation of classroom behaviors of retarded and autistic preschool children. *American Journal of Mental Deficiency.*

Garcia, E and DeHaven, E. (1974). Use of operant techniques in the establishment and generalization of language: A review and analysis. *American Journal of Mental Deficiency* 79:169-168.

Gesell, A. and Amatruda, C. (1947). *Developmental Diagnosis* New York: Harper and Row (Hober Medical Division).

————, Halverson, H., Thompson, H., Castner, B., Ames, L., and Amatruda, C. (1940). *The First Five Years of Life.* New York: Harper and Row.

Gray, B. and Ryan, B. (1973). *A Language Program for the Nonlanguage Child.* Champaign, Ill.: Research Press.

Hatten, J., Goman, T., and Lent, C. (1973). *Emerging Language.* Thousand Oaks, Calif.: The Learning Business.

Hewett, F. (1964). Teaching reading to an autistic boy through operant conditioning. *Reading Teacher* 17:613-618.

———— (1965). *Reinforcement Preferences of an Autistic Boy.* Unpublished manuscript.

————, Mayhew, D., and Rabb, E.W. (1967). An experimental reading program for neurologically impaired, mentally retarded and severely emotionally disturbed children. *American Journal of Orthopsychiatry* 37:35-48.

———— and Forness, S. (1967). *Education of Exceptional Learners* Boston: Allyn and Bacon.

Koegel, R. and Covert, A. (1972). The relationship of self-stimulation to learning in autistic children. *Journal of Applied Behavioral Analysis* 5:381-387.

Lenneberg, E. (1964). The capacity for language acquisition In J. Fodor and J. Katz ed. *The Structure of Language: Readings in the Philosophy of Language.* 579-603.

———— (1967). *Biological Foundations of Language.* New York: John Wiley and Sons, Inc.

Lewis, M.M. *Language, Thought and Personality.* New York: Basic Books, Inc.

Lovaas, O.I. (1966). A program for the establishment of speech in psychotic children. In J. Wing ed. *Early Childhood Autism.* New York: Pergamon Press.

———— (1966). Learning theory approach to the treatment of childhood schizophrenia. Paper presented at American Orthopsychiatric Association.

————, Freitag, G., Kinder, M., Rubenstein, B., Schaffer, B., and Simmons, J.Q. III. (1966). Establishment of social reinforcers in two schizophrenic children on the basis of food. *Journal of Experimental Child Psychology* 4:109-25.

————, Berberich, J., Perloff, B., Schaffer, B. (1966). Acquisition of imitative speech by schizophrenic children. *Science* 151:705-707.

————, Litrownik, A., Mann, R. (1971). Response latencies to auditory stimuli in autistic children engaged in self-stimulatory behavior. *Behavior Research and Therapy* 2:39-49.

Mecham, M.J. (1971). *Verbal Language Development Scale.* Minnesota: American Guidance Service, Inc.

Menyuk, P. (1971). *The Acquisition and Development of Language.* New Jersey: Prentice-Hall, Inc.

Mowrer, O.H. (1970). *Learning Theory and the Symbolic Process.* New York: John Wiley and Sons, Inc.

Ornitz, E.M. and Ritvo, E.R. (1968). Neurophysiologic mechanisms underlying perceptual inconstancy in autistic and schizophrenic children. *Archives of General Psychiatry* 19:22-27.

Osgood, C.E. and Sebeok, T.A. (1967). *Psycholinguistics: A Survey of Theory and Research Problems* Bloomington, Indiana: Indiana University Press.

Piaget, J. (1955). *The Language and Thought of the Child.* Translated by M. Gabain. Cleveland: Meridian Books.

Premack, A.J. and Premack, D. (1972). Teaching language to an ape. *Scientific American,* No. 4, 227:92-99.

Rabb, E.W. and Busch, J. (1968). Developing speech with nonverbal autistic children through reading. Paper presented at American Orthopsychiatric Association.

——— and Hewett, F. (1966). *Developing Appropriate Classroom Behaviors in a Severely Disturbed Group of Institutionalized Kindergarten-Primary Children Utilizing a Behavior Modification Model.* Unpublished manuscript.

Richey, V.E. and Flaharty, R.S. (1975). A cognitive-developmental approach to language acquisition in a mute autistic child. Paper presented at the Ninety-ninth Annual Meeting of the American Association on Mental Deficiency, Portland.

Rutter, M., Greenfield, D., and Lockyer, L. (1967). A five to fifteen-year follow-up study of infantile psychosis: II. Social and behavioral outcome. *British Journal of Psychiatry* 113: 1183-99.

——— and Sussenwein, F. (1971). A developmental and behavioral approach to the treatment of preschool autistic children. *Journal of Autism and Childhood Schizophrenia* 1:376-379.

Sailor, W., Guess, D. and Baer, D. (1973). Functional language for verbally deficient children: An experimental program. *Mental Retardation* pp. 27-35.

Sapir, E. *Language: An Introduction to the Study of Speech.* (1921). New York: Harcourt, Brace, & World, Inc.

Skinner, B.F. (1957). *Verbal Behavior.* New York: Appleton-Century-Crofts.

Stark, J., Rosenbaum, R., Schwartz, D., and Wisan, A. (1973). The nonverbal child: some clinical guidelines. *Journal of Speech and Hearing Disorders* 38:59-71.

Stokoe, W., Casterline, D., and Croneberg, C. (1965). *A Dictionary of American Sign Language.* Washington, D.C.: Gallaudet College Press.

Whorf, B.L. (1956). *Language, Thought, and Reality.* New York: Wiley and Cambridge, Mass: M.I.T. Press.

APPENDIX

Developmental Scale of Language Skills

Expressive Skills

	Pass	Fail	Comments
Level I – Neonate – 2 months			
Undifferentiated crying[1] (neonate – 1 month)			
One or two spontaneous vocalizations (.9 months)			
Differentiated crying[2] (1–2 months)			
Child cries in response to another child crying, especially if he can see the other child (1–2 months)			
Variety of non-crying utterances (1 months)			
Smiles in response to adult who smiles, talks, and touches child on abdomen (1.5 months)			
At least four spontaneous non-crying vocalizations (1.6 months)			
Level II – 2–5 months			
More than four non-crying vocalizations (2–3 months)			
Child may cry in response to angry voice (2–3 months)			
Smiles and vocalizes in response to adult who smiles, talks, and touches child on abdomen (2.1 months)			
Spontaneous vocalizations – two different sounds (2.3 months)			

	Pass	Fail	Comments
Child smiles on hearing a familiar voice, whether or not he can see the speaker (2.5 months)			
Child responds vocally to social approach (3 months)			
Child produces a wide variety of vowel and consonant sounds (3 months)			
Vocalizations are syllabic in nature (4–5 months)			
Spontaneous smiles, laughs, coos, and chuckles (4 months)			
Level III – 5–9 months			
Babbles frequently when alone or with others (5 months)			
Vocalizes in response to adult voice (5 months)			
Babbling may increase if adult uses same sound that child is uttering (5 months)			
Intonation of vocalizations expresses pleasure, displeasure, eagerness by change in pitch or intensity (5 months)			
Repetition of same sound— child repeats own vocal play (lalling) (6–8 months)			
Child vocalizes to his toys (6 months)			
Child vocalizes to his own image in a mirror (6 months)			

	Pass	Fail	Comments
Child vocalizes to initiate social approach (6 months)			
May "coo" to music (6 months)			
Child utters at least four different spontaneous sounds (7 months)			
Child combines several vowel sounds in one utterance (7 months)			
Vocalizes satisfaction after obtaining desired object (7 months)			
Vocalizations are intonated (pitch, intensity) in imitation of adult (8 months)			
Vocalized recognition of people and objects (8 months)			
Vocalizes to get attention (8 months)			
Child uses gestures while babbling (8 months)			
Child says "dada" or "mama" without meaning (8 months)			
Level IV − 9–12 months			
Babbles to others, as well as himself (9 months)			
Child imitates sounds, such as coughs, clicks, etc. (9 months)			
Says "dada," "mama," or other equivalent words, meaningfully (9 months)			

	Pass	Fail	Comments
Child imitates adult gestures and facial expressions (10 months)			
Child imitates many sounds, syllables, and words (echolalia) (10 months)			
Child uses one "word"[3] other than "mama" or "dada" (usually in response to adult stimulus) (10 months)			
Child imitates familiar vocalization by adult, both in sound and in number of times repeated (*e.g.,* adult says, "babababa" and child repeats exactly) (11 months)			
Imitates two tones sung by adult (11 months)			
Level V – 12–18 months			
Child uses holophrastic[4] utterances (12–18 months)			
Child uses vocalizations as a means of communication (12 months)			
Jabbers with or without gestures, but with adult-like intonation and definite meaning (12 months)			
Spontaneously uses one word (holophrase) (12 months)			
Imitates adult exclamatory sounds or familiar non-language sounds (*e.g.,* dog barking, clock ticking) (12 months)			

	Pass	Fail	Comments
Imitates simple words – usually those which have emotional importance to the child (13 months)			
Vocabulary of two words, other than "dada" or "mama," either spontaneously or imitatively (14 months)			
Jargon takes "sentence" form – in length, phrasing, and intonation of utterance (15 months)			
Indicates desires with pointing and/or vocalizations (15 months)			
Uses consistent two-syllable utterance for "thank you" (15 months)			
Vocabulary of four to seven words (15 months)			
Points to or verbally refers to place where particular object is routinely kept (as cookies, toys) (16–18 months)			
Verbally labels at least one object (17 months)			
Level VI – 18–24 months			
Vocabulary of ten to twenty words (18 months)			
Child responds to speech from others with verbal reply (18 months)			
Echos sounds and words when urged (18 months)			

	Pass	Fail	Comments
Uses words to express wants and needs (18 months)			
Verbally labels at least one picture (18 months)			
Uses "hello", "thank you", or other socially-oriented phrase (18 months)			
Fluent, conversational jargon is characterized by great sound variety and use in play (18 months)			
Echoes two or more words of adult phrase (21 months)			
Pulls a person by hand or arm to draw attention to object or event (21 months)			
Names two objects (21 months)			
Child connects two words in a phrase—must show two concepts (*e.g.*, "doggie there," not "all gone") (21 months)			
Child uses "yes" meaningfully (21 months)			
Child is able to refer verbally to a familiar situation (*e.g.*, "Where's doggie?") (21 months)			
Verbally labels three pictures (22 months)			
Level VII – 24–30+ months			
Child uses some prepositions pronouns, and articles (24–30 months)			

	Pass	Fail	Comments
Child's speech is socially-oriented (24–30 months)			
Child does not imbed negatives in sentence correctly (24–30 months)			
Verbally labels at least three objects (24 months)			
Verbally labels four body parts (24 months)			
Vocabulary of 275–300 words (24 months)			
Child combines three and four words in a phrase (24 months)			
Child's phrases are "telegraphic"— functionally, but not grammatically, correct (24 months)			
Child often talks while using gestures to illustrate his communication (24 months)			
Nouns, verbs, and adjectives predominate vocabulary (24 months)			
Jargon may have disappeared (24 months)			
Child uses pronouns I, me, you, but not always correctly (24 months)			
Child refers to himself by his given name (24 months)			
Child is able to talk about immediate experiences (24 months)			

Verbally labels at least five pictures (25 months)			
Vocabulary of 400 words (26–30 months)			
Child is able to refer simply to the future (26 months)			
Child is able to ask a yes/no question (26 months)			
Child carries on conversations with dolls (27 months)			
Verbally labels at least seven pictures (30 months)			
Verbally labels at least four objects, by use (30 months)			
Sentence averages three words in length (30 months)			
Child is able to use past tense (30 months)			
Child is able to give his full name (30 months)			
Vocabulary of 450 words (30 months)			
Child is able to ask an informational (wh) question (31 months)			

Receptive Skills

	Pass	Fail	Comments
Level I – Neonate–2 months			
Child gazes at speaker's face, when it is presented immediately before him (neonate–1 month)			
Responds to sound of bell or rattle, or other sharp sound (ceases activity) (neonate–1 month)			
Child ceases crying in response to soothing voice (neonate–1 month)			
Child shows pleasure in response to a lullabye and caress (1–2 months)			
Child shows social smile in response to adult talking, smiling, and touching him (1–2 months)			
Child shows anticipatory excitement at the approach of an adult (1–2 months)			
Turns to sound of voice–not always in right direction (1–2 months)			
Level II – 2–5 months			
Child responds discriminatingly to friendly or angry tone of voice (2–3 months)			
Child recognizes mother, visually (2 months)			
Child smiles in response to the sight of smiling adult (2 months)			
Child searches with eyes for sound (2 months)			
Child anticipates feeding at sight of food or dishes (bottle) (3 months)			

	Pass	Fail	Comments
Child focuses eyes directly on adult face (3 months)			
Child turns head to sound of bell, rattle, or other sharp sound (3–4 months)			
Child turns head toward speaker (4 months)			
Child sobers at the sight of a stranger (4 months)			
Child smiles at his own image in a mirror (4 months)			
Level III – 5–9 months			
Child responds to voice by turning his eyes and head (5 months)			
Child responds to fallen object (out of sight) by turning head (5 months)			
Child shows interest in sound production (bangs materials on table, etc.) (6 months)			
Child looks (actively) for fallen object (6 months)			
Child discriminates mother's voice from stranger's voice (6 months)			
Child turns to direction of unseen sound source (6 months)			
Child cooperates in hand-clapping games, etc. (may perseverate) (7–8 months)			
Child rings bell with direct purpose (7–8 months)			

	Pass	Fail	Comments
Comprehends parental gestures (7 months)			
Responds by raising arms when adult stretches out arms to pick child up (7 months)			
Pats own reflection in mirror (7 months)			
Child moves toward a familiar person when he is named (8 months)			
Level IV – 9–12 months			
Child responds to own name, "bye-bye," or "pat-a-cake" (9–10 months)			
Child retreats and cries upon seeing strangers and most other children (9 months)			
Child understands and responds to a simple verbal request (9 months)			
Child places a cube in a cup on request (9 months)			
Child shows a conditioned reaction to certain words and commands (*e.g.,* "hot," "bad") (10 months)			
Child imitates adult gestures and facial expressions (10 months)			
Child responds to "no" (10 months)			
Child shows interest in hearing isolated words associated with objects or activities important to him (11 months)			

	Pass	Fail	Comments
Level V – 12–18 months			
Child perceives and responds to (imitates) the emotions of others (anger, laughter) (12 months)			
Child is able to find concrete object when requested, even if the object is not immediately visible (13–15 months)			
Child is able to give a toy to an adult on verbal request accompanied by a gesture (13 months)			
Child pats pictures in book while looking at them (15 months)			
Child is able to find the picture of the "baby" in a larger picture (*e.g.,* a scene with other people) (15 months)			
Child is able to point to one article of clothing on verbal request (15 months)			
Child is able to follow a one-step direction (17 months)			
Level VI – 18–24 months			
Child is able to comprehend and respond to a simple question (18–21 months)			
Child responds to "sit down" and "stand up" (18 months)			
Child is able to point to three body parts (may include one article of clothing) (18 months)			
Child selectively looks at pictures in a book (18 months)			

	Pass	Fail	Comments
Child is able to point to body parts of doll (19 months)			
Child is able to selectively point to one picture (19 months)			
Child is able to selectively point to three pictures (20 months)			
Child understands and responds to "yes" (21 months)			
Child is able to selectively point to five pictures (21 months)			
Child is able to find object hidden under one of three cups (with verbal cue) (23 months)			
Child is able to point to four body parts (23 months)			
Level VII — 24–30+ months			
Child is unable to carry out a verbal instruction, if there is a slight delay between the instruction and action (24–30 months)			
Carries out four one-step directions with a doll (*e.g.,* put it in a chair, give it a drink) (24 months)			
Child is able to discriminate two parts of a complex scene (*e.g.,* "Where is the baby? Where is the doggie?" (24 months)			
Child is able to respond to "Put it (any object) in the box" (24 months)			

	Pass	Fail	Comments
Child is able to selectively point to seven pictures (25 months)			
Child understands two prepositions (28 months)			
Child is able to point to four objects described by use (30 months)			
Child is able to respond to "jump," "run," "walk," "throw it" (30 months)			
Child is able to give "all" the objects in front of him (30 months)			
Child understands and can repond to big/little (30 months)			
Child can point selectively to two pictures described by use (30 months)			
Child is able to give "just one" from several objects (30+ months)			
Child understands and can respond to three prepositions (30+ months)			

NOTES

1. Although each task is listed with a specific time of occurrence, these skills appear over a wide range of months. The values shown were drawn from developmental literature. The prescriptive language program is based on levels of functioning, rather than on a specific point within one level.

2. "Differentiated" crying contains those tonal qualities which make it possible for a mother to determine whether the child is crying because he is hungry or because of some other discomfort. Before the beginning of the second month of life, the child's cry sounds much the same in all situations.

3. The child's language from ten to twenty months of age is generally poorly articulated. When imitating or spontaneously uttering a one-syllable word, for example, the result will usually consist of the initial consonant and vowel sounds without the word ending sounds.

4. A "holophrase" or "holophrastic utterance" can be defined as one word which is used by the child to express any number of ideas. "Mama," for example, could not only mean "female parent," but also "Mama, come here," or "Help, I'm frightened," or even "I'm hungry. When are we going to eat?"

REFERENCES

Bayley, N. (1969). *Manual for Bayley Scales of Infant Development.* New York: The Psychological Corp.

Brown, R. (1964). *Social Psychology.* New York: Free Press.

DeVito, J. (1970). *The Psychology of Speech and Language: An Introduction to Psycholinguistics.* New York: Random House.

Doll, E. (1953). *Vineland Social Maturity Scale.* American Guidance Service, Inc.

Fry, D.B. (1966). The development of the phonological system in the normal and the deaf child. *The Genesis of Language: A Psycholinguistic Approach.* F. Smith and G. Miller eds., Cambridge, Mass.: The M.I.T. Press.

Gesell, A., Halverson, H., Thompson, H., Ilg, F., Castner, B., and Ames, L. (1940). *The First Five Years of Life*, Part II. New York: Harper and Row.

Goodenough, F. and Maurer, K. (1942). *The Mental Growth of Children from Two to Fourteen Years.* Minneapolis: University of Minnesota Press.

Lenneberg, E. (1964). The capacity for language acquisition. In J. Fodor and J. Katz eds. *The Structure of Language: Readings in the Philosophy of Language*, pp. 579-603: Englewood Cliffs, N.J.: Prentice-Hall, Inc.

——— (1967). *Biological Foundations of Language.* New York: John Wiley & Sons, Inc.

Lewis, M.M. (1951). *Infant Speech.* London: Routledge and Kegan Paul Ltd.

——— (1963). *Language, Thought, and Personality.* New York: Basic Books, Inc.

Lillywhite, H. (1958) Doctor's manual of speech disorders, *J.A.M.A.* Vol. 167.

Luria, A.R. (1964). Verbal regulation of behavior. *Readings in Child Behavior and Development.* Celia Stendler ed. New York: Harcourt, Brace, and World, Inc.

McCarthy, Dorothea. (1954). Language development in children. *Manual of Child Psychology* L. Carmichael ed. New York: John Wiley & Sons.

McNeill, D. (1966). Developmental psycholinguistics. *The Genesis of Language: A Psycholinguistic Approach.* F. Smith and G. Miller eds. Cambridge, Mass.: The M.I.T. Press.

—— (1970b). *The Acquisition of Language: The Study of Developmental Psycholinguistics* New York: Harper & Row.

Menyuk, P. (1971). *The Acquisition and Development of Language.* New Jersey: Prentice-Hall, Inc.

Naremore, R. and Hopper, R. (1973). *Children's Speech.* New York: Harper and Row.

Slobin, D.I. (1970). Universals of grammatical development in children. In G.B. Flores d'Arcais and W.J.M. Levelt eds. *Advances in Psycholinguistics.* New York: American Elsevier, pp. 174-84.

Templin, M. (1957). *Certain Language Skills in Children.* Minneapolis: University of Minnesota.

CHAPTER FIFTEEN

Educational Approaches at the Los Angeles County Autism Project

FLORENCE NEEDELS
COLLEEN JAMISON

For quite a number of years our county office, along with local districts, have been working with autistic children in a rather informal manner. Recently, we have approached this in a more formal way. In the Los Angeles County area alone there are three programs—an experimental program working with autistic and TMR children (some of whom are also emotionally disturbed) a school program based on sensory integration, and our language-based program for autistic children.

Our three sites are unique in that they are located at regular elementary schools. These facilities are leased from school districts and we operate the classes. Teacher/pupil ratios are one-to-two and serve children ages two through nine. The program is in the second year of a three-year grant, funded by a combination of EHA VI-B, state experimental and county funds.

PUPIL EVALUATION

All pupils referred to the program have a medically established diagnosis of autism. When an opening occurs, initial placement consists of a four- to eight-week assessment period. We term this "one-on-one." During this phase, the child attends class for approximately one hour a day. Several very important goals are achieved during this time. Base-line taping, parental completion of reinforcement surveys and questionnaires, identification of behaviors which interfere with learning and the start of elimination of these behaviors is undertaken. The language program begins

227

with phase-I commands (See Figure 1). We do not assume that the pupil has semantic competence for phase-I commands. Rather, we use gestures or other modes to teach them to respond to commands such as "Come here," "Sit down," "Look at me," "Hands down" (this later generalizes into readiness for learning), and "Give me." "Give me" is very important because we initiate our language program with the teaching of this response. We also assess each child in five developmental areas via a detailed criterion referenced curriculum. Once this is completed, psychologists and language specialists administer appropriate standardized tests. At this point, the pupil is placed in the actual classroom setting. The regular school day is from 9:00 A.M. to 2:00 P.M.

FIRST-YEAR ASSESSMENTS

Most of the children initially demonstrated the common behaviors and social disorders typical of autism. They had delayed social-emotional and academic development. Teacher evaluations generally agreed with parental evaluations in these areas. Initial standardized tests included the Leiter, the Merrill-Palmer, and Stanford-Binet. At the end of the year, retesting was done utilizing appropriate instruments. In terms of intellectual tasks, the children did best in areas of matching and counting but poorly on forms, color, block design, and completion progression subtest items. In terms of social tasks, as assessed by the Vineland, the children rated highest on *Occupation, Eating and General Self-Help*, and lowest on *Socialization, Locomotion, Dressing, Communication* and *Self-Direction*.

Twenty children were in the classes during the first year. Nineteen made obviously measurable gains in mental age. Nine gained at least one month developmentally for every month they attended school. Eleven gained less than one month per month in school, and were rated in the severely retarded range at the end of the year. Of the nine children who gained at least one month per month in school, seven received IQ scores below 100 and three were in the retarded range at the end of the year.

Of the twenty children, only eleven were in the program for the entire academic period of seven to eight months. Seven attended for five to six months and two for one to four months. As shown in Table I, gains were considerably greater than would have been expected on the basis of length of time in school. The fact that most gains occurred in the area of language is reflected by the improvement in the Stanford-Binet scores. A comparison was made between actual and developmentally anticipated gains over the academic year. The results are shown in Table II.

The IQ gains made were greater than would be expected on the basis of the highest post-test IQ scores. At the end of the year, 50 percent of the

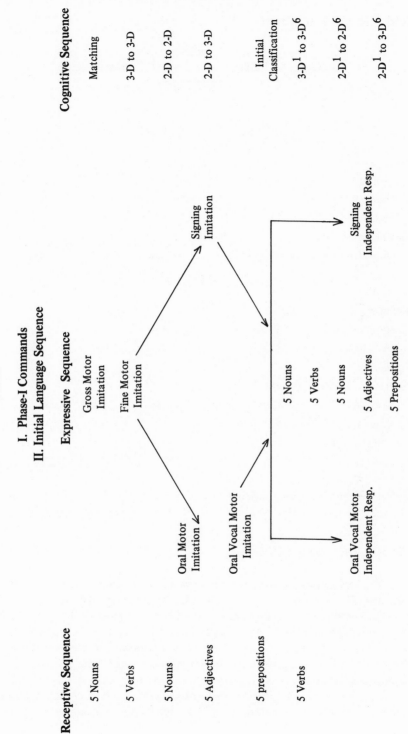

FIG. 1

I. Phase-I Commands
II. Initial Language Sequence

Receptive Sequence

5 Nouns

5 Verbs

5 Nouns

5 Adjectives

5 prepositions

5 Verbs

Oral Motor Imitation

Oral Vocal Motor Imitation

Oral Vocal Motor Independent Resp.

Expressive Sequence

Gross Motor Imitation

Fine Motor Imitation

5 Nouns

5 Verbs

5 Nouns

5 Adjectives

5 Prepositions

Signing Imitation

Signing Independent Resp.

Cognitive Sequence

Matching

3-D to 3-D

2-D to 2-D

2-D to 3-D

Initial Classification

3-D^1 to 3-D^6

2-D^1 to 2-D^6

2-D^1 to 3-D^6

229

Table I.
**Summary of Intellectual and Social Characteristics of
Twenty Pupils**

	Pre-test	Post-test	Mean Difference
Leiter			
Mean MA	56 mos.	61 mos.	5 mos.
Mean IQ	71	79	8
Number	10	13	
Stanford-Binet L–M			
Mean MA	44 mos.	54 mos.	10 mos.
Mean IQ	47	64	17
Number	4	7	
Merrill-Palmer			
Mean MA	30 mos.	37 mos.	7 mos.
Mean IQ	43	49	6
Number	7	9	
Vineland Social Maturity Scale			
Mean SA	42 mos.	45 mos.	3 mos.
Mean SQ	53	56	3
Number	16	19	

initial twenty children had IQ scores in the normal range (72 or above).
Seventy percent of the children gained at a normal expected rate.

PROGRAM STRUCTURE

We feel our pilot work to date has demonstrated that autistic children
can attend and benefit in a meaningful and measurable way in a public
school. We have also been concerned with developing a program which can
be duplicated in other school districts. Thus, we have a number of programs, including an itinerant teaching program, an inservice teacher training program, development of the language curriculum, and an extensive
parent and volunteer training program. These are all predicated upon our
highly structured diagnostic/prescriptive system. It includes a team approach to develop an individually designed pupil program with systematic

Table II.
Actual and Developmentally Anticipated IQ Gains

		Post-test Range			% In Normal Range	N gaining at normal rate	% gaining at normal rate
	N	TMR	EMR	Normal			
School A	8	1	1	6	75%	5 of 6	83%
School B	12	6	2	4	33%	4 of 7	57%
Total	20	7	3	10	50%	9 of 13	70%

data recording and review and revision process (See Figure 2).

We use behavior therapy techniques in all areas of our pupils' programs. A balanced program is provided for each pupil by always including one to three prescriptions in each of the following five curriculum areas:

(1) Social-Behavioral: We focus on decreasing motility disturbances and tantruming behavior. We strive to develop appropriate play, peer and social behaviors. By being on a regular school campus, opportunities for peer modeling and integration are readily available.

(2) Independent Living Skills: Programs are written and implemented to teach toileting, eating, dressing, hygiene and safety.

(3) Sensory-Motor: Fine motor and gross motor skills are taught with the assistance of remedial physical education specialists. One physical education instructor utilizes sensory integration techniques.

(4) Cognitive and Academic: Programs range from classifying by function and critical features, to reading, math and spelling. We also attempt to integrate appropriate pupils into regular classrooms.

(5) Language: A psycholinguistic approach to the development of highly structured receptive and expressive programs is used. They range from teaching single nouns to correct use of pronouns and other higher levels of language.

LANGUAGE PROGRAMS

A major focus of our efforts is directed toward developing programs in the area of language. We use a cognitive-psycholinguistic approach and emphasize the *semantic meaning* component of language and related cog-

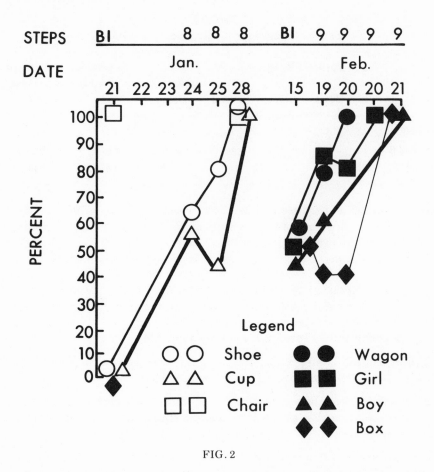

FIG. 2

nitive skills rather than articulation or speech. Of our initial twenty children, twelve did not have language.

To initially assess language, we use the Peabody Picture Vocabulary Test, Assessment of Children's Language Comprehension, The Northwestern Syntax Screening Test, the Illinois Test of Psycholinguistic Ability, language sample analysis, and an informal language screening survey.

The language criteria referenced curriculum is divided into three areas: (1) a phonemic or sound system, (2) a morphosyntactic system by which words are combined to produce grammatical forms, (3) a semantic system that specifies developmental levels of comprehension and use of meaningful symbolic language. For each of these systems, there is a sequence of objectives.

We assumed that the language curriculum was a finitely defined developmental sequence. However, twelve of the twenty children were functioning below testable objectives in all areas. Eight pupils demonstrated linguistic skill and deficit profiles that allowed placements at specific levels within the curriculum. The majority required approximately one year of intensive language training to reach the first step of the semantic component of the language curriculum.

Several of our severely impaired children were mute; the remainder were echolalic. Both the mute and the ecolalic pupils demonstrated severe oral apraxia. The apraxia of the echolalic children appeared to have an anomic-like feature. The common demoninator in *all* pupils was an *absence of functional language* due to their profound deficit in comprehension.

INITIAL LANGUAGE PROGRAM

A major focus of our language program was to develop an ordered sequence of criterion referenced pupil objectives. It consisted of specific learning steps that could bridge the information gap between entry skills and cognitive-linguistic skills (See Figure 1).

Programs in the initial language sequence were initiated after the pupil achieved mastery of phase-I commands. Two of these commands, "Come here" and "Sit down" are necessary for appropriate classroom behavior. "Hands down" and "Give me" are critical to all subsequent learning. The "Hands down" response generalizes to a readiness for attending. The "Give me" response, which is taught with only one noun object present, is utilized in all later receptive language programs.

The initial language program (Figure 1) consists of a receptive expressive and cognitive sequences of tasks. In the receptive language sequence, we arbitrarily decided to teach comprehension of five nouns, five verbs, five other nouns, adjectives and finally, prepositions. Single vocabulary items, such as nouns, are selected carefully. We include some that may be agents of action (mommy, daddy, baby, man). From these nouns we move to noun plus verb sequences such as mommy sitting, mommy sleeping, daddy sleeping. Some nouns like chair and block are selected because they can be described by various atttibutes such as color and size. Thus, the pupil can progress to adjective plus noun, or noun plus adjective sequences (blue block, red block, big block, big chair). Some nouns that can be placed in logical spatial relationships with one another were also selected. We could then move to noun plus preposition plus noun sequences (block on table, block under table, block beside chair). While the initial objective was to teach single vocabulary item comprehension, we found that some pupils generalized.

The expressive language sequence begins with gross motor imitation. Given the command, "Do this," the child is taught to imitate bilateral body movements (standing, sitting, arms above head). Next, fine motor imitation tasks are introduced (hands on shoulders, hands on head, hands on waist). We then teach unilateral imitative responses by requiring increasingly finer motor coordination. The purpose is two-fold. First, we teach oral motor imitation. The teacher says, "Do this," and models opening mouth or pulling lips together. Next, we teach oral vocal motor imitation. In this the child imitates isolated speech sounds and then speech sound sequences. For example, first is taught a reliable imitative response to "Say a," "Say m," then sequencing the two sounds "Say ma," and finally "Mama." At this point, visual reference (a picture of mommy) is introduced. The focus here is not on articulation but on facilitating volitional control of the oral speech mechanism. We also teach signing imitation. The pupil imitates the teacher's signed model while presented with a reference noun.

In both the oral vocal motor and the signing sequences, the goal is for the pupil to acquire independent labeling responses. For example, when presented with noun objects and asked, "What is this?" the child should be able to sign or say "cup," "baby," "shoe," etc.

The initial cognitive sequence consists of two objectives: first, matching a two-dimensional picture to a three-dimensional object and second, initial classification. The matching of identical three-dimensional objects progresses through a series of steps in which the child begins by matching identical two-dimensional pictures. Next he is taught to match a colored photograph of an object to the actual object.

In the initial classification program, the pupil progresses through a series of steps which require the matching of objects within a class (pictures of objects within a class that are increasingly dissimilar along such dimensions as color, size, and shape). Thus the pupil learns that when he hears one of the noun words (cup) or sees the sign for "cup," the label refers not only to the object used in his language program, but to others within his experience that have in common critical attributes of "cupness." The final goal is to introduce the concept that words label classes or categories of objects.

RESULTS OF THE LANGUAGE PROGRAM

As noted previously, twelve of the original twenty children began with no functional speech. Of these twelve, five acquired functional speech. Three acquired expressive language that was commensurate with their receptive language. However, their responses were dependent on cues in the training situation (a question). One is beginning to acquire expressive language using signs, but has not as yet demonstrated language comprehension or production via the auditory vocal system. The remaining three are at the point where they can imitate an oral-vocal model or the noun sign, but have not achieved an independent response level to those signs.

PART V

Management of Autistic Persons in the Community

CHAPTER SIXTEEN

Educational Approaches at the Behavior Research Institute, Providence, Rhode Island

MATTHEW L. ISRAEL

Behavior Research Institute (B.R.I.) is a private, non-profit organization whose primary activity is the operation of treatment center/schools for children, adolescents, and adults with severe behavior disorders. Most of the students at the Institute have been diagnosed as autistic, severely emotionally disturbed, schizophrenic, brain damaged, retarded, etc. The students currently range in ages from nine to twenty-one, but there is no actual upper or lower age limit.

The program has both day school and residential components. The day school operates 9 A.M.-5 P.M., six days a week, twelve months a year. All of the students are enrolled in this school full-time, except for a few who are only part-time students because they have progressed to the point of attending regular public school or college. Most of the day school students live at home, a few live in state institutions, and a few live in treatment-residences which the Institute operates.

The approach taken—both as to education and treatment—is thoroughly behavioral, growing out of operant conditioning concepts and research. Within this framework, each student receives an individualized program. Training is provided to the parents and siblings as well as to the students.

The Institute's goal is to provide sufficient treatment and education so that autistic persons can return to normal public education, avoid living in institutions or at home when they become adults, and instead live and work in as normal a fashion as possible. To this end, the Institute expects to involve itself in the development of normal work opportunities, community

239

residences, and sheltered workshops for autistic persons. A long-range vision of the Institute is some kind of therapeutic community for autistic persons, providing flexible, normalized living and working possibilities, with a behavior modification support system.

In addition to its day school and treatment residences, which are the primary activities of the Institute, the Institute also offers training to parents whose children are not enrolled in the B.R.I. school, conducts workshops for other professionals, and offers consultation services.

This chapter describes the education and treatment program currently operated by the Institute. It also proposes an integrated set of services for the autistic child, adolescent, and adult, that will enable them to lead dignified, non-institutional lives.

THE TREATMENT OF AUTISTIC CHILDREN

Group-Management Systems

The most effective treatment situation is that in which a treatment worker works on a one-to-one basis with a child. Consequently, the best strategy is to have most of the students functioning in a group or groups that are managed by a minimal number of treatment workers, thus freeing the remaining treatment workers to take individual students out of the group and work with them on a one-to-one basis. We label these two types of situations *group management* and *one-to-one*.

According to this strategy, the behaviors that must be taught first are those that will enable a student to function properly in a group of six to twelve students that is managed by a single teacher. The student must learn to sit in a chair without running away and without showing any major disruptive behaviors. Beyond these minimal requirements, it is desirable if the child can also work at some productive task on his own and can follow some basic instructions given by the teacher.

Many autistic students do not possess these behaviors when they first come to B.R.I. The behaviors have to be taught, and the best way to teach them is in one-to-one training. Thus, a student begins by receiving one-to-one training in those skills which will enable him to eventually function successfully in a group-management situation.

There are several possible ways to set up group-management situations. We use four basic types at B.R.I. Each type is scheduled for anywhere from one half hour to several hours each day.

Task-Reward Sequence

In this type of group-management, each student works independently at his own particular educational task while under the overall supervision of a teacher. In the task-reward sequence, the student does the first task, returns it to the shelf, takes his own reward, then gets his next task, does that next task, takes his reward, and so on.

Before a student is taught how to do the task-reward sequence, he should first be taught how to sit in front of some attractive rewards—such as candies or foods—and not take any unless he is given permission to do so by the treatment worker.

When doing the task-reward sequence, each student uses a set of 3x5-inch cards joined by a single ring. Each card contains a picture representing one particular educational task together with a printed word or phrase that is the name of that task. The student begins by looking to see what is on the first card. For example, the first card might have a picture of the stack-the-rings task and its name. The student then goes to the shelf, gets that particular task, and brings it back to his seat. He then does the task; he takes the rings off the pole and puts them back on in the correct order.

When he has finished the task, he returns it to its correct place on the shelf, returns to his seat, and then takes an immediate reward. This might be a piece of food, a penny, or a plastic token, depending on the student's particular program.

After taking his reward, the student turns to the next card, which contains a picture and the name of the next task that he is to do. It might, for example, be a picture of a buckle-board task. The student then goes to the shelf once more, gets the buckle-board task, and continues as before.

In teaching a student how to do the task-reward sequence, we start him on some fairly simple tasks, since our primary purpose at first is simply to teach him how to do the sequence correctly. Once the student has learned how to do the sequence itself, more and more difficult and educational tasks are inserted as the task components of the sequence. These are some of the tasks we have used in our task-reward sequence, arranged more or less in order of increasing amount of academic skills required.

    (1) Stack-the-rings
    (2) Playpax squares, rings, etc.
    (3) Large Lego blocks
    (4) Small Lego blocks
    (5) Number board
    (6) Buckle board, zipper board, button board, etc.
    (7) Wooden puzzles
    (8) Cardboard jigsaw puzzles
    (9) Association cards
  (10) Alphabet board
  (11) Teaching machines
  (12) Programmed instruction textbooks

Notice that a student can do task-reward whether or not he has learned to *read* in the usual sense of that word. He simply needs to learn to get a certain task from the shelf when he turns up a 3x5-inch card that has a picture of that task on it.

There are several benefits of the task-reward sequence. First, by teaching the student to do the sequence, one is also teaching him how to work on a task at a desk for sustained periods of time. This is valuable preparation for working in a sheltered workshop or other place of employment. Second, once the student has learned the task-reward sequence, it can be set up in the home and the parents can be taught how to maintain it. As a result, the student can be doing some useful work at home each evening. Equally important, his spare time can then be used profitably instead of being a time at which he may show various bizarre and inappropriate behaviors.

Programmed Opportunities

A second type of group management resembles the usual classroom procedure. In it, a treatment worker provides instructions, prompts, and consequences to a group of students who are seated in front of him. The treatment worker goes around the group from student to student giving each a turn. The treatment worker may give him an instruction, a prompt if needed, and an accelerating or decelerating consequence.

The particular instruction delivered to each student is determined by a form which the treatment worker has in front of him. It ensures that what he asks of each student is appropriate to that student's stage of progress in the particular skill being taught. In the case of one student, he may ask him to follow a simple direction; for another student, he may simply call his name and see if he makes eye contact. A third may be asked to repeat a word or phrase. The instruction is *individualized*, although the children are sitting in a group.

Supervised Teaching Machine Use

In this situation, one treatment worker closely supervises four to six children who are using teaching machines and programmed instructional materials. The treatment worker's role is to ensure that the student uses the machines properly, to ensure that he has the appropriate curriculum materials, to give him progress checks from time to time, etc.

Contracts

This situation is essentially the "contingency contract" system devised by Dr. Lloyd Homme and his associates. In our version of this system, it is necessary that the student be able to read some words and phrases and be able to carry on a meaningful conversation with the treatment worker as he discusses his contract.

The student begins by picking up an 8½x11-inch contract form at the beginning of the day. It looks like the form shown in Table I. The student then sits down with the treatment worker who is managing the contract group and chooses five curriculum areas which he would like to study that day. For each of these areas, one specific learning task is selected and entered in one of the boxes of the first column of the contract form.

Suppose the student decides that the first thing he would like to do is to work on his reading, and more particularly, to practice his reading in the *Sullivan Series Storybook 6*. This task would then be entered in the first box of the first row of the contract sheet as shown here:

Task

Read Sullivan
Storybook 6

The student then goes to the peg-board on which the charts showing his daily reading speed are displayed, finds the chart for his performance on Sullivan Storybook 6, and brings it back to the treatment worker. (We use the Daily Behavior Charts that are part of the Precision Teaching System devised by Dr. Ogden Lindsley of the University of Kansas.) Using the chart, the treatment worker and student now discuss what would be an appropriate criterion of mastery that the student will try to achieve on that particular behavior on that day. For example, they might decide that a reasonable target for that day might be to be able to read the story at 100 words correct per minute with zero errors per minute. This information would be written in the middle box as shown here:

Task   **Criterion**

Read Sullivan   Read at 100 w/p/m
Storybook 6   correct and at
                                  0 errors p/m

Next, the student and his treatment worker decide what the reward should be if he manages to reach the criterion in question on that day. It might be decided, for example, that the student will be paid 10 cents plus 50

Table 1. Contract Sheet

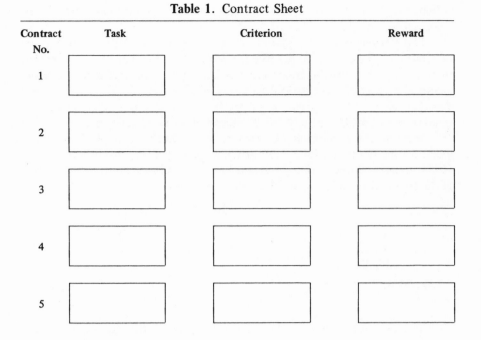

Contract No.	Task	Criterion	Reward
1			
2			
3			
4			
5			

paper money credits if he reaches the criterion. This information is entered in the third column, as shown here:

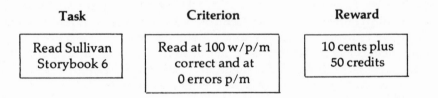

Task	Criterion	Reward
Read Sullivan Storybook 6	Read at 100 w/p/m correct and at 0 errors p/m	10 cents plus 50 credits

These same three boxes are then filled in for each of the other contracts on the page. When the page has been completed in this way, the student is ready to start to work on his first task.

Suppose that the first task is reading. The student gets the necessary materials, goes to his desk, does the reading, and then raises his hand when he has completed his task. The student then goes up to the treatment worker's desk, where he is given a one-minute test of his reading speed and accuracy to determine whether he has reached the criterion that was specified. If he does meet or better the criterion, he earns his reward. In the case under discussion, this consists, in part, of the payment of some special paper money credits. The student decides how much of this money he wishes to spend immediately and how much he wishes to bank for the future. If he wishes to spend some of it immediately, he might ask, for example, for a pass slip to go to a special reward room where he may select and enjoy a reward of his choice. Then he would return to the classroom and begin work on his second contract.

A beginning student in our school is first taught how to function in the task-reward or programmed opportunities systems. After mastering these, he moves on to the supervised teaching machine system, and then eventually to the contract system. In a sense, then, we have three groups of students, defined by what system of group management they are using. *Group 1*, the elementary group, makes use of task-reward or programmed opportunities systems. *Group 2*, the intermediate group, works in the supervised teaching machine group. *Group 3*, the advanced group, uses the contract system.

Self-Instructional Systems Used in Group Management

While a student is in a group-management system, it is important that his time be used as productively as possible. For this reason, we teach students how to use teaching machines and programmed instruction as quickly as possible. Supervised instruction in this is given in the supervised teaching machine situation (*Group 2*). When a student graduates to *Group 3*, the contract system group, he continues to make use of teaching machines and programmed instruction as tasks to be performed as part of his contracts. By that time, however, he is able to use the machines and materials correctly, and no longer needs the close supervision he received in *Group 2*.

The following is a brief summary of the various teaching machines and programmed textbooks that we currently use.

Multiple choice card machines

The student picks up a 5x8-inch card and puts it in the machine. The card contains a question, or stimulus, on the left side of the card and two possible correct answers on the right side. For example, the card might present a picture of a shoe (the problem) and two possible answers, such as the printed words *shoe* and *hat*. The student first looks at the problem (in this case the picture of a *shoe*), and then selects the correct answer, pressing a button that is near the answer of his choice. If he selects the correct answer, a signal light on the teaching machine automatically lights up. If he selects the wrong answer, the light does not light up.

Audio-card machines

We use these machines extensively in the teaching of reading, writing and spelling. There are two basic modes. In the first, the student picks up a card on which there is printed a letter, letter combination, or word. He tries to read aloud whatever is on the card. Then he inserts the card in the machine and the machine gives the correct pronunciation of whatever is on the card by "reading" a strip of prerecorded magnetic tape. By listening to the correct answer, he learns immediately whether he has read the card correctly or not. He then scores himself as right or wrong, places the cards he answered wrong in a special pile for further study, and then repeats this procedure with the next card.

In the second mode of using this teaching machine, the student begins by picking up a card that is blank on the side facing him. He then puts the card in the machine, which plays aloud whatever sound or word has been prerecorded on the card's magnetic strip. Then he tries to write down on a sheet of paper the letter, letters or word that spell out the sound or word he has just heard. After doing so, he turns over the card he has just played, and discovers the correct answer preprinted on the other side of the card. He then compares this preprinted correct answer with his own written answer, scores himself right or wrong, and goes on to the next card.

Cassette players

An ordinary cassette player serves as a third type of teaching machine. This is useful at the stage when a student can read words or sentences in a book. The student begins by attempting to read a word or sentence in a book. He then plays the cassette to hear the word or sentence read correctly. (The cassette contains a prerecorded version of the story.) After listening to see if he read the word or sentence correctly, he stops the cassette player, tries to read the next word or sentence in the book, then plays the cassette to check himself, and so on. As the student becomes more and more proficient, he uses the cassette merely to help with the more difficult passages.

3x5-inch flash cards

Much of our mathematics program is set up on 3x5-inch cards that have the problem on one side and the answer on the other. The student is taught to look at the problem, write the answer he thinks is correct on a sheet of paper, turn the card over to discover the correct answer, score himself as right or wrong, place the correctly done cards in one pile and the incorrectly done ones in the other, and then restudy the incorrectly done cards until he can do them correctly at an adequate speed.

Programmed textbooks

In a programmed textbook, the material to be learned is divided into a sequence of little paragraphs, each of which contains a question, or blank to be filled in, based on the material in that paragraph. The student reads the little paragraph, writes his answer, and then slides a mask down the side of the page so as to immediately uncover the correct answer. He then compares his own answer with the correct answer, scores himself as right or wrong, and advances to the next paragraph.

Through the use of these various group-management situations and the self-instructional machines and materials, a large number of children can be managed by a minimal number of treatment workers and can be learning useful things while being managed. On a typical morning in our Providence school, there might be a contract group of ten students, a task-reward or programmed opportunities group of five students, and a supervised teaching machines group of five students. Thus, a total of twenty students are educationally managed by only three treatment workers.

Opportunities and Accelerating and Decelerating Consequences Arranged in the Group-Management Situations

The treatment worker who manages a group-management situation is termed a *group manager,* to distinguish him from a treatment worker who does one-to-one work with the students. The latter is termed a *one-to-one worker.*

While the students are in a group-management situation, the group manager's responsibility is not only to oversee or direct the group-management activities themselves, but also to arrange various opportunities and consequences with a view towards achieving certain treatment or educational goals.

The consequences that the group manager arranges are of two types. A consequence that serves to *increase* the frequency of a behavior is termed an *accelerating* consequence. The closest lay term is *reward.* A consequence that *decreases* the frequency of a behavior is a *decelerating* consequence. The closest lay term is *punishment.* For example, while a student is doing his task-reward sequence, the teacher might notice Billy rocking and say, "No rocking, Billy! Pay a five cent fine!" Or, the group manager might notice Billy at a time when he is *not* rocking and might say, "Good for not rocking, Billy!" (or possibly, "Good sitting straight, Billy!") "Take a penny!"

The treatment worker might create an opportunity for a certain behavior. He might, for example, say, "Billy!" If Billy then looks up and makes eye contact, he might say, "Good looking at me when I say your name, Billy! Take a penny!"

In carrying out this function of arranging opportunities, and accelerating and decelerating consequences, the group manager is guided by a Daily Recording Sheet that is prepared daily for each student. This sheet is an individualized treatment plan for the student. It lists the behaviors which should receive accelerating consequences, and those which should receive decelerating consequences. It also lists certain opportunities (stimuli) that should be arranged, the behavior that is sought in such situations, and consequences (accelerating or decelerating) that the treatment worker should arrange. The form also provides a space in which the treatment worker is to record each consequence that he administers—both accelerating and decelerating. Each group manager records his consequences in a different colored pencil so that, at the end of the day, the frequency with which different treatment workers have administered opportunities and consequences can be tallied and compared.

Accelerating Consequences Used in Group-Management

It is critically important, in a behavior modification treatment program to have effective accelerating and decelerating consequences.

Foods

To make food more effective as a consequence, we often ask the parents not to serve the student breakfast at home. Instead, the student earns it, bit by bit, over the course of a morning. The same is true of lunch, and even supper, in the case of students in our residential program.

Money tokens or points

Often we use food as the preferred accelerating consequence when a student first enters the program. Then, as he learns how to work for money, tokens, or points, these latter items are substituted as the immediate consequence and are exchanged for food (or other accelerating consequences) from time to time, when the student has accumulated a certain number of pennies, tokens, or points.

Activities

Another type of accelerating consequence is the special activity. Some examples are:

        (a) Watching television
        (b) Crayoning, using Pla-Do, or finger painting
        (c) A chance to look out the window
        (d) A chance to relax in a lounge, listen to music, etc.

    (e) A chance to feed the gerbils

    (f) A tickle

    (g) A swing in the arms of the treatment worker

    (h) A fan on a hot day.

Each of these activities are available for a specified number of minutes.

Reward menu

From time to time in our school, and sometimes in home programs, we have made use of a reward menu to display the various accelerating consequences that are available and prices of each. Typically, the reward menu consists of a bulletin board with 3x5-inch cards on it that represent the various consequences available. Each card contains a picture of the item, its printed name, and its price in tokens or pennies.

The student might gain access to the reward menu by accumulating a certain number of tokens or by demonstrating some desired behavior. When he approaches the menu, this is a good opportunity for the treatment worker to teach the student some useful conversation and the meaning and use of money. The interaction between treatment worker and student at this point might go like this:

Treatment Worker:	"What would you like to buy?"
Student:	"I'd like to watch T.V., please."
Treatment Worker:	"Do you see how much it costs?"
Student:	"It costs five cents."
Treatment Worker:	"Do you have five cents?"
Student:	"Here it is."
Treatment Worker:	"Okay! Enjoy it!"

Those students who are unable to say words may simply point to the accelerating consequence they want or may make a *sign* designating that item—if they are learning signs. If a student is just learning to make his first one or two sounds, we might ask him to make one of his sounds to "ask for" the item.

Choice of Accelerating Consequences

Currently, we make frequent use of foods as accelerating consequences. They have an advantage in that they are quickly administered, so that the student can get back into the treatment work immediately. This is particularly important when a child is receiving one-to-one treatment. They are also quite powerful when a child is suitably hungry. Generally, the immediate accelerating consequence is the receipt of a penny, and when the student has accumulated five, ten, or twenty pennies, he buys a small food reward.

The more advanced students in our contract group generally work for some kind of activity as the accelerating consequence. With them, the fact that a consequence may take five to fifteen minutes is of less importance, since their need for intense treatment is somewhat less than that of the beginning students.

Decelerating Consequences Used in Group Management

We always work on two "related" behaviors at the same time—for example, *rocking* and *not rocking* (or *standing still* and *sitting still*). We apply an accelerating consequence to the desired behavior (for example, *not rocking*) and at the same time arrange a decelerating consequence for the undesired behavior (*rocking*).

Hierarchical procedure to determine needed level of aversiveness

During the first few days a student is in our program, we try to find the least aversive consequence that will be effective and efficient in decelerating the student's inappropriate behaviors. On the first day or two of the program, we simply film the child's various behaviors. No consequences, either accelerating or decelerating, are applied at this time, so in effect this stage is similar to the process of ignoring the inappropriate behaviors. We record and plot data throughout the day in half-hour intervals to determine something about the level of the various behaviors and the extent that they may be changing simply through being ignored. Usually the decrease in inappropriate behaviors that occurs through this type of ignoring is either not evident or too slow to satisfy us.

The next thing we usually try is the combination of a reward system for the behaviors we wish to accelerate and a loud "No!" as in "No rocking!" for the opposite behaviors we wish to decelerate. We continue to record behavior data to determine whether this procedure is effective. With some children it is.

If it is not, we might next try a token fine (combined, of course, with a reward program for the desired behavior). Whenever the student shows an inappropriate behavior, he must pay back one or more tokens or pennies that he has either earned previously, through his desirable behaviors, or that he has been given free at the beginning of the school day. In the case of autistic children who have just entered the program and have not yet learned the meaning of tokens, we might skip this step of the token fine. On the other hand, for many of our advanced students, the token fine has become very effective, and with them we may never have to resort to anything more aversive.

If the loud "No!" or the token fines do not serve to decelerate the inappropriate behaviors reasonably quickly, we try some physical aversive consequence (still combined, of course, with a reward program for the opposite, desired behaviors). For most students, one or more spanks administered to the buttocks is sufficient to decelerate the problem behaviors.

In some cases, we have used decelerating consequences of the "activity" type, such as "time outs." These are often effective but have a disadvantage similar to that of the activity type of accelerating consequence—their administration takes up a lot of valuable time, and we would much prefer that the student spend that time in some positive treatment experience.

With judicious use of the decelerating consequences we have managed to avoid having to use electric shock on any of our students, and it is our hope that we can continue to be this fortunate. This has been true in spite of the fact that we deal with very severe cases who have failed to respond to other forms of treatment. Indeed, we have never refused admission to a child or excluded a child because of the severity of his behavior disorders.

Other Decelerating Consequences

With most students, physically aversive consequences are needed primarily in the early stages of treatment. As the student progresses, less aversive kinds of decelerating consequences, such as a disapproving shake of the head, come to be effective.

One consequence that we often use, and that is often effective without being physically aversive, is requiring the student to repeat the correct form of the behavior a number of times. For example, if a student uses a pronoun incorrectly, we might ask him to say the sentence correctly and to repeat that sentence ten times correctly. This procedure has the dual effect of serving as a decelerating consequence for the undesired behavior, as well as strengthening the alternative, correct form at the same time.

Controls on the Use of Decelerating Consequences

We employ a variety of controls to ensure that decelerating procedures are used carefully and properly. The various controls we are currently using include the following.

(1) There is a training program for the staff in the theory and practices of behavior modification. The program takes about a year to complete, and

by demonstrating mastery of all seven steps, the trainee can increase his salary, incrementally, by a total of $2,600 per year.

(2) We obtain the informed consent of the parent or guardian whenever possible. This includes actual demonstration of the procedures, together with a discussion of the advantages and disadvantages. If a student resides in an institution, the administrative, nursing, and ward staff are kept fully informed.

(3) The staff is required to record each instance of the administration of a decelerating consequence on the Daily Recording Sheet.

(4) All treatment takes place in one large classroom. Thus, the administration of decelerating consequences is overseen by the principal and several other treatment workers in the same room.

(5) Decelerating consequences that are physically aversive are presented to a Human Rights Committee that is independent of the school and its parents for review. The State Department of Mental Health has its own Human Rights Committee, which also oversees physically aversive procedures.

(6) The specific policies and procedures relating to decelerating consequences are written down in a manual which is filed with the relevant state agencies and is read and studied by all treatment workers before beginning work.

(7) Whenever possible, the family physician is consulted to insure that there are no special reasons *not* to use a specific contemplated procedure.

(8) The classrooms are open to unscheduled visits by representatives of the relevant state agencies (education and mental health) at all times.

(9) The ratio of accelerating to decelerating consequences administered to each child is tallied and reviewed daily by the principal. The ratio is kept very high. Currently in our school, it ranges from 10:1 to 40:1, even when a token fine is counted as a decelerating consequence.

(10) A special staff member, whose role is staff behavior recorder, is particularly responsible for overseeing the use of decelerating procedures and insuring their proper use.

(11) All staff members sign an affidavit affirming that they will report any suspected misuse of decelerating procedures immediately to the director.

(12) All decelerating procedures are specified in advance, in writing, on an individualized basis for each student.

(13) Behavior data is reviewed on a daily basis to determine whether a given procedure is working or not and whether a change in procedure is needed.

Charting

The group manager records each accelerating and decelerating consequence that he arranges. Because the group manager arranges a consequence for desired and undesired behaviors each time they occur, the number of accelerating and decelerating consequences given out also give us data on how often the behaviors occurred.

To measure our progress in increasing or decreasing each behavior, we use the Daily Behavior Charts designed by Dr. Ogden Lindsley. A separate chart is kept for every single behavior of every single student, and data is entered on the chart on a daily basis.

For example, consider the chart for Peter's behavior of nagging. The chart shows that, on his first day with us, he nagged about 250 times in a four-hour period—a rate of about one nag per minute. After treatment was started, the rate of nagging decreased to zero within five or six weeks and has remained at that level since then.

For each student, there are three groups of charts—one set for the student's behaviors in the group-management setting, one set for the behaviors he is working on during his one-to-one time, and one set for the behaviors he is working on at home. We have also found it useful to keep a chart that shows the daily total of all of a student's inappropriate behaviors grouped together. Periodically, charts are also kept on the behaviors of our treatment workers. For example, we sometimes chart the rate at which each group manager arranges accelerating and decelerating consequences, opportunities (stimuli), etc. We measure whether any favoritism toward particular children has crept in. If one group manager is managing five or six students in the group-management situation, we sometimes chart the total of all of the inappropriate behaviors shown by all of his students grouped together.

The One-to-One Curriculum

The various group-management situations function like the student's "homeroom." They are where he is normally, and he is taken out of those situations for his one-to-one work. Each student has an individualized teaching and treatment program to be covered during his one-to-one time. For each student there is one one-to-one treatment worker assigned to be a specialist for that student. This specialist contracts, every one or two weeks, with the principal, to achieve certain specified results in the one-to-one work he will do with his student during the next week or two. At the end of that period, there is a review to determine whether the specialist has met his goals. At that time, his performance in reaching his contract goals is rated, and his ratings become part of his professional record at the Institute.

During a student's one-to-one teaching time, the curriculum is devoted, first, to teaching him those behaviors which will help him to function successfully in whatever group-management situation he will start in. Thus, during a student's first days and weeks in school, he learns such skills as doing various tasks, operating the teaching machines and programmed textbooks, doing the task-reward sequence, following the contract system, using the reward room, and so on.

In addition to these skills, each student undergoes a special one-to-one teaching and treatment curriculum designed for autistic persons. The steps in this curriculum are summarized below. The student starts at whatever level is appropriate. The progression is not strictly linear, but the order is more or less as follows.

Good sitting

This means sitting with good posture. The student's feet are on the floor and still, his hands are folded, his head is up and steady, his mouth is closed with no talking, and his eyes are making eye contact with the treatment worker. We arrange accelerating consequences for each of these behaviors as necessary and arrange decelerating consequences for deviations from these behaviors or for any bizarre or otherwise inappropriate behaviors that may occur in the course of the training. It is in this training, as well as in the group-management situations, that the student learns to stop doing most of the bizarre, self-injurious, and otherwise inappropriate behaviors that he had when he started our program.

Our policy is to get rid of all bizarre and inappropriate behaviors as soon as possible, preferably before we start to work seriously on the various academic, social, and self-care deficits the student may have. The good sitting behaviors are like "readiness" behaviors. Once the student accomplishes good sitting, he is more ready to profit from the remaining curriculum of one-to-one instruction. If he has *not yet* learned good sitting, then our treatment workers find themselves having to devote a lot of valuable one-to-one time to behaviors that interfere with the student's receiving and attending to the lesson.

Following simple directions

The student learns to understand and follow simple directions, particularly those relating to movement, such as "Stand up," "Sit down," "Come here," etc.

Non-verbal imitation

The treatment worker says, "Do this," and then points to his own nose, touches his own head, claps his hands, etc. The student's job is to imitate the action precisely. After learning to imitate such actions, the student may be asked to imitate movements of the mouth, teeth, and lips. Once a student is able to imitate such actions well, instruction in a whole variety of curriculum areas, particularly that of making speech sounds correctly, may be facilitated.

Speech and language skills

> (a) Making sounds
> (b) Imitating sounds
> (c) Imitating words
> (d) Imitating phrases and sentences
> (e) Using sentences to ask for and describe things
> (f) Conversation

Other standing and sitting skills

> (a) Good standing (similar to above, but involving standing rather than sitting)
> (b) Good walking
> (c) Casual sitting (sitting in relaxed, casual manner)
> (d) Casual standing (standing in a casual position)

Relaxation

The student learns to systematically tense and then gradually relax various muscle groups in his body.

Covert conditioning

The student imagines himself in certain situations, then imagines himself responding to the situation with certain appropriate or inappropriate behaviors, and then imagines a certain rewarding or aversive situation.

(In teaching our staff how to teach these techniques and in how to teach relaxation, we have consulted with Dr. Joseph Cautela, of Boston College, who has originated many of the covert conditioning techniques.)

Signs

Students who are deaf or who do not progress quickly in learning oral language are taught some signs with which to communicate basic needs and to make basic responses.

Reading, writing, and mathematics

We have developed our own curricula in each of these basic areas, which form the heart of our academic program. The key features of these curricula are:

Behavioral analysis Each curriculum is based on a behavioral analysis of what the minimum component skills are that are required for mastery, what the stimuli are that should cue the behaviors, and what the appropriate order is in which the skills should be mastered.

Discrete skills mastered one at a time Each curriculum is divided into discrete sets of skills, each of which requires only one more behavior than was required in the previous set, and each of which must be mastered before starting to work on the next set in the series. Thus, if the student does poorly on a given set, we know exactly what behavior is lacking in his repertoire and can remedy the situation immediately.

Use of card systems Each set or subsection of the curriculum is made up of a group of cards, each of which contains the stimulus for the behavior on one side and the correct response on the other. The same cards can be used for self-study as well as testing and, because of the flexibility that the use of cards permits, the student need only study those skills he has not yet learned.

Precision teaching Precision teaching methods, including the Standard Behavior Charts, are used to measure progress. The student must achieve a certain individualized rate correct and rate incorrect before it is considered that he has mastered the skill covered by a given set of curriculum cards.

Programmed instruction and teaching machines Once basic reading skills and math facts are learned, programmed instructional materials and teaching machines are used to carry much of the remaining teaching load whenever possible.

Interpersonal skills

We devote considerable attention to teaching our students to be warm, to be able to hug and kiss, to express thanks, to be friendly, and to smile. At one time, for example, we noticed that Billy, one of our students, did not smile much. We began prompting him to laugh and smile by tickling him. Then we taught him how to tickle himself, in order to get himself to laugh and smile. Now he can smile pretty well by himself without special help.

Self-management

We teach as many of our students as possible how to pinpoint behaviors, how to record behaviors on a wrist-type golf counter or in a notebook, how to chart their frequencies on a graph to determine whether the behaviors are changing as desired and how to try different techniques—such as new stimuli, and accelerating and decelerating consequences—in order to get the behaviors to change. (Here, too, we are indebted to Dr. Ogden Lindsley for his work and inspiration in this area.) In this way we try to transfer as much of the control of a student's behavior as possible to the student himself, and thus try to teach him the age-old goals of self-control and self-management.

Other curriculum areas

(a) Using and understanding money
(b) Telling time, setting timers, etc.
(c) Self-care skills—washing, brushing teeth, dressing, making bed, shopping, cooking, cleaning up, etc.
(d) Eating skills—eating various foods, eating nutritious foods, good table manners
(e) Social skills—greetings, introductions, conversations, dancing
(f) Classroom skills—listening and paying attention to a teacher who is addressing a classroom of students at the same time
(g) Typing
(h) Behavioral psychology
(i) Sex education
(j) Athletic skills
(k) Functioning in public areas, such as restaurants.

Casual Consequences

In addition to the accelerating and decelerating consequences delivered to students during the group-management and one-to-one situations, we also try to maximize the consequences arranged throughout the day when he is in other situations—for example, in the hallway, in the bathroom, on his way out of the school, etc. We sometimes refer to these as "casual consequences."

To make it easier for all members of our staff to arrange appropriate casual consequences, we require each student in our school to wear a name tag that lists a few behaviors he is trying to increase or decrease. This immediately gives any member of our staff who may interact with the student—including the secretaries, the bookkeeper, and the maintenance man—a few behaviors that he can reinforce the student for when he encounters him. To encourage this even more, we have experimented with distributing an envelope of tokens to every member of our staff each morning, with the rule that he must give out those tokens to the students as casual rewards during the day for behaviors designated on their tags.

This rule concerning name tags has been applied to our staff as well. Each is required to wear a tag identifying behaviors he is working on. This makes it easier for staff members to reinforce each other and even for students to reinforce the staff.

The parallel treatment of staff and students regarding name tags raises an important point. In selecting our staff members, we particularly look for individuals who are interested in and committed to the application of behavioral techniques to their own lives as well as to the treatment of the children. We have found that such persons make excellent treatment workers, are good models for the students, treat their job as more than a 9 A.M.-5 P.M. activity, and stay with us for longer periods of time.

Parent Training

Parent training is an important part of our program. Our staff works a thirty-seven-and-a-half hour week in our school. The remaining two and a half hours of each treatment worker's time is available for parent training assignments in which we send the treatment worker into the home to teach the parents how to apply behavioral procedures.

One approach to parent training that we have tried is to set out a range of options for the parents as to the degree of training that they may wish. Some parents may simply sign up for once-a-month group meetings. Some may want regular in-home visits by a treatment worker as well. Some may also want to learn self-management skills. Some may want to learn the full range of group-management and one-to-one skills that we impart to our staff.

Whatever the training option a parent selects, he is asked to sign a contract in which he makes a money deposit—$25.00 in some cases. He then earns back the deposit by showing certain agreed-upon behaviors. In some cases, this may mean just coming to meetings. In other cases it may mean setting up and maintaining certain specific procedures in the home. In other cases it means all of that plus charting behaviors, arranging stimuli and consequences, changing consequences according to what the charts show, and doing one-to-one work. In cases where we ask a parent to make a deposit which is then earned back by his showing specified behaviors, we also ask that our own staff members do likewise.

A minimal goal that we set for each home is that the parents arrange for each student to have a homework period after supper in which the student does a special task-reward sequence or contract system specifically designed for the home. During this period the student continues his academic learning by working on his teaching machines and programmed instruction textbooks. We ask that each parent provide a teaching machine and other self-instructional materials for his child in the home. Included also in the task-reward sequence or contract system can be various chores to help out around the house.

A major problem in parent training is motivating the parents. The procedure described simply accepts the level of motivation that the parent may have and offers him appropriate training. An alternative approach that we are considering is to make the student's opportunity to attend the Saturday program depend on whether the parents have earned a sufficient number of points in their parent training program. In this design, the treatment worker who goes into the home on a regular basis would work out with the parents things they would undertake to do during the coming week. If they did those things, they would earn points, and with a sufficient number of points, their child could attend the next Saturday session.

In training parents, just as in training our own staff, we find that introducing parents to the techniques of self-management is most helpful. All of our staff members are expected to set up and maintain various self-management projects. The parents and staff who have tried self-management have successfully lost weight, stopped smoking, and improved their interpersonal behaviors. Such successes greatly strengthen and enhance a favorable attitude toward behavior modification.

Residential Program

The residential program associated with our Providence school is operated in a normal, six-bedroom house in a semirural suburb of Providence called Seekonk, Massachusetts. Currently, four children live in the house and attend our day program. Each evening and on Sunday, two treatment workers are assigned to do treatment work with the children. A treatment worker is also assigned overnight, both to care for the children and to carry out various programs designed to eliminate bed-wetting, etc. The house also serves as a place of residence for one member of our staff.

The treatment work that goes on in the house during evenings and Sundays focuses on self-care and independent-living skills and on the productive use of the student's spare time. Each student's program is designed by the principal of our day school, who works one night a week at the residence. The staff is trained in our day school to begin with and then moved to the residence program when their skills are adequate. Our director of training provides further in-service and on-the-job training to the staff at the residence on a weekly basis.

When a student becomes sufficiently trained, he may graduate from the treatment residence and move into a less intense, more normalized living experience. For example, one of our students, Billy, was able to move out of an intensive residential program after two years. He now shares an apartment with one of the members of our staff and pays his own way.

Work Training

We have a number of students in their middle and late teens and have instituted several types of work training for them. Many of the students have been given maintenance, clerical, and even group-management responsibilities in the school. As a result of such training, one student has graduated from the status of student to that of staff member; he is employed as an assistant maintenance man.

We have made arrangements with several sheltered workshops to which we have been permitted to send in one or two of our students accompanied by one of our treatment workers. Eventually, when the students are able to work on their own, the treatment worker "fades" himself out of the picture by being present for shorter and shorter periods each day until the students are completely independent.

On Saturday, our head maintenance man takes a crew of four to six students and teaches them how to do maintenance work and how to do lawn and garden care. We plan to get some actual jobs for this work crew, both in the maintenance and lawn-care industries. We believe that this concept of a work-crew of autistic persons that is guided and accompanied by a normal treatment person is a valuable concept for developing job opportunities.

Community Reintegration

The goal of any treatment center should be to graduate students, whenever possible, into more normal avenues of education, work and residence. We call this "community reintegration." We have been able to accomplish this, either partially or wholly, in the case of several of our students. A few of these cases are described below.

Billy, age twenty-one, was our first student. He started with us at the age of eighteen, having been excluded from the private schools that

Massachusetts had sent him to, having become impossible to live with at home, and having been eventually placed in a state mental hospital. Today he has a full-time job in our school as an assistant maintenance man and is financially independent of his family. (His case history is told in detail in the last section of this chapter.)

Bertha had inappropriate behaviors from her earliest years. At the age of eleven she began to scream. This caused her to be excluded from public school and to have to live at home. The school sent a private teacher to her home.

Bertha began treatment with us in 1972 at the age of thirteen. On her first few days she screamed hundreds of times per day, she murmured constantly, her speech was so unclear it was hard to understand, and she occasionally slapped her own face and struck other people and objects.

She began her treatment on the third or fourth day in the program. She recorded each scream on a wrist-type golf counter and made contracts with her treatment worker to go without screaming for periods of time that gradually increased in length. Within a few days she was able to stop all screaming, and she has not screamed since then. Then she went to work in the same way to stop her urges to scream and her murmuring. She succeeded within a few weeks.

In the fall of that year (1972), which was only a few months after starting treatment, she started to attend one class of regular public high school. Gradually she increased the number of classes she took until, in the spring of 1974, she was able to handle a full day of school. Today she is only a part-time student in our school, attending for only the last few hours of the day after attending high school.

Wayne, age nineteen, scored in the upper 700s on his college entrance exams, but his autistic behaviors prevented him from attending college. As a result of his participation in our program, he is now attending Rhode Island College as a full-time student and is majoring in biology. He, too, is now only a part-time student in our school.

Frank, age sixteen, had been living at home before he started our program due to his various autistic behaviors. He has now progressed to a point where he is taking several classes in vocational education each day at his local public high school. He attends our school as a part-time student for the remainder of the school day.

Our work with older students such as these proves that parents need not give up hope when their child reaches his teens. Behavior modification procedures appear to work at any age when they are applied properly and consistently by well-trained persons.

To help persons appreciate the full impact of the progress our students have made, we have prepared video tapes and films that show these case histories and the techniques and curriculum we use. (Interested persons should write to the author for information concerning the possibility of renting or borrowing these films and video tapes.)*

A PROPOSAL FOR THE FUTURE OF AUTISTIC CHILDREN

The Problem

In recent years it has become clear that a consistent, well-executed behavior modification treatment and educational program can help autistic children to make remarkable gains. They can be taught to eliminate most of their bizarre and disruptive behaviors, and to acquire useful speech, academic, self-care, and social behaviors.

However, the very success of these techniques raises further, bothersome questions. What will happen when these children grow older? Will they still have to be institutionalized when their school-age years are over? Having spent a considerable amount of money to educate the autistic child, will society allow that investment to be wasted by failing to insure that the child be able to live and work in the society-at-large rather than vegetate in institutions or at home?

To a director of a school for autistic children, these questions must be a particular personal concern. Am I wasting my time and energies in educating the autistic child? Will there be a productive future available to these children?

To these questions, society might reply, "We'd like to help. We think all children are entitled to an education. But is it realistic to think that autistic children can ever live and work on their own? Are there any such children who have been able to do so—even when appropriate education and training has been made available?"

The Case of Billy

When we started our school for autistic children at Behavior Research Institute, the only students were we able to get, at first, where those that other, more established schools had discarded. They were discarded either because the students were too old or because they were too bizarre and disruptive.

So it was that we met Billy, a seventeen-year-old autistic boy. Billy had been autistic since birth and had attended a number of private schools with

---

*See page 271

Table II.
Total Time Observed: 14½ hours

How Bill Spent his Time	
Rocking	34% of his time
Aimless sitting and wandering	37%
Investigation of surroundings	13%
Flittering with objects	5%
Eating	7%
Math	4%
	100%

Episodes of Certain Behaviors in One Day	
Fingers in ear	327 times
Pinching self	170
Screeching	262
Echolalia	137
Mumbling	1,816
Demands	92
Shirt to nose	72
Yelling/tantrums	6

the aid of funds from the state of Massachusetts. He had learned some reading and writing at one of these schools, but as he grew older, it had become increasingly difficult to teach him anything in school, to take him out in public, or to manage him at home. As a result, his parents were forced to place him, at the age of sixteen, in the Foxboro, Massachusetts, State Mental Hospital. There he was eventually placed in a locked ward that had no one his own age; there was no program for him. He spent most of his time rocking, mumbling, screeching, and doing nothing. At that point, he had no future prospects except to spend the rest of his life in Foxboro State Hospital, rocking back and forth, and showing his other bizarre and inappropriate behaviors.

In January of 1972, we took Billy, then seventeen, out of Foxboro State Hospital and placed him in the comprehensive day and residential program of behavioral treatment described in the first part of this chapter. The first thing we did was to measure his various bizarre and inappropriate behaviors so that we could document the changes we expected to make. Table II shows a record of how he spent his time and of how often he showed various bizarre behaviors. We also made various films and tape recordings of Billy's behaviors at that time. From the data recorded in Table II and from our various audio visual recordings, we could easily see that Billy was an autistic young man.

The next thing we did was to teach him to stop showing the bizarre and disruptive behaviors listed in Table II and to be able to sit appropriately at a table and do productive, educational work. He learned these things quickly, and after Billy's first three months in the program, we were able to move him into a sheltered workshop for the retarded in Cranston, Rhode Island.

At first, Billy received close supervision and assistance from a treatment worker from our school who went to the workshop with him. Later, the treatment worker began to remove himself slowly from the picture as Billy became able to work more and more on his own. By the spring of 1974 (two years into treatment), Billy could work for a full day, entirely on his own, at a sheltered workshop. At this point, he tried out for a regular factory job in competitive employment and proved he could do the work at competitive speed and accuracy. In November of 1974, a job opening was offered him at the factory where he had done the trial day work. However, by that time, we had come to think so highly of his work that we hired him as a full-time assistant maintenance worker at our school.

While Billy was learning to work, he also was learning to improve his speech. When he started in our program, his only means of communication had been to shout out one-word guttural demands. As a result of treatment, he has learned to speak in sentences, look at the other person as he does so, carry on small conversations, use a pleasant tone of voice, and make his needs known through appropriate speech. Billy has also learned to take care of himself. He can now prepare his own meals, wash the dishes, do some of the housekeeping chores, make his bed, mow the lawn, cross streets safely, etc.—all of which he was unable to do three years ago. Billy now shares an apartment with one of our staff members. That staff member can now drop Billy off at home after work and leave him alone for the evening. He will make his own meal, do a few chores, relax and listen to music, take a shower, and go to bed—all by himself.

In short, Billy today is a very different person—with bright prospects—compared to what he was three years ago. He can work at a job, earn a living wage, and live in a dignified and satisfying way in a near-independent status in a normal residence in the community. That is not to say Billy is "cured" of autism. He still has numerous handicaps that are quite evident if you spend some time with him. His conversation is limited and unsure. He still swings his arms in a slightly odd way when he walks. And he is unsophisticated in a great many nuances of living, dressing, behaving, etc.

Indeed, I think it is fair to predict that, although Billy will continue to make progress throughout his life in all of these behaviors, he will always have certain autistic-type behavior deficits. And I think it true, therefore, that Billy will always need a little bit of assistance from others. Nonetheless, the important thing is that the behavior deficits that Billy has today are no longer so gross as to foreclose the possibility of a normal, non-institutionalized life. In fact, the deficits are now quite small and get smaller each day with continued training. As a result, Billy's need for continuing assistance is also small and gets smaller all the time.

The Assistance that Billy Needs

Now let us look at the continuing assistance which Billy and other autistic persons like him will probably always need. There are a few important things to note about it.

First, the assistance should be "behaviorally informed"—it should be given by persons who understand and use the principles of behavior modification in responding to him. If he continues to receive this type of assistance, he can hold onto the gains he has made so far and can progress even further. Without, he may regress in some respects and fall back into older, inappropriate habits.

Second, as noted earlier, the assistance that Billy needs gets smaller and smaller as he learns more and more skills. Indeed, he is rapidly becoming more and more of a positive help to others, rather than simply being a person to be helped.

Third, the assistance that Billy requires now is so small that he is able to pay for it, as well as for his room, board, clothes, etc., out of the money he earns from his job.

The fourth point is perhaps most important. Billy is now such a pleasant, interesting individual that everyone seems to *like* to help him. The staff members of our school, and even their friends and spouses, are always asking me if they can take Billy home with them for an evening, an overnight, or a weekend. There is something about being with, teaching, and helping an individual like Billy that is very enjoyable and satisfying. This was not always the case. When we first began working with Billy, one treatment worker refused to even eat at the same table with him because it was such an exhausting, frightening, and messy experience.

Some Economic Points

Billy's story has some interesting economic implications. If Billy had continued to live in the Foxboro, Massachusetts State Hospital, he would have cost the State of Massachusetts somewhere between $500,000 and $1,000,000. This assumes that he would live for another fifty years and that the cost of a bed in a state mental hospital is between $10,000 and $20,000 per year. Instead of being an enormous drain on the taxpayer for the rest of his life, Billy is now self-sustaining.

Is Billy a Special Case?

Is Billy a special case? Can other autistic students make similar progress? We think so, because we have produced comparable changes in other students, some of whom were worse than Billy in the behaviors they presented when we first began their treatment.

If other autistic children can make progress comparable to Billy's, what kind of program is required? How many years of training will be necessary? How many of these should be in an intensive day program? How many in a residential program? What should the package of services look like?

Deficits of Autistic Children and Their Remedies

In order to answer these questions, let us first consider what the major deficits of an autistic person are. Then we can make some estimates concerning the time required to remedy each.

It may be useful to divide the deficits of an autistic person into the following three areas:

(1) *Has miscellaneous bizarre and inappropriate behaviors.* Also lacks self-care, independent living, and work skills. With two years of intensive day and residential treatment, most autistic students can be taught to at least work successfully in a sheltered or competitive work situation, to live at least in a group home or apartment that is given supervision, and to get rid of his major bizarre and inappropriate behaviors.

(2) *Lacks the ability to communicate effectively with others.* To remedy this, as for example, by teaching a repertoire of signs, would require two additional years of intensive day treatment.

(3) *Lacks basic reading and writing skills.* This, too, would require two additional years of intensive day treatment.

Table III summarizes these points and presents additional details concerning the deficits and corresponding appropriate treatment.

Table III suggests that a minimal period of treatment would be two years in an intensive residential program. This would enable the average autistic student to avoid institutionalization, to work at least in a sheltered workshop, and to live in some kind of community-based group residence that is provided with some supportive services. (This was the case with Billy, the student described earlier. He had the set of deficits which are termed Type 1 deficits in Table III.) Ideally, these two years of intensive treatment would be given between the ages of fourteen and sixteen, so that the student could be graduated into a sheltered or non-sheltered job at the age of sixteen.

Table III. Major Deficits of Autistic Children,
and Curricula and Time Required to Remedy Them

Type	Behavior Deficits	Curriculum Needed	Estimated Time Required to Remedy the Deficits
1	Miscellaneous Autistic Behavior Deficits (a) Has some speech (e.g., can imitate words and sentences) but needs improvement. (b) Does not follow simple directions. (c) Has bizarre and inappropriate behavior. (d) Cannot work efficiently at a task for long periods of time. (e) Needs various self-care and independent living skills. (f) Cannot follow simple token reward and fine system. (g) Does not understand money. (h) Cannot tell time. (i) Needs social skills. (j) Needs sex education. (k) Needs a job and specific training for that job.	Needs a general curriculum for the treatment and education of autistic children.	Two years of a complete residential program would enable student to at least work in a sheltered workshop and live in community-based group home.
2	Speech Deficit Cannot speak. Cannot make any sounds; or can make only a few sounds.	Needs to learn a system for communicating basic requests – through speech, by signing, by pointing to pictures, or writing.	Additional two years of an intensive day program
3	Literacy Deficit Cannot read, write, or do simple mathematics.	Needs to learn to read at a level that permits reading signs, work assignments, labels, recipes, schedules, etc. Needs writing to a level that permits writing name, writing up own work "contracts," etc. Needs simple mathematics to a level that permits using money, making purchases, telling time, etc.	Additional two years of an intensive day program.

If, in addition to the Type 1 deficits, the student also has no speech (Type 2), another two years of treatment would be desirable, but these could be day-treatment services. This would be in addition to the two years of residential treatment mentioned above. Such a student might be in a day program from twelve to fourteen, and in a residential program from fourteen to sixteen.

If a student also cannot read or write (Type 3), another two years of day treatment would be desirable. For this student, then, a total of six years would be desirable, of which two would be full residential treatment and four would be day treatment. This student could be in a day program from age ten to fourteen and in a residential program from fourteen to sixteen.

If this program is implemented, most autistic persons could be helped to live a near-independent and normalized existence. The phrase "near-independent" is used advisedly. Like Billy, most autistic adults are likely to need a certain amount of continuing help from their environment. The continuing assistance that is needed will include the following items.

(1) There should be a system of residence opportunities with varied levels of independence possible so that the autistic person can move toward increasingly independent living if he wishes to.

(2) Sheltered workshops should be available that will accept autistic persons and use behavior modification techniques.

(3) Competitive, nonsheltered jobs should be available.

(4) Social opportunities should be available to enable autistic persons to meet persons of the opposite sex and to enjoy a social life.

(5) Recreation opportunities should be available with appropriate supervision.

In summary, the total set of services that an autistic person needs can be viewed as having three parts: a day school in the early years; a residential program in the middle teens; and, a program of continued assistance in the late teens and adult years. These three components of the total program that are needed are shown in Table IV.

COORDINATION OF CHILD, ADOLESCENT, AND ADULT PROGRAMS IN A THERAPEUTIC SYSTEM

It would be helpful if the various components—child, adolescent training, and adult programs—were well coordinated. For example, it would obviously be desirable if the directors of adolescent programs know what type of residence and work opportunities would be available to the autistic adult, for then the adolescent program could be geared to train the individual for those opportunities. The same is true in the relationship of the day program that the child might be in during his younger years and the residential program he might be in during his middle teens.

Table IV. Three Phases of Proposed Program

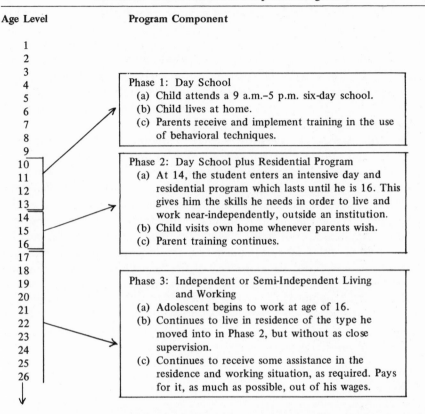

Age Level	Program Component
1	
2	
3	
4	Phase 1: Day School
5	(a) Child attends a 9 a.m.–5 p.m. six-day school.
6	(b) Child lives at home.
7	(c) Parents receive and implement training in the use
8	of behavioral techniques.
9	
10	Phase 2: Day School plus Residential Program
11	(a) At 14, the student enters an intensive day and
12	residential program which lasts until he is 16. This
13	gives him the skills he needs in order to live and
14	work near-independently, outside an institution.
15	(b) Child visits own home whenever parents wish.
16	(c) Parent training continues.
17	
18	
19	Phase 3: Independent or Semi-Independent Living
20	and Working
21	(a) Adolescent begins to work at age of 16.
22	(b) Continues to live in residence of the type he
23	moved into in Phase 2, but without as close
24	supervision.
25	(c) Continues to receive some assistance in the
26	residence and working situation, as required. Pays
	for it, as much as possible, out of his wages.

Behavior Research Institute has as one of its objectives the establishment of just such a set of integrated and coordinated services for autistic persons. The overall goal of this system would be to help autistic individuals to avoid institutionalization and to lead dignified and meaningful lives.

We envisage the possibility of creating a kind of therapeutic community, which might contain education, work, and residence components. It might even be made attractive enough so that some of the staff members themselves would choose to live in such a community on an integrated basis with the autistic persons.

It is important that such a community not be designed as an isolated, self-contained facility. Rather it should be open, normalized, and closely integrated with the community-at-large. For many of the autistic persons it would serve merely as their home base, or place of residence, from which they would go out each day to places of work, education, and recreation in the community-at-large.

For reasons stated earlier in our account of Billy's progress, it is crucially important that the proposed environment make a consistent and comprehensive use of behavior modification. This is needed if the autistic adults are to hold onto, and to continue to add to, their repertoire of appropriate behaviors. One of the goals of Behavior Research Institute is the creation of a set of behavioral systems and services to help normal persons reach their maximal potential. Since the autistic adult also needs a set of behavioral systems and services to assist him, we are considering the possibility of interrelating these two goals.

In other words, the persons needed to operate various educational, treatment, and adult-support services could be drawn largely from those who wish to create behavioral systems and services for their own lives. There could be certain advantages in doing this. Many of the same behavioral systems could serve both the non-autistic staff as well as the autistic persons, and this might result in certain savings and efficiencies.

More important, however, those providing services to the autistic adults would be excellent role models and would be personally committed to the maintenance and development of the behavioral services that the autistic persons most need. This would help assure the maintenance of appropriate therapeutic care for the autistic persons on a long-term basis and would help to prevent the system of care from degenerating into an uncaring and uninvolved custodial service of the type we see so often in our public institutions for the retarded and mentally ill.

SUMMARY

Over the past ten years, powerful behavioral education and treatment methods have been developed to help autistic children eliminate their bizarre and self-injurious behaviors, improve their speech, learn to care for themselves, and live semi-independently. One such education and treatment system is currently operated by Behavior Research Institute, with both day school and residential components.

The success of such efforts raises the question, "What is to be done when autistic children become adults?" It is clear that in order to maintain the gains they have made in intensive treatment programs such as the Institute's, there will need to be some system of continued behavioral support for most autistic adults, if they are to avoid having to live in institutions or in their parents' home during their adult years.

It is proposed in this chapter, that the typical autistic person needs a therapeutic system with three parts: a day school program when he is young; two years of a full residential program when he is in his mid-teens; and, a continued-support system during his adult years. Each of these parts should make comprehensive use of behavior modification. Behavior Research Institute hopes to develop such an integrated set of services.

One possibility for autistic adults might be an open, non-isolated therapeutic community in which autistic adults might live and from which they might go out daily to places of work or recreation. If such a community were properly developed, some of the staff that provides education and supporting services might be attracted to live in an integrated fashion with the autistic persons. It would be desirable that such a staff be personally committed to the use of behavioral procedures if the quality of care is to be maintained on a long-term basis.

REFERENCES

Lindsley, O. *Direct measurement and prosthesis of regarded behavior.* (Rev. ed.) University of Oregon Curriculum Bulletin, 1969, 25.
Lindsley, O. Experimental analysis of social reinforcement: Terms and methods. *American Journal of Orthopsychiatry*, 1963, 33:624-633.

For information write to:

MATTHEW L. ISRAEL, Ph.D.
Director
Behavior Research Institute, Inc.
240 Laban Street
Providence, Rhode Island 02909

CHAPTER SEVENTEEN

Primary Responsibility: With Whom Should it Rest?

EDWARD R. RITVO

THE PROBLEM

Several recent books by parents of autistic children eloquently indict medical and educational professionals. These biographies portray in heart-rending terms the systematic neglect these parents meet when attempting to obtain proper diagnostic and remedial help for their children. I for one feel these indictments should stand and if brought to trial, we would be found guilty on many grounds.

I have personally witnessed how individual physicians, psychologists, and special educators have mismanaged autistic persons and their families. Some of the reasons for this are as follows:

(1) *Ignorance of the condition*—It is easy to stop learning. One cannot diagnose nor properly treat conditions one cannot recognize. Much of what is now known about autism has been learned over the past decade and many professionals simply do not keep abreast of the current research.

(2) *Systematic avoidance of autistic patients*—"OK, your child is autistic but there is nothing which can be done about it, so good-bye and good luck." This is the "love 'em, bill 'em, and leave 'em" approach to management. Obviously there is no place in our professions for these attitudes.

(3) *Inappropriate recommendations*—"Crazy kid equals crazy parents—Rx: psychotherapy for mother, psychotherapy for father, psychotherapy for child"—or "obviously your child has brain damage so we must quiet him

down with some drugs and when you get tired of putting up with his behavior at home, warehouse him in an institution, but don't come back here with your problem."

Local, state and Federal agencies have played musical chairs with families and autistic persons in these ways:

(1) *Pediatric Clinics*—"Your child is just a little slow developing but if you wait, everything will be all right." "Oh! That's what we said last year when he wasn't speaking and he's three years old? Well, I guess he's retarded so go down the hall, turn left and knock on the door labeled B."

(2) *Mental Retardation Clinic*—"Your child is not testable on our tests so we can't tell how retarded he is but he obviously has some problem with his brain function, so you should go down the hall, turn left and knock on the door labeled C."

(3) *Pediatric Neurology Clinic*—"Our test doesn't show anything except a few funny wiggles on the EEG, so it's *obvious* that your child *probably* has no specific form of brain disease which we can diagnose. Therefore, we suggest you go down the hall, turn left and enter door D."

(4) *Psychiatric Clinic*—"Well, your child is too sick to be tested for emotional problems but has some form of retardation and brain damage as indicated by these wiggles on the EEG report. Since there's nothing we can do for him we suggest you go down the hall, turn left and enter door E."

(5) *Special Education Clinic*—"Your child is obviously too sick to fit into our school programs so we suggest you go down the hall and enter door A where the doctor will diagnose and treat him. When and if he gets better, then come back to school."

Unfortunately, no amount of laughter at this not too hypothetical scenario can assuage the suffering nor give back the lost hours to parents who have been shuffled around this professional merry-go-round.

THE SOLUTION

Each autistic person and his family must have a primary physician who is responsible for establishing the diagnosis and maintaining long-term-overall management. He must be knowledgeable about all the medical ramifications of the disease and abreast of the "current state of the art" with respect to new therapies and management techniques. He is the first line of emotional support. He must also be able to function as the captain of a multidisciplinary therapeutic team. Periodic medical re-evaluations are essential as we now know that seizures or other evidence of central nervous system dysfunction may appear in autistic children as they grow older. Other periodic re-evaluations are also necessary to reassess such factors as educational placement and social development.

A qualified child psychiatrist (Diplomate of the American Board of Psychiatry and Neurology with specialty training in psychiatry and child psychiatry) is usually best trained to fulfill these functions. Some pediatricians, pediatric neurologists, and family practitioners are also qualified to fulfill this role for autistic children and their families. The individual doctor's interest, dedication, and overall attitude are much more important than his professional label.

I am often asked by parents how they can locate qualified child psychiatrists, pediatric specialists or appropriate clinics in their communities. The answer, of course, depends upon the nature of their community. If there is a medical school available, a call to the chairman of the department of psychiatry will usually produce a list of faculty members and qualified people. Each county has a local medical society from which similar information can be obtained. A third source of referral would be the American Academy of Child Psychiatry at 1800 R Street, N.W., Suite 904, Washington, D.C. 20009. Finally, the National Society for Autistic Children's Information Service should be mentioned. Their current Director, Mrs. Ruth Sullivan, will provide the specific address for this service in chapter twenty. Dr. and Mrs. Lapin also point out in their chapter (See Chapter Nineteen) that several local branches of the National Society have referral services with detailed knowledge of local facilities.

CHAPTER EIGHTEEN

Parents As Paraprofessionals

B.J. FREEMAN
EDWARD R. RITVO

Training parents of autistic patients to administer behavior therapy at home has recently emerged as a major approach to management. One could say that parent training is the "Zeitgeist" of the times. Looking toward the future, we predict that it will become increasingly widespread. The traditional model of parents bringing their child for treatment is giving way to the more practical model in which parents are trained, as paraprofessionals, to administer treatment to their autistic child at home. This chapter will introduce behavior therapy to parents. We shall begin with a brief overview of the theory of behavior therapy and then explain certain terms which describe its techniques. Next, we shall discuss specific ways in which parents have been trained within the paraprofessional model to treat their children at UCLA as well as elsewhere. In conclusion, we shall present some examples of specific behavior therapy programs which parents of our patients have learned to administer successfully at home.

BACKGROUND

The theoretical foundations of behaviorism were established by several famous psychologists, namely Thorndike, Watson and Skinner. Their students used these theories to develop practical ways of defining behavior, its antecedents, and its consequences, and to develop methods of modifying behavior. These methods are called "behavior therapy." One type which is particularly applicable to autistic patients is operant therapy.

In 1961, Ferster published a now classical report in which he demonstrated that behavior therapy could be applied to autistic patients. Many others (e.g., Lovaas, 1967; Risley and Wolf, 1967) have since confirmed his observations and refined treatment techniques. Research in this area has now demonstrated conclusively that specific behaviors in autistic patients can be predictably modified by manipulating their consequences. This is the hallmark of operant conditioning therapy.

PRINCIPLES OF OPERANT THERAPY

A first principle of operant therapy is that *the future strength of a specific behavior is influenced by its consequences.* Consequences are the *immediate* conditions which exist after the occurrence of a behavior. They may lead to one of three results; they can strengthen, weaken, or have no effect on the initiating behavior. Initiating behavior is strengthened if it is immediately and consistently followed by reinforcement. Reinforcement is defined as anything which causes behavior to be strengthened and can be either of the positive type or of the negative type. An example of positive reinforcement is giving a patient something he likes, while an example of negative reinforcement is taking the patient away from a situation which he does not like. In both instances, the patient will be more likely to repeat the behavior which was followed by the reinforcement.

Anything a child likes—including the presence of his therapist—can serve as a potential positive reinforcer. Positive reinforcement is the type most often used to teach autistic patients new behaviors. Simply stated, it involves giving the child a "goodie" for performing a behavior defined as desirable by the therapist. After many presentations of the reinforcer, the behavior will be strengthened. Those of us who practice behavior therapy are often ridiculed about the ubiquitous "M and M." However, we also use many other positive reinforcers.

Punishment, or the presentation of aversive stimuli, was at one time extensively studied as a possible means for eliminating undesirable behaviors. Research proved, however, that it had many bad side effects. Recently, as operant technology has become more sophisticated, other methods to eliminate undesirable behaviors have proven more effective than punishment. For example, if one assumes that many things in an environment are reinforcing to a child, then removing him from this environment may weaken or diminish the frequency of a given behavior. Techniques based on this assumption are called "Time out from positive reinforcement." They involve taking the child away from all reinforcers and would be the equivalent of making the child "stand in the corner," in the usual household setting.

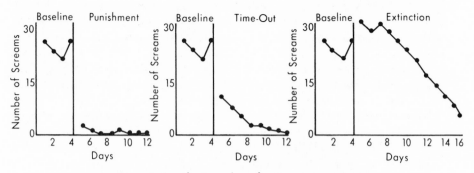

Figure 1   Specific Procedures for Decreasing Behavior

Another treatment procedure used to reduce the frequency of a behavior is called "extinction." This technique requires taking away a positive reinforcer for a specific behavior. It is used with autistic children most often when analysis of the child's behavior reveals that it is being reinforced unwittingly by an adult's attention. When an extinction procedure is used, it involves ignoring the behavior.

To illustrate these points further let us take the example of a behavior commonly exhibited by autistic children, namely screaming, and show how these three techniques are used. First, one could actively punish, using slapping as the punishment. An idealized graph of response is pictured in Figure 1. On the left of this figure is the frequency of screaming when no intervention is made. This is labeled the *base line condition*. When screaming is punished by slapping, it decreases quickly. The screaming would be expected to increase again to the base line levels if the slapping was discontinued. Essentially, the same thing happens when *time out* is used. However, it is a slower process. It can be made more effective if positive reinforcement for good behavior (not screaming in this example) follows the time out. *Extinction* of the behavior involves ignoring the child while he is screaming and paying attention to him only when he is quiet. An extinction procedure usually first produces an increase in screaming, prior to the decrease. The extinction procedure, though the slowest of the three, has proven to be very effective with many types of behaviors in autistic children. This is due to the fact that many of their behaviors are unwittingly maintained by adult attention.

A RATIONALE FOR TRAINING PARENTS

A common and often justified criticism of behavior therapy is that beneficial effects may not continue from one part of a child's life to the next.

In more technical terms, therapeutic changes may not *generalize*. This has raised many questions regarding the clinical application of operant therapy and gave initial impetus to training parents as paraprofessionals. For example, if an autistic child is involved in a school program which uses operant techniques, would it not be better if the same techniques were applied to his behavior at home? The obvious answer to this question is "yes." This is the basic justification for training parents in the application of behavior therapy techniques. Furthermore, since parents spend the most time with their children, they are in the best position to train them (Hawkins, 1972). In addition, the trained parent will be able to maintain a difficult-to-manage child at home for a longer period of time. Another factor which has given impetus to training parents is logistics. There are a vastly greater number of autistic children in need of treatment (Lindsley, 1966) than there are professional therapists. Training parents to work with their child in his natural environment provides a source of potential therapists as great as the number of patients.

In 1974, O'Dell summarized the general advantages of teaching parents behavior therapy. His list of advantages, while not specifically aimed at parents of autistic patients, is readily suited to this group and is summarized as follows:

1. Parents can easily learn operant principles and carry out treatment programs at home.

2. Behavior therapy is based upon easily-observed phenomena and thus is readily acceptable to parent-trainees.

3. Many parents can be taught simultaneously.

4. Relatively short training periods are required.

5. Professional staff have more treatment impact by training parents than by working in one-to-one treatment sessions.

6. Parents more readily accept treatment models which do not imply parental pathology.

7. Many autistics have well-defined behaviors which respond to behavior therapy.

8. Successful behavior therapy increases the chances of an autistic child remaining at home.

While some of these advantages are self-evident, others are based on research. The most important such evidence has demonstrated that parents can successfully carry out behavior therapy with their own children. Despite this, some misgivings have been expressed in this regard (Hawkins, 1972). We are not concerned as to the possibility of the misuse of behavioral techniques by trained parents. Our philosophy has been summarized by Hawkins (1972) as follows: "It is not a matter of whether parents will use behavior modification techniques to manipulate their children or not, but rather whether they will use these techniques unconsciously with an unknown, unchosen, and unhappy result, or use them consciously, efficiently, and consistently to develop the qualities they choose for their children."

For those who may still have reservations concerning the ethical implications of training parents in the paraprofessional model, let us construct an analogy to children with diabetes. While medical science has not delineated the exact cause of diabetes, and no specific cure exists, there are symptomatic treatments such as the injection of insulin. Similarly, autism is a disease of the central nervous system, the exact cause of which is still unknown, and for which we do not have a specific cure. However, as in diabetes, we have symptomatic treatment, such as behavior therapy. Routinely, the parents of childhood diabetics are trained as paraprofessionals to give insulin, under the supervision of a physician. Similarly, parents of autistic children can be trained as paraprofessionals to administer behavior therapy to their child under the direction of a trained behavior therapist.

METHODS FOR TRAINING PARENTS

Several methods have been developed to teach parents. Two review articles recently appeared which summarize research since 1968 (Goodall, 1972; O'Dell, 1974). The techniques involved have been of three primary types. First is the didactic or lecture type. Second is a modeling approach in which the teacher demonstrates specific techniques for the parents to imitate. In the third approach, the trainers direct the parents using feedback to instruct them while they are working with their child. The radio receiving device commonly referred to as the "bug in the ear" is used by the trainer who observes the parents via a one-way mirror. We are unaware of any studies undertaken to demonstrate that one of these techniques is superior to the other. However, in our clinical experience, we have observed that success depends not only on the technique used, but to a great degree on the enthusiasm and persistence of the trainer. It has also been necessary that the trainers give parents continuing positive reinforcement. Follow-up work must be conducted in each case so that behavior therapy techniques can be modified when the child progresses and his needs change.

To improve the quality of parent training, we must develop studies which include the following:
1. Careful assessment of demographic and personality characteristics of parents;
2. Precise medical and behavioral descriptions of each patient;
3. Precise description of the parents' role in their child's training;
4. Precise description of the trainer's role in relation to the parents' description of the specific behavioral technologies employed;
5. Precise description of the experimental designs employed with

delineations made between base line, experimental, and follow-up stages;
6. Information on the cost of programs in order to allow comparisons of efficiency (O'Dell, 1974).

In summary, we wish to stress that: (1) parents of autistic patients can and should be trained in the paraprofessional model in order to extend treatment for their child into his home setting, and (2) systematic research is needed to identify those variables which will increase the success of parents working with their children.

BEHAVIORAL ANALYSIS

Next, we shall illustrate how behavioral analyses are used to design and implement treatment programs for autistic patients at UCLA. This process begins once the medical diagnosis has been established in the manner described in detail by Ornitz and Ritvo (1968). Then, a behavioral diagnosis is formulated which takes us many steps beyond the usual labeling of patients. Such labels as "autistic with retardation, autistic without retardation, autistic with or without evidence of brain damage, etc." are completely replaced by a precise description of each child's specific developmental skills, deficits, and arrests.

The behavioral diagnosis is based only on clinical observations and the patient is observed in as many situations as can be arranged and he is given IQ tests appropriate to his general developmental level as described by Freeman and Ritvo (Chapter Three). These observational data are pooled and levels of function determined within a framework of developmental theory. Thus, a given patient's behavioral diagnosis includes as many areas as we can assess, and each area of behavior is graded from normal on down, depending upon severity of impairment. This approach is not unique to our program. It has also been emphasized in the literature by Schopler and Reichler (1971) and Rutter and Sussenwein (1971).

Once we have determined a child's current behavioral status in this manner, we are in a position to design specific behavioral programs geared to his developmental level. When behaviors are absent, we can attempt to build them in or teach them through the use of positive reinforcement. When bizarre behaviors are present, we can attempt to suppress or eliminate them.

Target Behaviors

Our experience indicates that certain behavioral deficits are particularly amenable to behavior therapy. First are social and self-help skills.

These include feeding, dressing, toileting, and personal hygiene. Usually, these behaviors can be taught by using positive reinforcement. When treating an autistic patient who is extremely negative and refuses to co-operate, we stress to the staff and parents that *they* are training the child, *he* is not training them. Thus, in practice, whenever a patient is physically able to make a response, we require him to do it. One problem which staff and parents must deal with when they are teaching self-help skills, is not to expect too much too soon. One has to divide a task into small steps and teach one step at a time. For example, when teaching how to dress, one would not begin by requiring a child to go to his bureau, select his clothes, and put them on before receiving reinforcement. Rather, one would begin by completely dressing the child except for pulling up his pants. The child would be required to do this by himself; then he would be given a positive reinforcer. After he has mastered this step, a new one would be added. Following such a step-wise procedure insures a slow progression towards the final goal with much positive reinforcement for both child and parents along the way. Technically, this procedure is referred to as "backward chaining."

A second behavioral area which receives much emphasis in our therapy programs is language. A majority of young autistic patients are either mute or echolalic and it is often assumed that only a highly trained speech therapist can implement language programs. This is not true. Following an adequate speech evaluation we have designed language programs which have been implemented by parents. For example, we have successfully instructed parents to positively reinforce babbling and in methods of shaping new sounds. As mentioned before, one important goal of using parents as paraprofessionals is to have their child's school program continue when he is at home. This has proven particularly helpful in fostering language development in autistic patients.

A third area is the development of motor skills and appropriate play behaviors. Walking, holding feeding utensils, holding crayons and other writing instruments, throwing and catching balls, are skills which can be built in by the patient application of step-wise positive reinforcement programs.

Regarding play behavior, many autistic patients have to be taught what to do with toys. In the usual case, the young autistic patient will use a toy to obtain repetitive perceptual inputs. For example, he will flap a doll or ball before his eyes, he will lick, taste and smell pets (not always to their liking), and he will spin or stare at spinning objects. Beginning with simple items, more appropriate play behaviors can be built up by step-wise positive reinforcement.

SUMMARY

In this chapter we have presented an overview of operant therapy, the rationale for training parents as paraprofessionals, and given a few examples of how we design and implement behavior therapy programs.

In training parents, we always emphasize: (1) be realistic and use common sense whenever you are teaching your child; (2) implement only programs which are close to your child's developmental level; (3) use positive reinforcement and gradually increase increments of expectation to maintain a "happy" situation for both you and your child. Patience is a golden virtue and one must not expect too much too soon; (4) keep objective written records in order to monitor your child's progress; (5) maintain consistency of your behavior programs from day to day and from situation to situation; (6) whenever possible, follow through at home with the behavior programs which have been instituted at your child's clinic or school.

REFERENCES

Ferster, C.B. (1961). Positive reinforcement and behavioral deficits of autistic children. *Child Development* 32:437-56.

Goodall, K. (1972). Shapers at work. *Psychology Today* 6:53-63, 132-38.

Hawkins, R.P. (1972). It's time we taught the young how to be good parents. *Psychology Today* 6:28.

Lindsley, O.R. (1966). An experiment with parents' handling behavior at home. *Johnstone Bulletin* 9:27-36.

Lovaas, O.I. (1967). A behavior therapy approach to the treatment of childhood schizophrenia. In J.P. Hill ed. *Minnesota Symposium on Child Psychology* 1, University of Minnesota Press.

O'Dell, S. (1974). Training parents in behavior modification. *Psychological Bulletin* 81:418-33.

Risley, T. and Wolf, M. (1967). Establishing functional speech in echolalic children. *Behavior Research and Therapy* 5:73-88.

Rutter, M. and Sussenwein, F. (1971). A developmental and behavioral approach to the treatment of preschool autistic children. *Journal of Autism and Childhood Schizophrenia* 1:376-97.

Schopler, E. and Reichler, R.J. (1971). Parents as co-therapists in the treatment of psychotic children. *Journal of Autism and Childhood Schizophrenia* 1:87-102.

PARENT-TRAINING MANUAL

Alvord, J.R. (1973). *Home Token Economy*. Champaign, Illinois: Research Press.

Baldwin, V.L., Fredericks, D.B., and Brodsky, G. (1972). *A Training Program for Parents of Retarded Children*. Springfield, Illinois: Charles C. Thomas.

Bannatyne, A. and Bannatyne, M. (1972). *How Your Child Can Learn to Live a Rewarding Life*. Springfield, Illinois: Charles C. Thomas.

Becker, W.C. (1971a). *Parents Are Teachers: A Child Management Program.* Champaign, Illinois: Research Press.

—— (1971b). *A Group Leader's Guide for Parents and Teachers.* Champaign, Illinois: Research Press.

Beltz, S.E. (1971). *How to Make Johnny Want To Obey.* Englewood Cliffs, New Jersey: Prentice Hall.

Carter, R.D. (1971). *Help! These Kids Are Driving Me Crazy.* Champaign, Illinois: Research Press.

Deibert, A.N. and Harmon, A.J. (1970). *New Tools for Changing Behavior.* Champaign, Illinois: Research Press.

Galloway, C. and Galloway, K.C. (1970). *Parent Groups with a Focus on Precise Behavior Management.* Nashville, Tennessee: Peabody College.

Guerney, G.B., ed. (1969). *Psychotherapeutic Agents: New Roles for Non-professionals, Parents and Teachers.* New York: Holt, Rinehart and Winston.

Hall, R.V. (1971). *Managing Behavior.* Volume 3. *Behavior Modification: Applications in School and Home.* Lawrence, Kansas: H. & H. Enterprises, Inc.

Hunter, M. and Carlson, P.V. (1972). *Improving Your Child's Behavior.* Glendale, California: Bowmar.

Kozloff, M.A. (1972). *Reaching the Autistic Child: A Parent Training Program.* Champaign, Illinois: Research Press.

Larsen, L.A. and Bricker, W.A. (1968). *A Manual for Parents and Teachers of Severely and Moderately Retarded.* Nashville, Tennessee: Peabody College.

Madsen, C.H. and Madsen, C.K. (1970). *Teaching Discipline: Behavioral Principles Toward a Positive Approach.* Boston, Massachusetts: Allyn and Bacon.

Madsen, C.K. and Madsen, C.H. (1970). *Parents, Children, Discipline: A Positive Approach.* Boston, Massachusetts: Allyn and Bacon.

McIntire, R.W. (1970). *For Love of Children: Behavior Psychology for Parents.* Del Mar, California: CRM Books.

Patterson, G. (1971). *Families.* Champaign, Illinois: Research Press.

—— and Gullion, M.E. (1968). *Living with Children.* Campaign, Illinois: Research Press.

Smith, J. and Smith, D. (1966). *Child development: A program for Parents.* Ann Arbor, Michigan: Ann Arbor Publishers.

Williams, D.L. and Jaffa, E.B. (1971). *Ice Cream, Poker Chips, and Very Goods: A Behavior Modification Manual for Parents.* The Maryland Book Exchange, College Park, Maryland.

Valett, R.E. (1968). *Modifying Children's Behavior: A Handbook of Psycho-educational Resource Programs.* Belmont, California: Fearon.

—— (1970). *Prescriptions for Learning: A Parent's Guide to Remedial Home Training.* Belmont, California: Fearon.

Von Helscheimer, G. (1970). *How to Live with Your Special Child.* Washington: Acropolis Books.

Walder, L.O., Cohen, S.I., Breiter, D.C., Warman, F.C., OrmeJohnson, D., and Pavey, S. (1971). *Parents as Agents of Behavior Change.* Greenbelt, Maryland: Behavior Service Consultants.

Wittes, G. and Radin, N. (1969). *The Reinforcement Approach: Helping Your Child to Learn.* San Rafael, California: Dimensions Publishing Company.

Zifferblatt, S. (1970). *You Can Help Your Child Improve Study and Homework Behaviors.* Champaign, Illinois: Research Press.

CHAPTER NINETEEN

The Plight of Parents in Obtaining Help for Their Autistic Child and the Role of the National Society for Autistic Children

HARVEY LAPIN
CONNIE LAPIN

We are the parents of an autistic child—and speak to you from this point of view. While medical experts describe and discuss autism, we feel it and know it in another way. To us, autism is our little boy who once seemed to be developing normally—and then stopped. It is our little boy who screamed for hours and could not be comforted, whom we could not toilet-train, who said words and then has never said them again, who runs right past us and his loving grandparents without paying notice, our beautiful little Shawn who cannot understand the world around him.

Autism to us is confusing, challenging, and heart-breaking. One problem we shared, unfortunately with other parents, was that it was mis-diagnosed early when we and Shawn most needed help. The time of diagnosis is particularly crucial to parents. When we were finally given the correct diagnosis it was as if we were told the child we thought we had died and that we had a new child in his place—a new child whom we had to understand, whom we had to learn all over again to live with and to love. We and other parents need time to mourn and to adjust to dealing with the new reality of having an autistic child.

What we and all parents need is a definite statement from the doctor that our children have autism and not some mumbo-jumbo about "funny development," or "slow development," or "he'll outgrow it," or "possible retardation with autistic features." Most certainly, we don't need to be told we have disturbed kids because *we* are uptight or neurotic.

Each professional we deal with needs to bear in mind, particularly, that we parents often have false hopes for our children and conflicting ex-

287

pectations of how they can help us. If an expert doesn't know what the diagnosis is, he should have the honesty, the guts, to say so and send us to someone who does. What we most need is honesty, frankness, and sharing of information—with no secrets being implied or held back. Shielding parents only causes confusion.

We parents of autistic children are aware that we have been falsely accused of having psychopathology by some professionals and of having caused our children's disease. These professionals have misunderstood our normal reactions to the stress of having a seriously disabled child and all the heartaches and headaches which go with this tragedy. One statement which Dr. Ritvo and his research colleagues have made, and for which we are grateful, is that *parents do not cause autism.*

Once given the diagnosis, our next problem was knowing where to go for help. When we finally received Shawn's diagnosis, we had never seen a poster for the National Society for Autistic Children nor heard public service commercials advertising the Society. We did not know that there were many other parents like us looking for help for their children. We felt so alone. Such isolation need not exist. There is now, fortunately, a National Society casting light in these lonely corners. It is dedicated to the education of families of autistic children and all children with severe disorders of communication and development. It is an organization of parents and professionals who are interested in sharing what knowledge we have about these children, in fostering programs in legislatures to guarantee that these children receive education, and to foster programs of research into the cause and development of new treatments. We know that unless we find the cause and develop a true cure, we, our children, and future generations of autistic children and their parents will continue to suffer.

One way we implement these goals is via the National Society for Autistic Children's annual meeting to which all parents and professionals are invited. Furthermore, we have established a national information and referral bureau. (Mrs. Ruth Sullivan is in charge of this service at present.) The National Society also has an honorary board of distinguished citizens from the fields of law and government, and a professional advisory board. Dr. Ritvo has recently been appointed Chairman of this committee and we are grateful for the voluntary contribution of time and effort by him and other professionals in the field.

We would now like to discuss what we parents need most for ourselves and our children. The first thing parents need is to find a professional, (a child psychiatrist, a pediatrician, a psychologist, a teacher) who really cares about our children—one whom we trust and one who will hang in for the years of help we need.

Second, *we need public school education for our autistic children.*

Recently in California, specific legislation was enacted which makes it mandatory for school districts to either provide classrooms for autistic children or give a school district money so that special education can be arranged. Autism has recently been defined as one of the "developmental disabilities," thus allowing for our children to receive federal and state funds earmarked for such programs.

Third is *the need for centers which can accurately diagnose children who are not developing on schedule,* or who are known to be at high risk because of physical problems which occurred during pregnancy or in their early months of life—centers where specialists will be available to help our local doctors and clinics.

Fourth, *preschool programs have to be established.* It is commonly agreed among the medical experts that the earlier autistic children are diagnosed and treated, the better their prognosis may be. Too often our children miss important learning years because preschool programs simply do not exist.

Fifth, *after-care day programs are a necessity.* Autistic children do not come home from school and play as normal children do. They must have supervision around the clock. If parents need to work, and most often they do, they need the peace of mind of knowing their child is being properly cared for.

Sixth, *pre-vocational training programs must be made available which teach independent living skills and basic self-help skills.* Very few autistic children we know are able to live in society on their own. Those who can, must be given every chance possible.

Seventh, *training programs to instruct teachers and other professionals how to work with autistic children are necessary.* Many of us have had the problem of taking our children to clinics for tests or schools for evaluations and being told that the teachers don't know how to work with autistic children and thus won't even try.

Eighth, *parental counseling and training programs are necessary to help us learn to live with our autistic children, and to adjust to the problems created within our families by having to live with our severely handicapped children.* In many instances, brothers and sisters also need counseling on how to get along with their autistic sibling.

Ninth, *respite care programs are necessary in order to give families a chance to live without their autistic child for periods of time.* No family should be ashamed to ask for a time out, a period to recharge their batteries. How many times have we talked with parents who have never been away for even a minute from their autistic child for five, ten, or fifteen years.

In summary, we want to stress that professionals and parents alike must educate themselves as to what autism is and how best to live with an autistic child. During the years in which we have worked with the National Society for Autistic Children, it has been gratifying to watch the boundaries of knowledge extend. But they have only moved inches in terms of the miles we yet have to progress. How many doctors and psychologists have never heard of autism, how many schools exclude autistic children just because they are autistic, how many research programs will not study autism because it is not thought to be important enough or a psychological problem? We need programs which are geared for all-aged autistic children and for those with all degrees of severity. Parents need to be made part of the therapy team. No blackmail therapy should ever be pushed. This refers to programs which will not take a child unless his parents acknowledge that they have some kind of emotional disturbance and consent to psychotherapy.

Don't throw our autistic children away. All children are potential learners. Help us bring them up and educate them as best we can. There is always some realistic hope for a meaningful life, whether it be in a sheltered environment or as a partly responsible citizen. When it comes right down to it, our son Shawn is still just a six-year-old little boy. He needs to be educated like all six-year-old little boys need to be educated. He needs to be loved like all six-year-old little boys need to be loved. Shawn did not ask to be born autistic; he has the same rights as anyone to live a meaningful life, with dignity, despite and within the bounds of his handicap.

CHAPTER TWENTY

Autism: Current Trends in Services

RUTH CHRIST SULLIVAN

About a dozen years ago, the mother of a newly-diagnosed autistic child called the local Mental Health Association in the large eastern city where she lived for information about the new term which had just come into her family's life. Two staff members had never heard of autism and transferred the call to the association's executive director, whose reply was, "Oh, yes. For information on that, call the Institute of Art and History."

With appreciation of the progress made in the last twelve years that same mother will now discuss current trends of service for autistic children in the United States. In 1970, Harriet Mandelbaum, one of the prime movers in the founding of the League School in Brooklyn and the mother of an autistic son who was then twenty-seven years old, addressed the second National Society for Autistic Children's annual meeting and conference in San Francisco with these words, "It is less difficult, I think, to be a parent of a mentally ill child today, but probably even more frustrating. Easier, because the diagnosis has been refined, because you can find and work with other parents who share the problem. More frustrating, because in an atmosphere of greater hope and knowledge, facilities are still tragically few."

Things have improved dramatically since Harriet Mandelbaum realized that she had an autistic son. Even since 1970, there has been remarkable progress toward opening doors for autistic children everywhere.

The recently concluded 93rd Congress introduced a record number of bills (over fifty-five) affecting the handicapped—including a significant number specifically for handicapped children, notably P.L. 93-380 (the ESEA amendments). Congress is moving into a second generation of support, that is, from funding for seed and catalytic programs to funding for direct service programs as part of the federal commitment. There is growing congressional support for full and appropriate education for all the handicapped.

Even more important is the fact that some of the most powerful men in both houses of Congress are deeply committed to better services for the handicapped and are lending their full support to some of the most exciting new legislation ever enacted for the nation's handicapped population.

But this legislation did not just happen; it is the result of a strong and effective movement of consumer-citizens (parents) to organize into militant pressure groups and to demand services for their children as a *right*. The day has passed when parents feel they are asking for special gifts of charity when approaching legislatures, school boards, and other community agencies for special services. Bolstered by recent court decisions in their favor, new federal and state laws, and by a rising consciousness about responsibility for serving the handicapped, parents (with the help of a growing body of professionals and other friends) are pressing for full services for their handicapped children.

Another very significant change is the swell of interest in biophysical answers to the cause of autism. Just recently NSAC (founded in 1965), through our national president, Mary Sweeney Akerley, sought and received a commitment from the National Institute of Neurological Diseases and Strokes (NINDS, HEW) to do research. Today, there is a strong and rapidly moving trend away from a purely psychogenic explanation of autism.

In spite of whatever credit we parents are tempted to give ourselves for this progress, we must recognize that we are fortunate enough to have come upon the scene at a time when there is a new enlightenment about the rights of all the handicapped. There is a new recognition in Congress, state legislatures and the courts of the basic human rights of the handicapped; in the last few years there has been a steady movement to correct past injustices.

It is probably safe to say that there are no handicapped citizens who have been subjected to more discrimination or received fewer community services than those labeled "autistic." They are the last to be included, last on the waiting list—the "hard core" handicapped. Parents of autistic children are painfully familiar with the phrase, "He doesn't fit our program." Few facilities make any effort to make their programs fit the autistic child. And once admitted, he is too often only tolerated. His parents are told that, if he upsets the other children, or the routine, or the teacher (or therapist), he will be dismissed. Too often, in fact almost inevitably, he does one or all three, and the facility then can report, "He is unable to benefit from our program," thereby placing the onus of failure on the child, not the facility. The parents then continue their search for help, often exhausting their financial, physical and psychological resources, seldom finding an adequate program suited to their and their child's individual needs.

The increasing visibility of the National Society for Autistic Children and its Information and Referral Service, along with the expanding number of diagnosed cases of autism, led to a contract with the National Institute of Mental Health to publish *U.S. Facilities and Programs for Children with Severe Mental Illnesses: A Directory.* The survey was finished in August 1973, and was published by NIMH in August, 1974. It lists over 500 facilities in the United States which say they take autistic or autistic-like children and persons.

In the course of collecting data for the *Directory*, we surveyed the United States and all its territories and have been able to detect trends and compile new statistical information which we feel is significant. We can report that the desperately sad plight of autistic children is at last beginning to improve, and it is doing so rapidly. (For instance, seven weeks after our cut-off date for inclusion of new facilities in the *Directory*, we received fifty-seven new listings!) Some observations can be made from our data, and the development of trends can be seen from the following findings:

(1) *With few exceptions, new programs have a strong educational base, where the main "interveners" are teachers.*

This corroborates a statement by Dr. Michael Rutter (1970) of England when he wrote, "Perhaps the biggest change in the last ten years in the treatment of autistic children has been the increased emphasis on the importance of education." Because autism was "found" by a psychiatrist, Dr. Leo Kanner (1943), and because until the last ten to fifteen years most professional writing on the subject was done for psychiatric-psychological publications, the condition became known as a "psychiatric disorder." The literature reflected the prime interveners as mental health "therapists" who conceived themselves in the role of persons skilled in the psychiatric-psychological treatment of mental disorder. Unfortunately, for all involved—therapist, child, and family—little progress was made in correcting the seemingly inevitable outcome of this grave and inexorable condition. Though articles about these children appeared with increasing frequency, it seemed the writers wrote more to *describe* than to *prescribe*. It was as though having been intrigued for a while by a fascinating, albeit pathetic, group of children, the practical decision was made that time might be better spent on more easily treatable forms of mental disorder.*

Today there are few psychiatrists who spend a large portion of their

*The 1961 Report of the Joint Commission on Mental Health, though it almost completely ignored children, reported that psychiatrists spend most of their time on the milder forms of mental illness and neurosis.

time on autistic or autistic-like children. Indeed, there is indication that the profession does not consider this problem to have priority at all.

It is not surprising then that in the last twenty years, beginning with founding of the League School in Brooklyn in 1953, a small but growing number of facilities have been established which use education as the main therapy, "making a clean break," as Dr. Carl Fenichel (1969) subsequently reported, "with the deep-rooted official doctrine that psychotherapy was the number one prescription in any comprehensive treatment program for disturbed children." However, as late as 1967, other special educators—even some well-known ones—were still saying that autistic children did not belong in special education until they "worked through their emotional problems."

It was not until the emergence of the National Society for Autistic Children, founded in 1965 by Bernard Rimland, Ph.D., that a nationwide concerted, intensive and continuing effort was made to counteract the theory that autism is the result of noxious mother-child relationship. Dr. Rimland's book, *Infantile Autism* (1964) and his many articles (especially "Freud is Dead," 1970) began to dispel the iatrogenic guilt suffered by parents who were unfortunate enough to have borne autistic children during those early years when, almost without exception, professionals blamed parents— especially mothers—for their child's autism and when psychotherapy (even psychoanalysis) was the preferred treatment. Though there are still some of those professionals around, no really important ones continue to express a purely psychogenic theory. Attempts to treat the autistic child through treatment of his parents or isolation from them ("parentectomy" is imperative in Dr. Bettelheim's (1967) Orthogenic School in Chicago) are based on the idea that parents caused the condition. Dr. Ornitz (1973) of UCLA says, "Such notions are no longer accepted . . . and are now only of historical interest."

It is no wonder that parents turned to educators. Having painfully witnessed and experienced the psychotherapeutic process and its very expensive and limited success with their autistic children, parents found that a teacher "who fosters self-discipline, emotional growth, and more effective functioning is (also) doing something therapeutic" (Fenichel, 1966). There was a renewed interest in Dr. Jean Marc Itard's (1962) account of a feral boy written in the early 1800s. Too, it was a new experience for most parents to be considered part of the solution instead of part of the problem. Dr. Eric Schopler's (1973) program (TEACCH) in North Carolina is among those which recognize parental authority and responsibility and which consider the parent as a co-therapist. And education, though quite expensive for most families, costs less than psychotherapy. The success of a good, structured educational environment, including systems of behavior therapy, has by now been well established and is probably the most effective method of amelioration now known for severely behaviorally disturbed children.

I have dwelled on the development of education in the treatment of autistic (and, of course, all other handicapped) children because it seems to be the most sharply delineated trend confirmed by our data. It is also the most important single rallying point for handicapped children's parents. New coalitions of parent groups are demonstrating their consumer power. Their determined and energetic lobbying activities are getting the attention of education administrators, lawmakers, and the community. They are being rewarded with new state mandates for their children's education and favorable decisions from the courts. There is a new awareness of violations of the children's basic human rights. Education for handicapped children, even autistic children, is becoming the new frontier.

(2) *A large majority of programs have been started within the last five to ten years.*

Many of the directors have either established the programs themselves or are the first directors, demonstrating how young the schools are. Most programs are small. Only a few have as many as thirty or forty students, and these are usually found in the older facilities which have had time to expand. Even programs in state hospitals have only a few children.

(3) *Almost all of the programs established within the last five years list be-havior modification as part of their curriculum, sometimes as the major method of working with the children.*

This is especially true of programs which admit mostly or only autistic and autistic-like children. The few programs based on psychogenic theory are usually attached to a large university with a medical school.

(4) *Few programs (probably less than 25 of the 500 listed) are primarily for autistic children.*

Most "will accept," with a variety of stipulations (e.g., must be toilet trained, self-feeding, self-dressing, verbal). Some will allow only a certain percentage of autistic children in their program. Some will accept autistic children only as an exception.

(5) *There are still a significant number of mental hospitals (both public and private), even some with children's and adolescent's units, which will not admit autistic children.*

In many states there is *not one* facility which will take an autistic child as a matter of policy!

(6) *The cost of care, especially in residential centers, is usually beyond the means of most parents.*

We found one facility which costs $29,000 per year. Even in the few facilities which offer scholarships, tuition is still too high for most families. The Civilian Health and Medical Program of the Uniformed Services (CHAMPUS) and welfare are the most common outside sources of funds for parents. CHAMPUS's educational benefits terminated in December 1973, and most families are not eligible for welfare. Except for the few public school classes and other types of community programs, the average annual cost of residential education and care is approximately $12,000.

(7) *The more parent involvement in policy-making, the longer and more flexible are the hours of service.*

For instance, a few parent-founded facilities operate 9:00 to 5:00 six days a week, twelve months a year. A notable exception is one state hospital program whose director invites parent participation. Her program offers weekend respite care to children who go to community special education classes and live at home all week. A few other facilities offer residential programs during the week with children home on weekends. Although the in-and-out arrangement has many advantages for children and families, it creates a hardship for parents who do not live within easy commuting distances. We have had reports of parents, usually the mother, driving over 200 miles a day.

(8) *Most public school special education programs who responded to our questionnaire operate between ten and twelve months a year.*

Public school programs is our fastest growing list.

(9) *The preponderance of our listings, day programs for preschoolers and pre-adolescents form the largest group.*

(10) *There is a sudden drop in the number of available programs, both day and residential, once a child reaches puberty or late adolescence.*

(11) *Suitable programs for adult autistic persons are so rare as to be practically nonexistent.*

(12) *Only a few residential camps (and a slightly larger number of day camps) will accept autistic children.*

(13) *Some programs still insist, sometimes as an admission criterion, that parents become involved in "psychotherapy." Even public school programs are numbered among these.*

The psychogenic theory that parents are part of the problem dies hard.

(14) *Some residential facilities do not allow parents in their children's sleeping or eating quarters. A number of day facilities stipulate, "No parents allowed on premises without permission."*

(15) *Some residential programs do not allow parent visitation for as long as six months after admission; one facility prohibits visitation for one year!*

(16) *Seven facilities reported they use electroconvulsive therapy on children.*

(17) *Most programs, both public and private, receive at least some government funds.*

(18) *A few educational programs receive some funds from state departments of mental health.*

(19) *Most programs have a long waiting list, one for as long as three years.*

(20) *Most states do not have an accreditation or licensing agency for these schools. Most need only fire-marshal approval.*

These are some of the outstanding findings. As we are able to work with the data we hope to make a more comprehensive report. The information we have is, as far as we know, the first to be collected on a comprehensive national survey, based on a questionnaire designed not only to get general data, but also to get special information dealing with the questions often asked by parents.

Among the most interesting trends is the growing sophistication and concurrent militance of parents. They are clearly taking a leading role in pressing for research, education, respite care, and other services for their children. The Ralph Nader idea of consumer participation is already full-blown in the lives of many crusader-parents who will no longer sit by whimpering while the Provider tells him to put his child away and forget he was ever born. Parent expectation is rising. As they become co-therapists, co-teachers, co-workers, co-operators with the professionals, it seems likely the spin-off can only *help* the autistic child.

(For those of you who are interested, the current address of the Information and Referral Service of the National Society for Autistic Children is 306-31st Street, Huntington, West Virginia 25702 Tel: 304-697-2638.)

REFERENCES

Bettelheim, B. (1967). *The Empty Fortress—Infantile Autism and the Birth of the Self.* New York: Free Press.

Fenichel, C. (1966). Psycho-educational approaches for seriously disturbed children in the classroom. *Intervention Approaches in Educating Emotionally Disturbed Children.* New York: Syracuse University, Division of Special Education and Rehabilitation.

——— (1969). Keynote address delivered at annual meeting of the National Society for Autistic Children, Washington, D.C.

Itard, Jean-Marc-Gaspard. (1962). *The Wild Boy of Aveyron.* New York: Appleton-Century-Crofts.

Kanner, L. (1943). Autistic disturbances of affective contact. *Nervous Child* 2:250.

Ornitz, E.M. (1973). Childhood autism—a review of the clinical and experimental literature. *California Medicine* 118:21-47.

Rimland, B. (1964) *Infantile Autism.* New York: Appleton-Century-Crofts.

——— (1970). Freud is Dead. University of Southern California Distinguished Lecture Series in Special Education June.

Rutter, M. (1970). Autism: concepts and consequences. *Special Education* 59:2.

Schopler, E. (1973). Current approaches to the autistic child. *Behavior Disorders.*

Index